I0793044

IMAGES
of America

ARIZONA'S HISTORIC TRADING POSTS

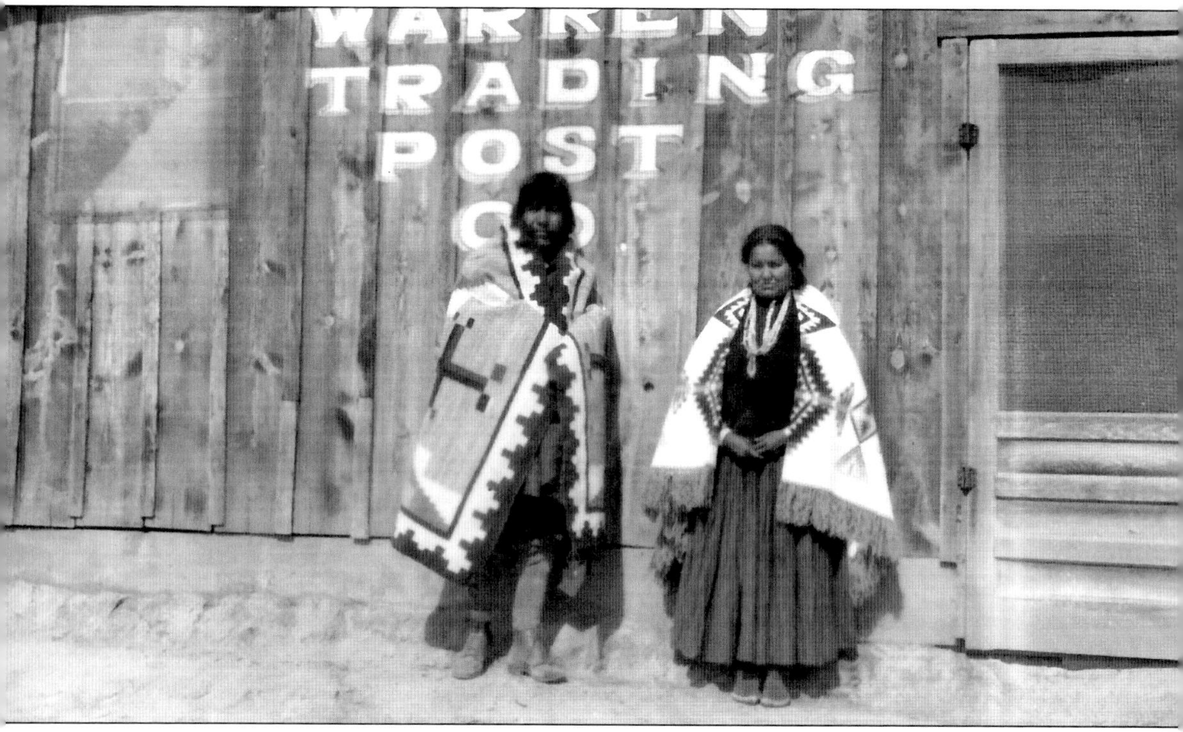

John and Sue Bradley were photographed in front of Warren Trading Post at Kayenta about 1930. John is wrapped in one of Sue's weavings, while Sue is wearing a Pendleton blanket. (Courtesy of the author.)

On the Cover: Tracy's Trading Post on the Tohono O'odham Indian Reservation was a center for accomplished basket makers. In this 1934 image, Wilma Coplen, granddaughter of Marion and Goldie Tracy, is surrounded by a collection of O'odham baskets. The swastika symbols on the baskets and the blanket hanging behind Wilma are ancient Native American symbols representing the four directions, the celestial star, and prehistoric migration routes. (Courtesy of Neil Sutherland.)

IMAGES
of America

ARIZONA'S HISTORIC TRADING POSTS

Carolyn O'Bagy Davis

ARCADIA
PUBLISHING

ISBN 978-1-4671-3249-7

Published by Arcadia Publishing
Charleston, South Carolina

Printed in the United States of America

Library of Congress Control Number: 2014938564

For all general information, please contact Arcadia Publishing:
Telephone 843-853-2070
Fax 843-853-0044
E-mail sales@arcadiapublishing.com
For customer service and orders:
Toll-Free 1-888-313-2665

Visit us on the Internet at www.arcadiapublishing.com

A lifelong trader, Byron Hunter made this book possible. Thank you for your help, your photographs, and your patient answers to my questions.

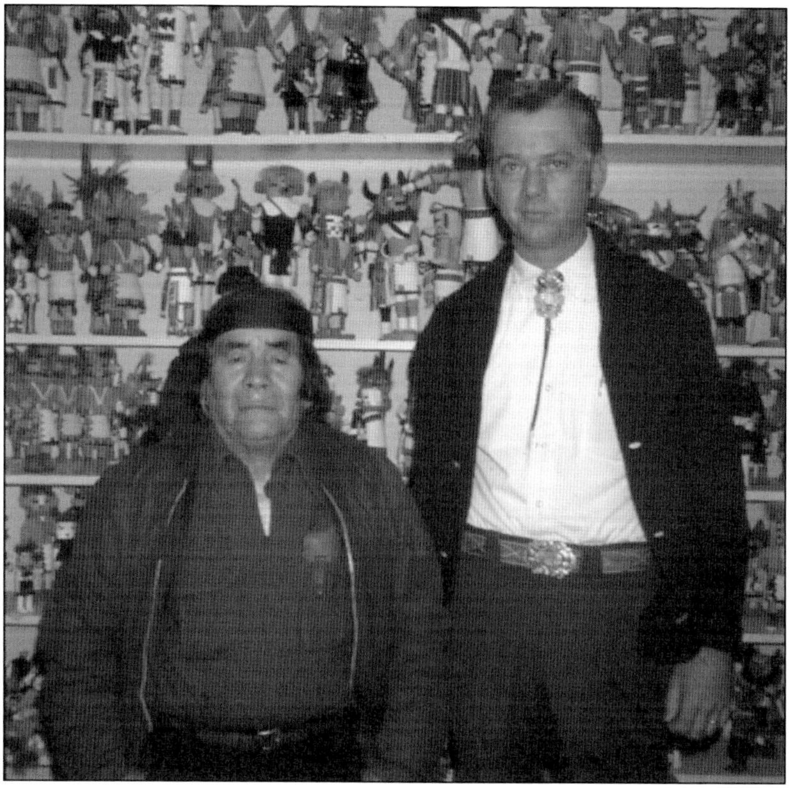

Bryon Hunter managed Polacca Trading Post on First Mesa from 1963 to 1970. He is shown here (right) about 1968 with Hopi artist Otis Polelonema. (Courtesy of Byron Hunter.)

Contents

ACKNOWLEDGMENTS

For their generous help and support, I wish to thank the Arizona Historical Society, Jim Babbitt, Mary May Stiles Bailey, Bill Beaver, Harry and Isabelle Benally, Hank and Victoria Blair, Bruce and Virginia Burnham, Edgar Busch, Cynthia Cobb, Tom Collins, Anthony Cooley, C. Burton Cosgrove, Joseph and Janice Day, Catherine H. Ellis, Mary Tate Engels, Alan Ferg, Henry Golas and Frashers Fotos, Kenneth Headrick, Nina Heflin, Eleanor Means Hull, Byron Hunter, John W. Kennedy, Bernice Klohr, Edythe Headrick Klopping, Nathan LaFont and Goulding's Trading Post and Lodge, Allan Lagumbay and Pomona Public Library, Harvey Leake, Martin Link, Billy Malone, John McCulloch, Clifton and Betty McGee, Lois McMindes, Russell Mead and Mead Publishing, Florence Crannell Means, Richard Mike, Hannah Morris, Laura O'Bagy, Victor Ochoa, Bruce and Delna Powell, Veran Steckel, Neil Sutherland, Kara Tanoue, Bertha S. Thomas, Edison and Karen Tootsie, and Betty Rodgers Worthey.

Thanks go to Matthew Smith, who helped locate many wonderful photographs in the Southwestern National Photograph Collection, Western Archeological and Conservation Center (WACC), Tucson, Arizona. Additionally, Jannelle Weakley, curator of the photographic collections at Arizona State Museum, University of Arizona, and Ann-Mary J. Lutzick, director of Old Trails Museum/Winslow Historical Society, both spent valuable time locating images and stories. Unless otherwise noted, all images are from the author's collection.

Special thanks go to Richard C. Berkholz, author of *Old Trading Posts of the Four Corners*, who answered questions, shared information, and graciously allowed me to quote from his informative book.

And to Al and Margaret Grieve, thank you for allowing me to be a part of your trading post.

Introduction

By the 1860s, Eastern settlers were moving into traditional Navajo lands in northern Arizona. As clashes between Navajos and the newcomers became more frequent and violent, the US government sent troops into the country to capture the Navajos and to place them on a reservation at Bosque Redondo in New Mexico. Thousands of Navajo people were then forced to march to New Mexico in what became known as the Long Walk. Hundreds died on the way. Finally in 1868, the government relented and allowed them to leave the barren, hated land and return to their traditional homeland.

Years of living in a different land, eating government rations, and being exposed to Anglo goods resulted in their desire to obtain Anglo foods and materials, such as sugar, salt, coffee, white flour, pots and pans, and bridles and saddles. As a result, early traders traveling through the area sold these goods from their wagons. Trading posts began to appear in northern Arizona about 1870, when traders built primitive but permanent posts, usually located on trade routes near water sources. In 1900, there were about 80 trading posts on the Navajo Reservation; by 1930, there were 154 stores, plus additional trading posts located just off the reservation. Trading posts were also built on other reservations around Arizona in the early 20th century as more Native Americans were exposed to new goods and found markets for their arts. There were hundreds of trading posts located across Arizona—many more than could be illustrated in this book, which is intended to give a flavor of an old-time way of life and of living in remote and isolated areas of the Southwest.

These stores evolved into trading and social centers where wool, sheep, rugs, and Native arts were exchanged for food and other merchandise. On the Navajo Reservation, trading posts typically had a raised counter around three sides of the store, and the trader stood behind the counter on a floor raised 6 to 12 inches above the central store area, also known as the bull pen. A woodstove in the middle of the floor provided heat for the trading post. Canned goods lined the walls behind the counter (canned tomatoes with crackers was considered a treat), bags of flour were stacked on the floor, and ropes, tools, and bridles hung from the ceiling. Several traders noted that orange or strawberry soda pop was also a favorite with visiting Navajos, but they preferred it room temperature and not chilled. At some stores, a bag of peanuts poured into the soda bottle was an added favorite.

Most traders had a can of loose tobacco nailed onto the counter, with additional nails pointing upwards so that only enough tobacco to roll a cigarette could be taken from the can. Bolts of velveteen, satin, and calico were also stocked, and many traders' wives recall that Navajo ladies came to the trading post to use their sewing machine to stitch up their shirts and voluminous skirts. Traditional Navajo women wore gathered skirts made with 6 to 12 yards of fabric (in earlier times, fabrics came in narrower widths than today). Typically, they also wore two or more skirts.

Even today, it is not uncommon to see an older Navajo woman wearing a traditional gathered skirt with the fabric of a second skirt peeking out below the hem. Pendleton blankets also became popular, and it is common to see them on shelves in reservation stores. Vintage black-and-white photographs show women wrapped in the stripes and zigzags of Pendleton blankets.

Navajo trading posts are best known, but trading posts existed on every reservation in Arizona. Traders became the intermediaries between Native peoples and the outside world, providing not only hard goods, but other essential services, including translating, writing letters, providing emergency transportation, helping in times of sickness, and donating food to ceremonial gatherings and holiday celebrations. Because Navajos traditionally had a fear of death, when a family member was dying, they often put him outside of the hogan, away from the dwelling. Shonto trader Elizabeth Hegemann told of a little girl put out in a brush shelter "under the night sky to await the end." If someone died in a hogan, it would be abandoned due to fear of the resulting evil spirits. Consequently, traders were often summoned to bury the deceased, saving family members from having to go through a four-day purification ceremony. There are many stories of traders building simple caskets with wood from Arbuckles Coffee crates and traveling to a hogan to bury a person. Traders also had to be watchful that there was never a death inside their trading post, even physically carrying out a person who was ill or injured. If someone died inside the store, the business would be gone, as no Navajo would venture inside again.

The commissioner of Indian Affairs through the Department of the Interior had the sole power to appoint traders. Furthermore, no non-Indian could live and work at a trading post without approval from the commissioner. That approval, as well as a license to trade, had to be renewed every year. Traders were also prohibited from selling guns and ammunition. And not only was it illegal to sell alcohol to an Indian, having alcohol in the store or in the trader's living quarters was prohibited as well. According to the 1927 trader's regulations booklet, traders could not "sell, give away, or use any opium, chloral, cocaine, peyote or mescal bean, hashish or Indian hemp or marahuana [*sic*]." There was to be no gambling, and all stores were required to close on Sundays.

The regulations also stated that if credit was given, it was at the trader's own risk. The government would not help to collect debts. It soon developed that most stores did give credit (and some still do), which was not surprising considering that in earlier times, especially on the rural reservation land, there was very little cash and most people used barter and trade among themselves. Leatherwork or a load of wood would bring a bag of groceries. The collectible local arts, pottery, baskets, and weavings would bring a higher credit. Among the Navajo, credit also was associated with a widely used pawn system. Jewelry, rugs, Pendleton blankets, baskets, rifles, and saddles could be pawned for cash plus interest, for a certain amount of time. Pawn has been called the Navajo Banking System. For many, it was practical: banks seldom gave small loans, especially when there was little collateral and no formal employment to ensure repayment. Most honest traders kept pawn items well beyond the required time, giving families time to reclaim the item. It was generally not even a moneymaker for the trader, to have so much money tied up in merchandise that could not be sold. Pawn and credit were usually settled up twice a year, once in the spring when wool was sold to the trader after sheep shearing and then again in the fall when lambs and livestock were sold.

Pawning a valuable item was also sometimes a way to keep it safe. Living in a hogan, with no door to lock and many people going in and out, made it impossible to protect valuables. But pawn rooms in trading posts generally had barred windows and heavy doors, or even a vault. Thus, having pawn at a trading post was like having a safety-deposit box at a bank. There are stories of traders loaning back pawn items, such as pieces of jewelry, if the owner wished to wear them to a special gathering or ceremony, and then returning them afterward. In the 1970s, the Federal Trade Commission held hearings regarding the trading post business and came out with new regulations that impacted the continued existence of the traditional trading post. Pawn mostly came to an end; although, in many areas it just moved off the reservation. Today, only Van Trading Company in Tuba City still has a pawn room, but just off the reservation in the Gallup, New Mexico, area, there are many businesses that operate heavily in pawn. In a different and state-regulated form, pawn is still the Navajo Banking System. On a recent visit to one store, the pawn area held 8,000 Pendleton blankets, 2,000 saddles, hundreds of rifles, baskets, pelts, and an entire room of jewelry.

One consequence of operating a trading post, and having valuable pawn, is that the stores and the traders were often at risk for robberies and killings. Trading posts would have the only money in the area, in addition to the store's inventory, and there are many stories of robberies and shootings in the isolated stores. In 1922, Tolchaco trader Carl F. Steckel wrote, "Indian traders life is very lonely and the howl of the wolf to moon makes it moreso lonely." For most traders, their safety, and their social life, relied on the security of the store, but more important were the good relations with their customers and local community. Successful traders saw their customers as their neighbors. Therefore, their help went beyond selling goods. They contributed to local celebrations, nursed the sick, promoted the arts; they spoke the local language, and they often explained or intervened with laws and decrees coming from a distant Washington.

Trading posts generally passed into history after the 1973 Federal Trade Commission issued new regulations. It was also a time when tribes were taking control of their lands, and the businesses operating within their borders. But there were other causes for closing the trading posts. In earlier years, a 10- or 20-mile trip to the trading post took a day or more of travel by wagon or horseback, but automobiles and paved roads made towns and large stores more accessible and convenient. And the traders were changing as well. Where before, trading was generally a family business with sons and daughters taking over a store that had been in the family for one or two generations, now children and grandchildren moved to town, attended college, and had very different life goals. As the old-time traders passed away or retired and moved to town, which they were required to do because as non-Indians they could not remain on reservation land, the stores closed one by one. The empty buildings were soon vandalized and, eventually, removed. Most traces of the old trading posts have now vanished.

The stores taken over by the tribes are now mostly "C-stores," convenience stores that sell snacks and gas. The few trading posts still operating are owned, at least partly, by a native tribal member; although, there are a rare few that are still operating under long-term leases through the tribes. At those stores, there is sometimes a lingering whisper of those earlier times, when the trading post was a part of the romance of the vast Southwest.

As an endnote to the reader, it is important to mention that most trading posts, or the ruins or original sites, are on tribal land. That land is private, and it is illegal to go onto these lands without permission or a local guide. Some sites can be seen from roadways, but please respect the privacy of tribal members, and of the tribal boundaries, and do not venture onto those lands.

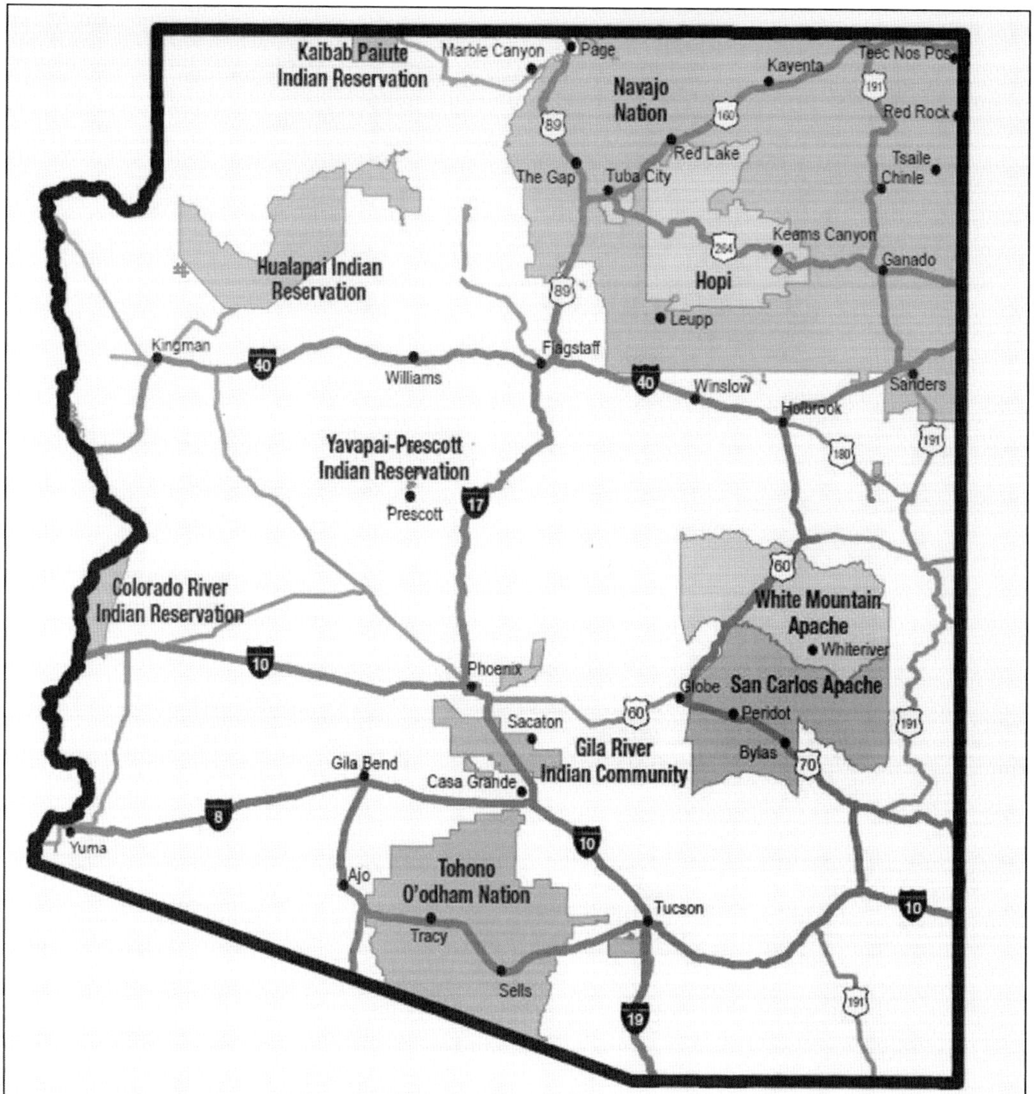

This map of Arizona, created by Hannah Morris and Kara Tanoue, shows the locations and established boundaries of Arizona's tribal lands.

One

Diné Bikéyah
Navajoland

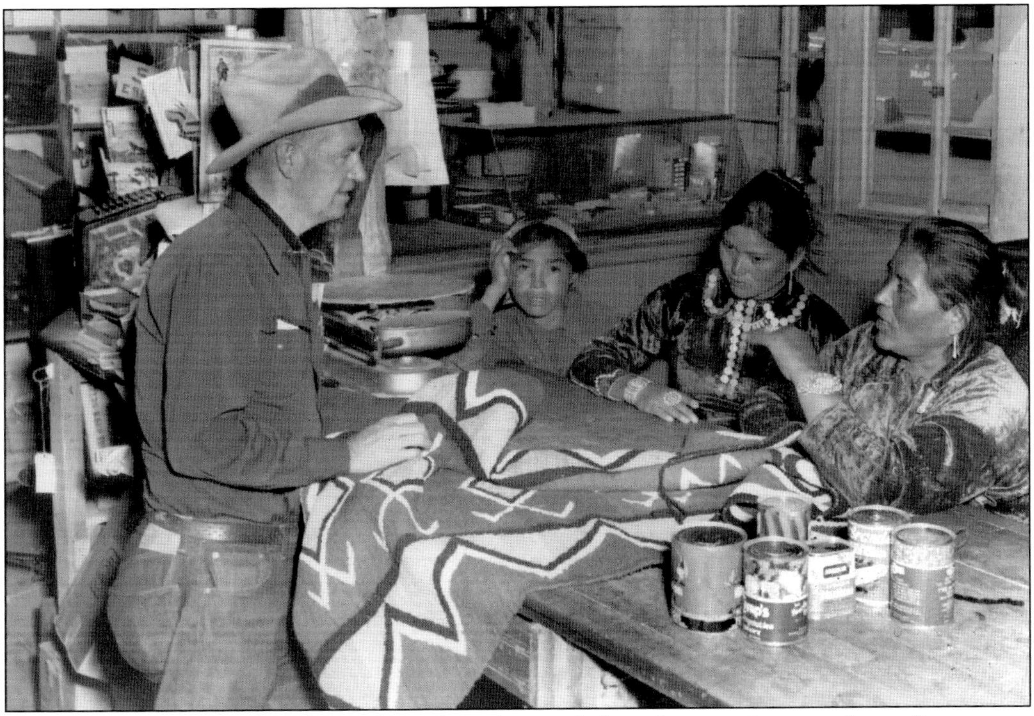

Navajo women did much of the trading when they took their sheep and rugs to the trading post to exchange for groceries and other necessities. This weaver at Goulding's Trading Post is negotiating a rug price with Harry Goulding. The ladies are standing in the central area known as the bull pen, in front of a high counter with a raised floor behind it. (Courtesy of Nathan LaFont and Goulding's Trading Post and Lodge.)

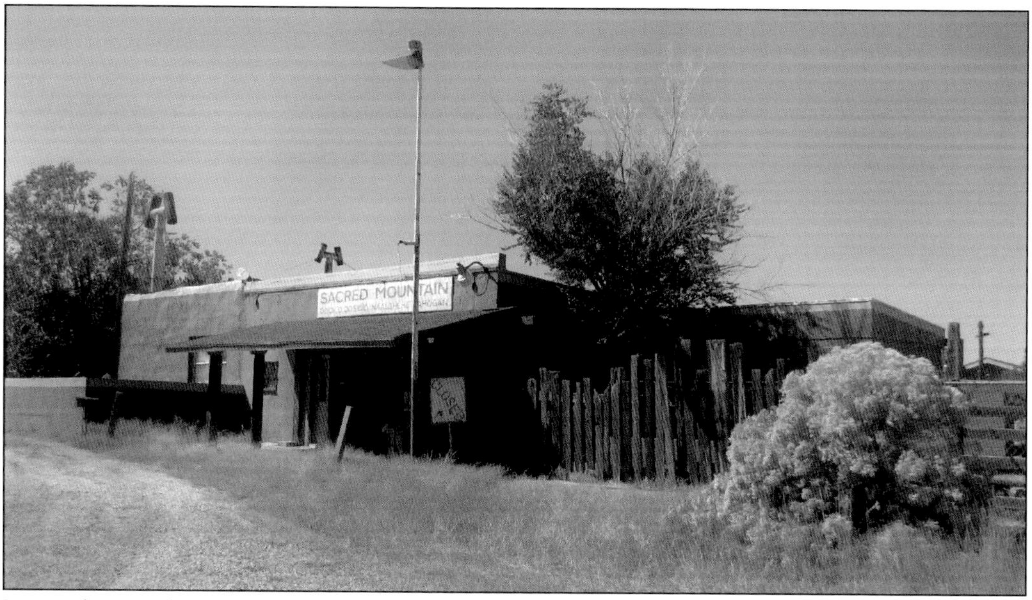

Located on Highway 89 north of Flagstaff, Sacred Mountain Trading Post was built in 1915 and was known as Deep Wells Trading Post. Trader William Beaver had worked at Shonto Trading Post from 1950 until 1960, when he bought Deep Wells and renamed it Sacred Mountain. Beaver spoke fluent Navajo, and until his passing in 2009, he worked to promote the revival, and survival, of Navajo pottery. One Navajo artist from the Cow Springs area who often worked with Beaver is Louise Goodman, who is known for her whimsical pottery bears.

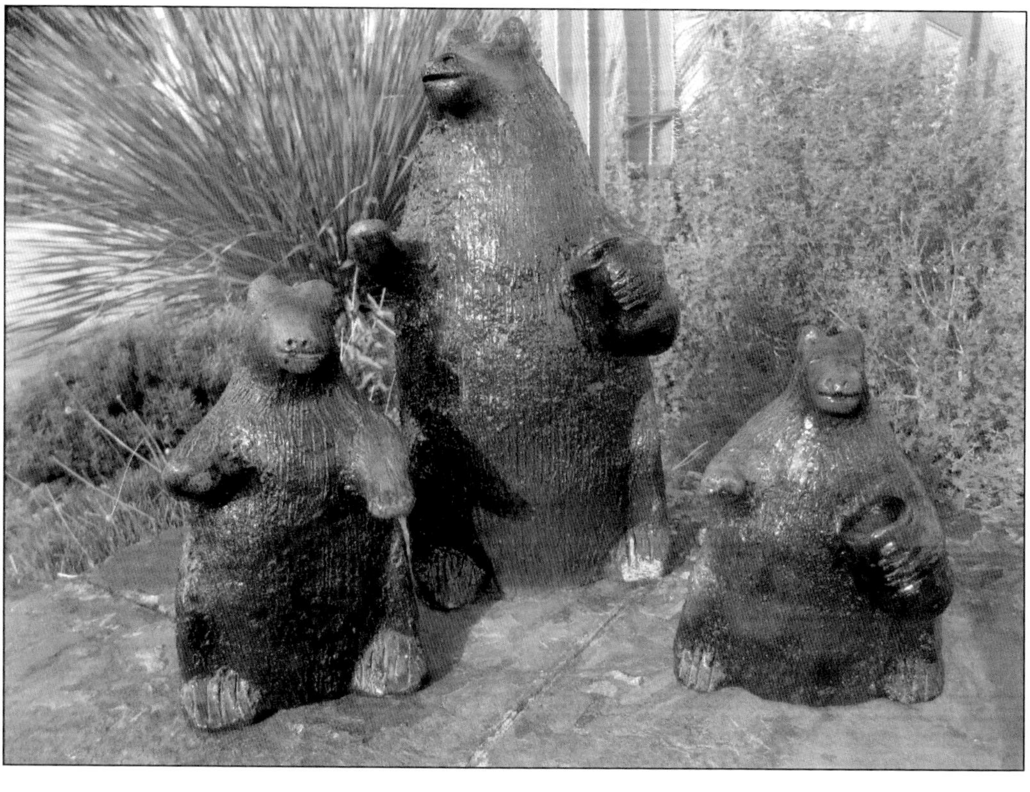

The five Babbitt brothers came to Flagstaff from Ohio beginning in 1886. They worked together to build a business empire that included ranches, mercantile stores, automobile dealerships, and dozens of trading posts on the Navajo and Hopi Reservations. The family business still manages many of those original enterprises.

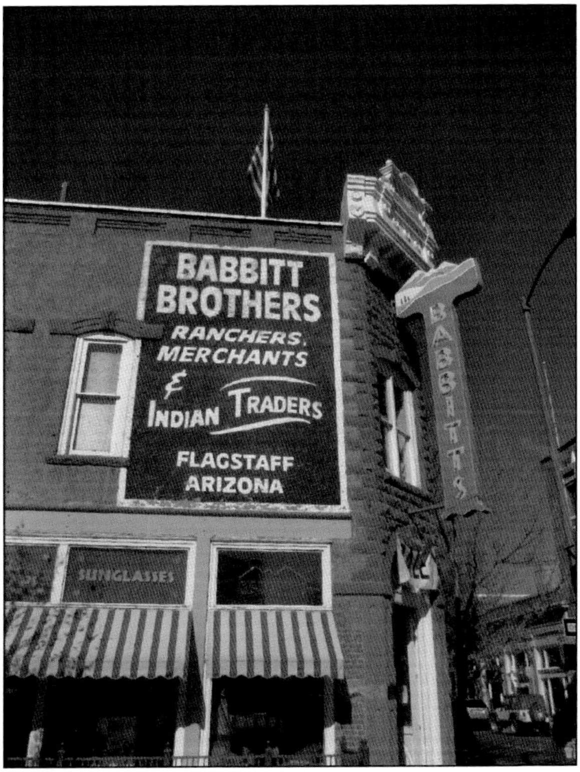

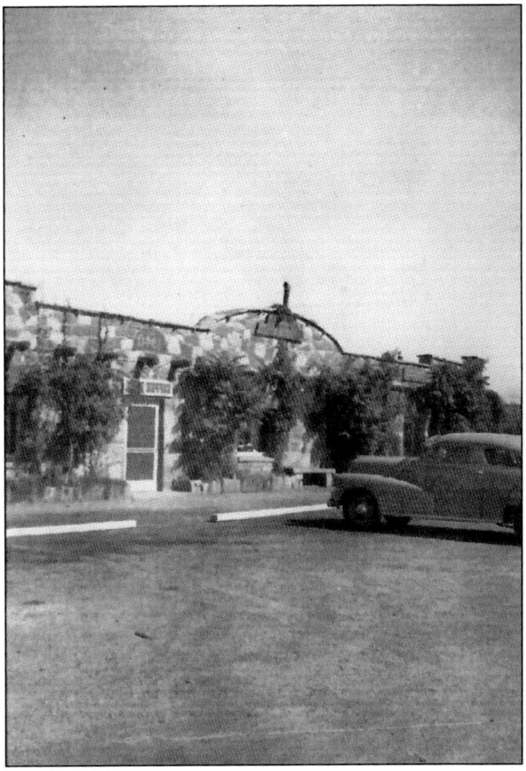

Gray Mountain Trading Post on Highway 89 north of Flagstaff had a restaurant for tourists traveling north to the Grand Canyon. The restaurant walls were painted with nearly life-size kachina figures. Gray Mountain rises to the northwest toward the Grand Canyon. Apollo 15 astronauts trained at Gray Mountain because the area has a moonlike landscape. (Courtesy of Martin Link.)

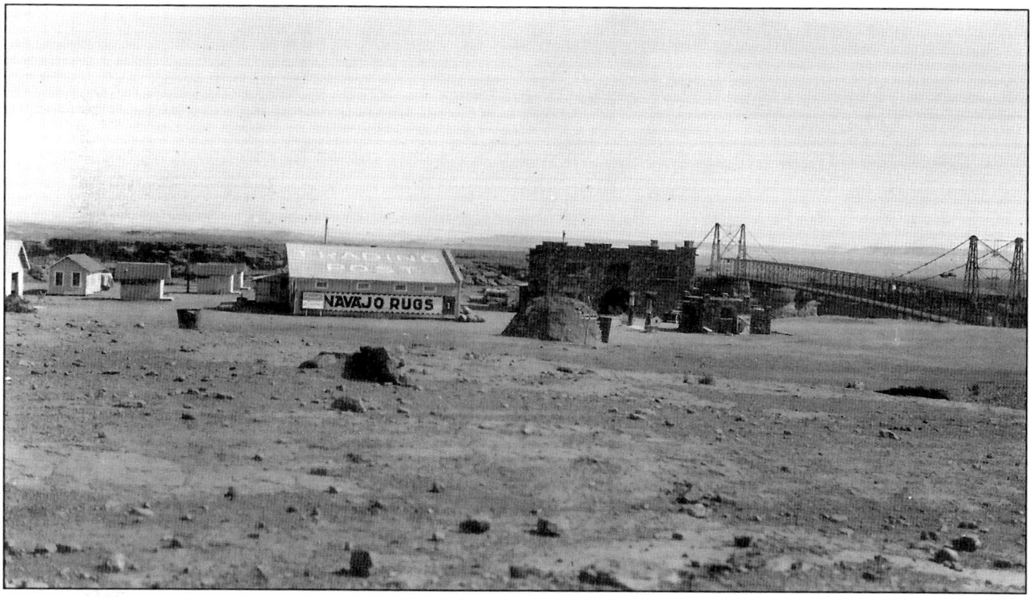

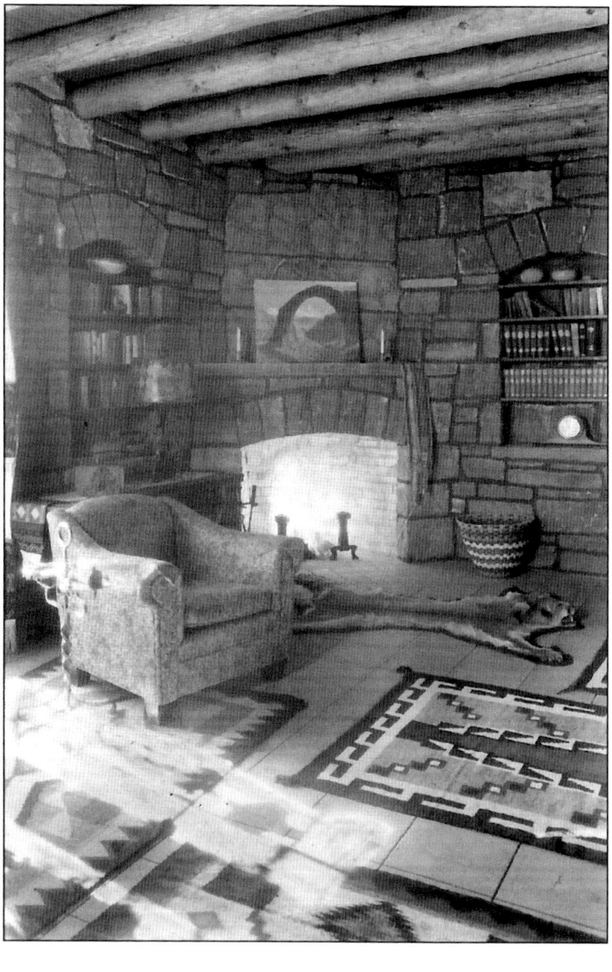

Samuel Preston built Cameron Trading Post in 1910 when construction started on a one-lane bridge over the Little Colorado River. Hubert Richardson enlarged the store, but in 1925, his nephew Gladwell visited and described the post as "a drafty, wooden store building and four small, one-room-shack cabins overlooking the bare river canyon. Not only did the cool weather turn colder, but the Navajos' 14 kinds of wind blew downriver all night long." In later years, the lobby at Cameron Trading Post, left, was inviting and comfortable, decorated with Navajo rugs and baskets. A striking painting of Rainbow Bridge hangs above the fireplace.

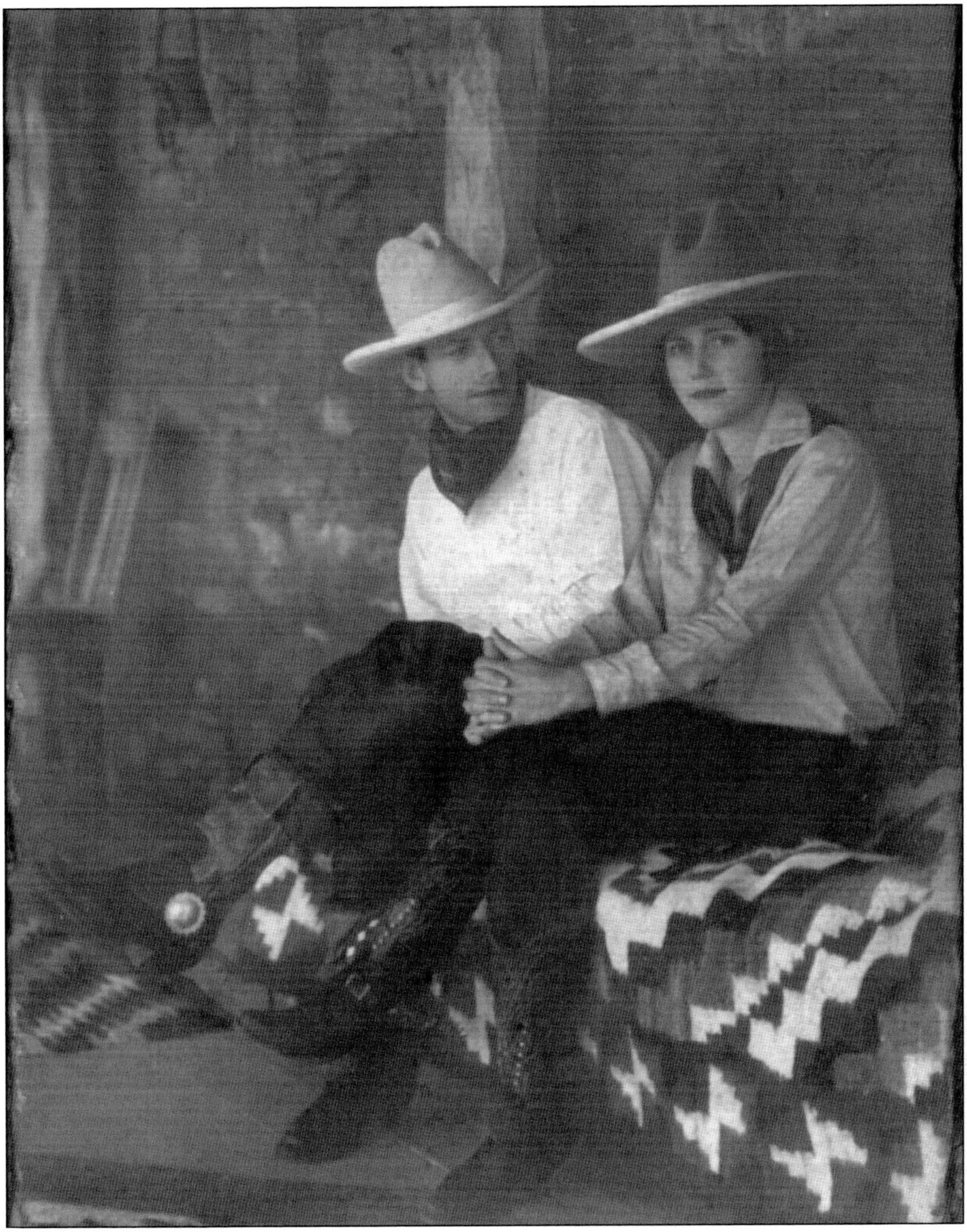

Two of the several managers of Cameron Trading Post were Stanton and Ida Mae Borum. Ida Mae was known to always wear a wide-brimmed hat and Navajo jewelry, including a silver-and-turquoise squash blossom necklace. In 1926, preacher Shine Smith married Wes and Billie Case in the middle of the bridge across the Little Colorado River, and not a single automobile had to be stopped during the ceremony. Many famous people visited Cameron; the guest registers were signed by Zane Grey, Errol Flynn, and John Wayne, among others. Today, Cameron Trading Post thrives as a popular tourist stop with a restaurant, hotel, gallery, and gift shop. (Courtesy of Old Trails Museum.)

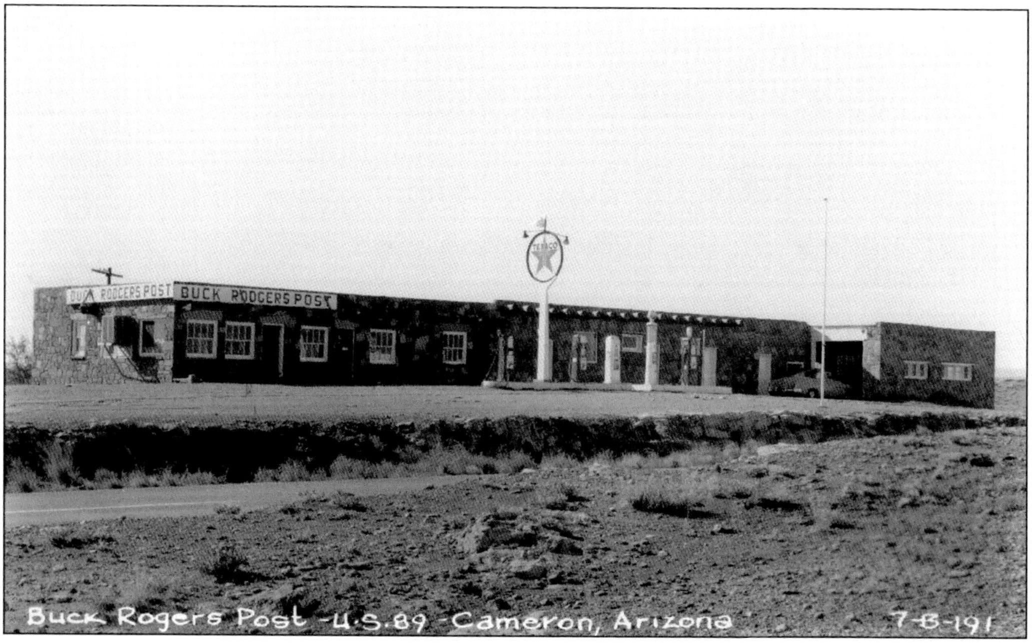

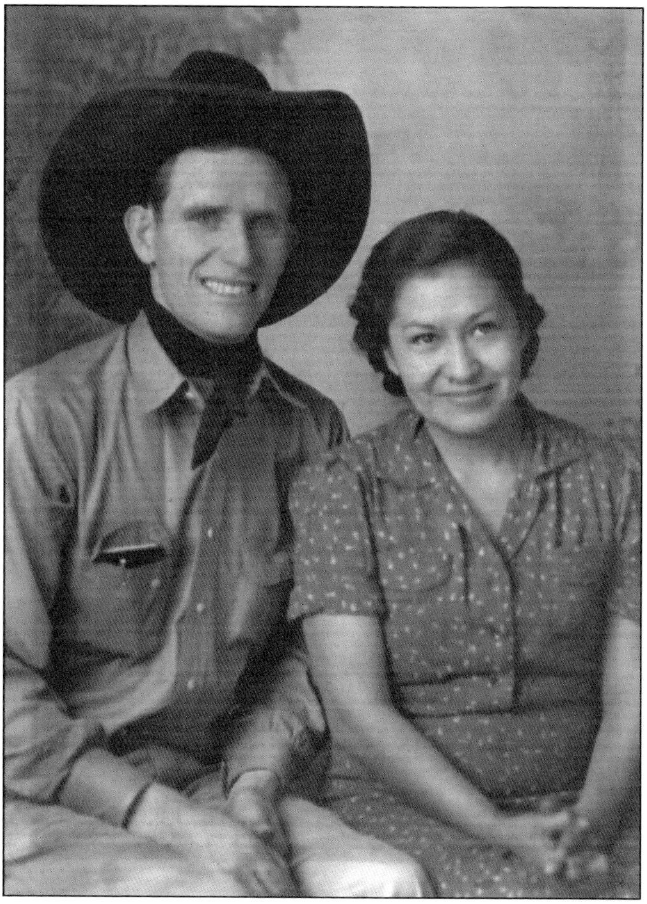

Buck Rodgers began building his trading post in 1936, and while it was under construction, he lived in a tent. The store was located on Highway 89, fifty miles north of Flagstaff, at the junction with Highway 64 leading to the east entrance of the Grand Canyon. Buck was from Texas, but his wife, Betty, was Navajo and also the foster daughter of Kayenta traders John and Louisa Wetherill. There was a lawsuit when the government tried to take the store from Buck and Betty, but the Rodgers prevailed because Betty was Navajo. Betty's daughter remarked that her mother's heritage kept them from being evicted. Buck and Betty had five children, and growing up, they all helped in the store. Buck Rodgers Trading Post had a hotel for tourists, groceries, and hand-pumped gasoline tanks. (Above, courtesy of Tom Collins; left, courtesy of Harvey Leake.)

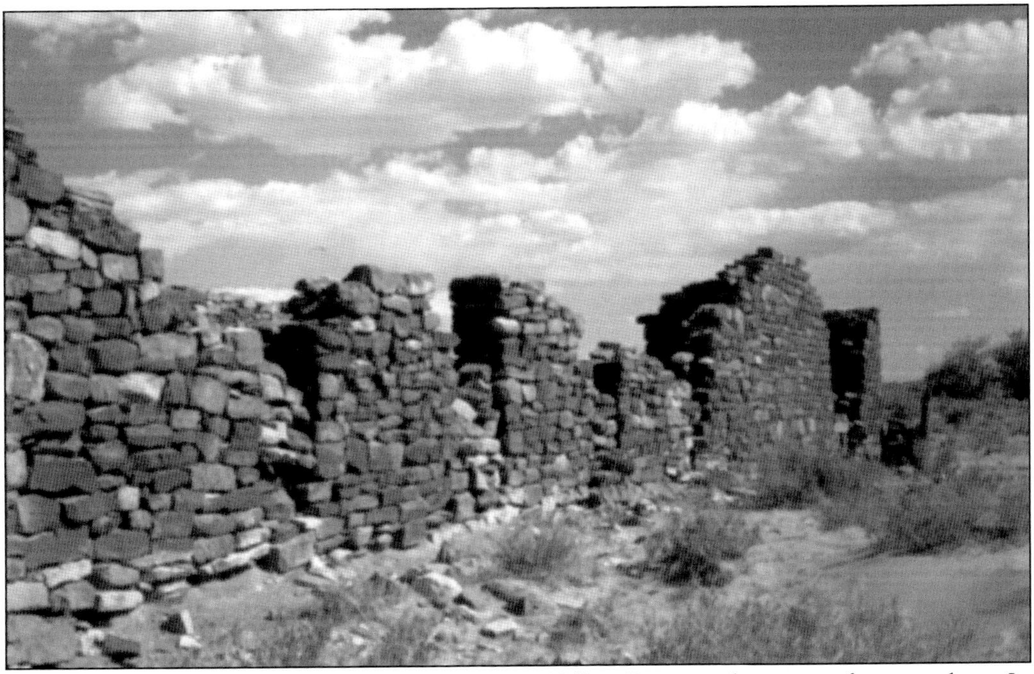

In 1876, John Bigalowe operated the first store at Willow Springs, closing it a few years later. In 1885, George McAdams, partnering with the Babbitt Brothers Mercantile Company, reestablished the post, which was in operation for the next 20 years. Willow Springs Trading Post was located just off of Highway 89, north of the turnoff to Tuba City and below Moenave. The post was located along the ancient Hopi Salt Trail, as well as the Honeymoon Trail, the route used by Mormon settlers in Arizona traveling north to St. George, Utah, to have their marriages solemnized in the Mormon temple. Both Hopis and Mormons left inscriptions on the nearby boulders.

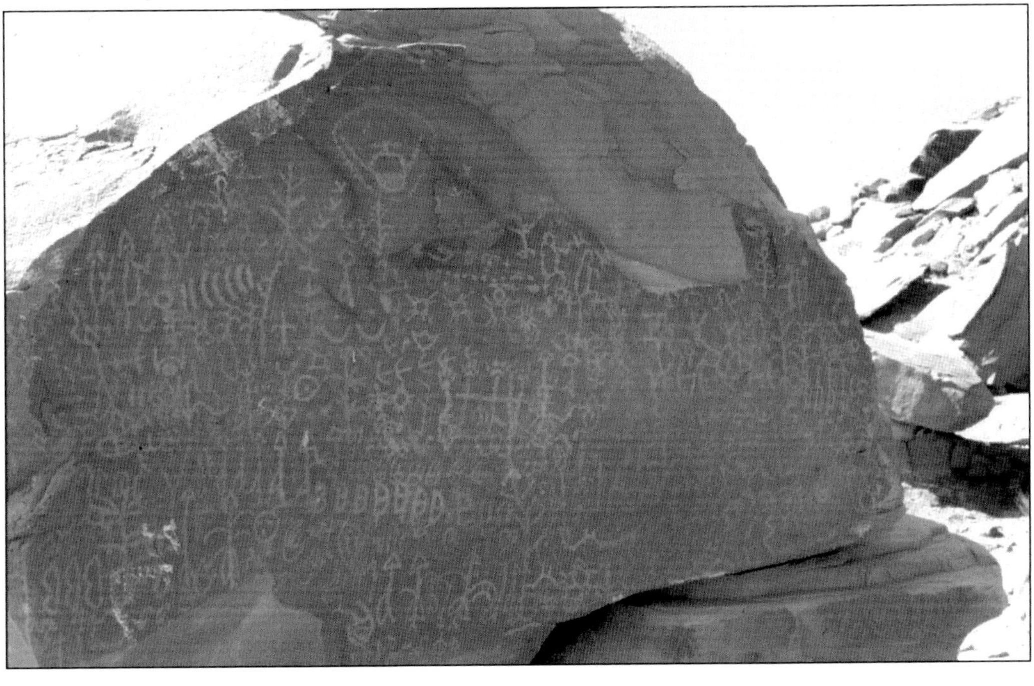

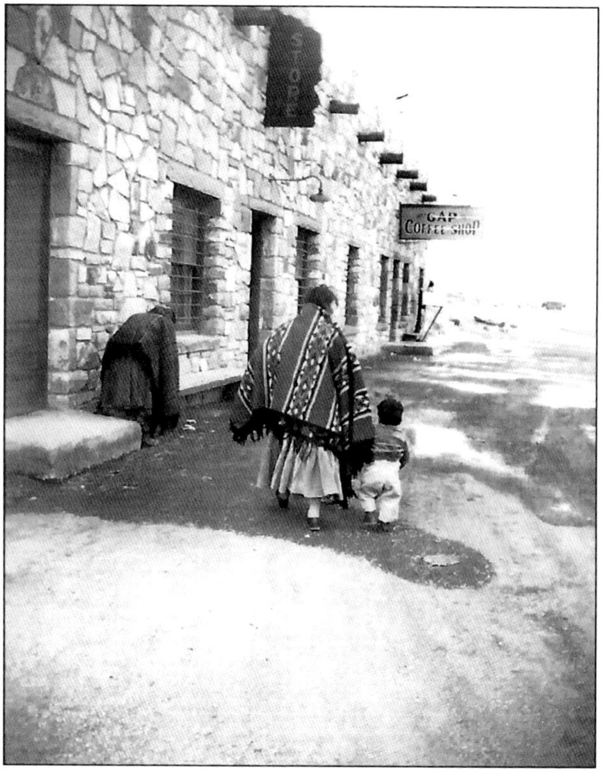

The Gap Trading Post was named for a nearby break in the Echo Cliffs and was originally operated in buildings abandoned by copper miners. Anglo traders J.C. and Laraine Brown and Joe Lee bought the store in 1921. According to a 1940 *Desert Magazine* article, J.C. was known as Hosteen Bitzeen, "Thin Man," and Laraine was "Thin Man's Fat Squaw [*sic*]." In 1924, a Hollywood film company asked the traders to find 300 Navajos to appear in *The Last Frontier.* The Navajo actors were paid every night with three $1 bills, and every evening, there would be a crowd of Navajos waiting outside the store to spend their wages. Soon, there were so many single bills that Lee nailed a sack to the wall to hold them. Below, Myles Headrick trades with Navajo customers. (Left, courtesy of Martin Link; below, courtesy of Edythe Klopping.)

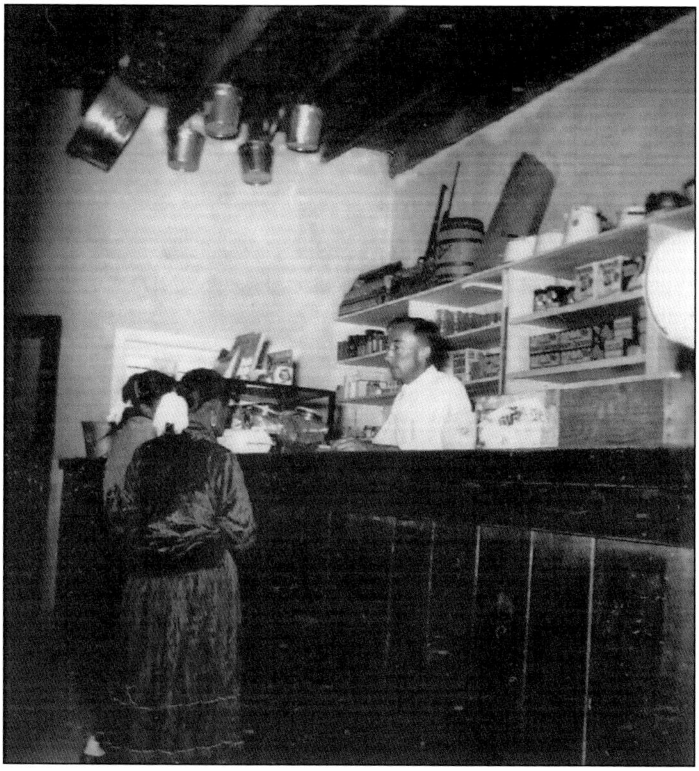

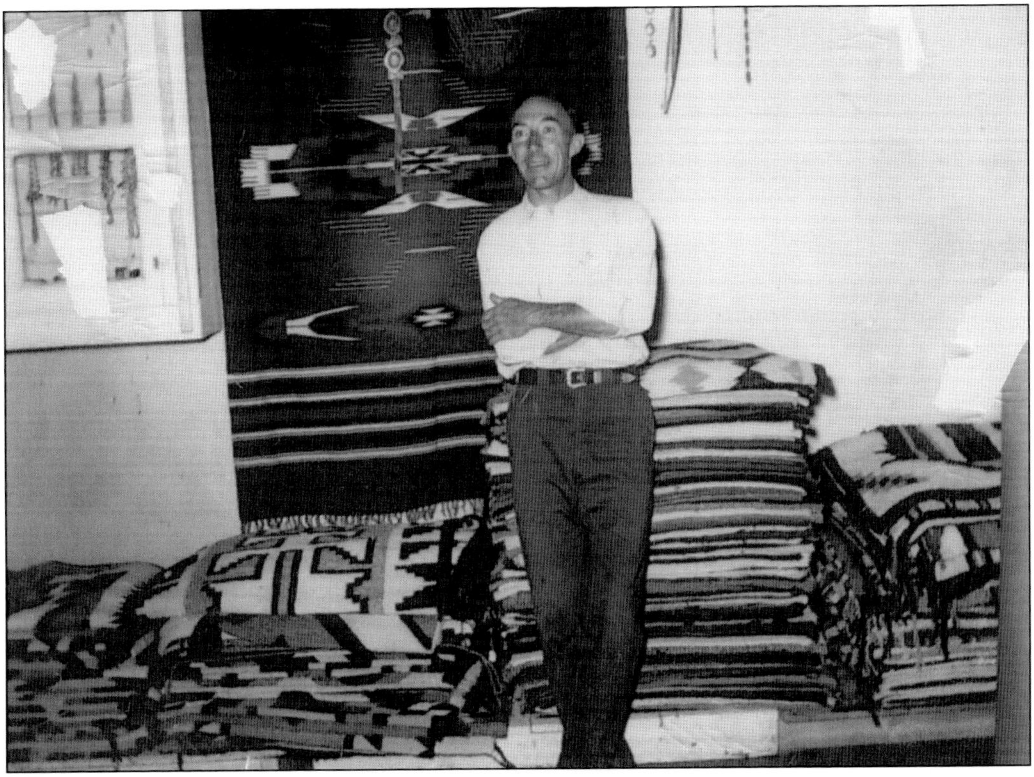

Myles and Doris Headrick managed The Gap Trading Post beginning in 1947, moving there from Little Red Lake Trading Post. Navajo weavers at The Gap are known for their tree of life rugs. Above, Myles is standing in the trading post rug room. The Headrick family photograph, at right, shows, from top to bottom, Myles, Myles "Bob," Doris, Edythe, and Kenneth. The Headrick children loved growing up with the freedom of the trading post setting. They walked on homemade stilts, rode bikes on the unpaved Highway 89 in front of the store, and explored the hills behind their house. (Both, courtesy of Edythe Klopping.)

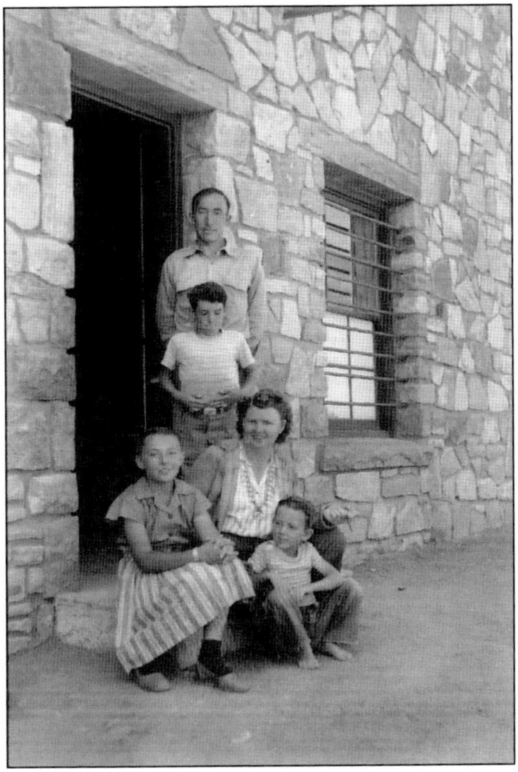

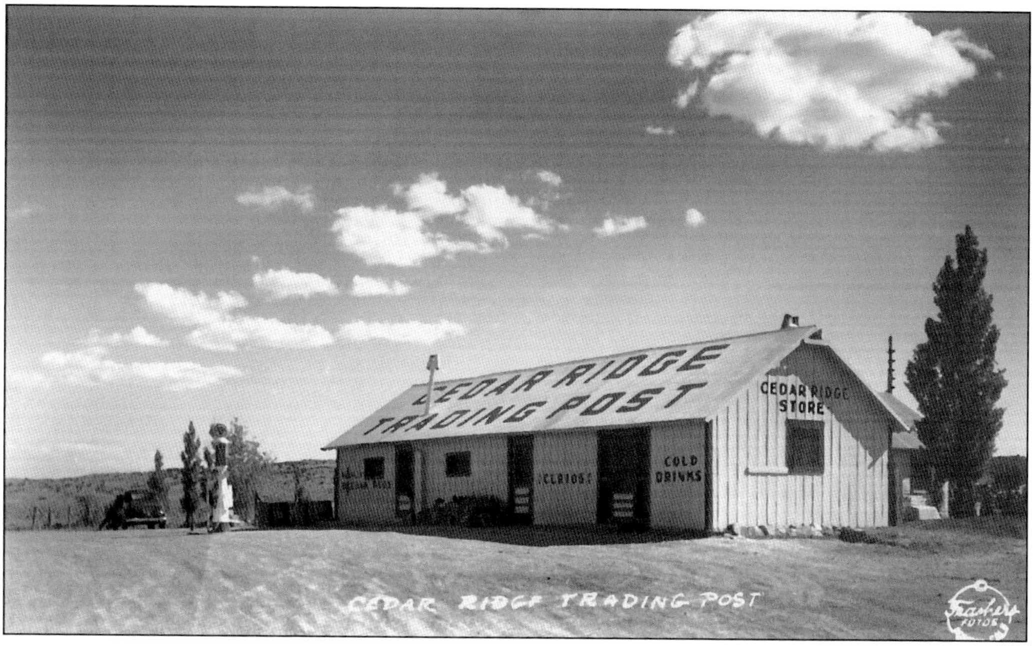

Cedar Ridge Trading Post was seven miles north of The Gap Trading Post on Highway 89. The post was founded by C.H. Algert in 1890 and later purchased by Babbitt Brothers. Keith and Hazel Warren managed the store from 1935 to 1949. Cedar Ridge was a "dry post"; it depended on rainwater runoff from the store's tin roof, as well as water hauled from The Gap. Shonto trader Elizabeth Hegemann referred to the store as "the last stop in civilization for a long, long way north." There were four guest hogans behind the store. At the front door, Hazel built a stone flowerbed that needed no water as it was made with colorful petrified wood. In the photograph below, Hazel and Keith Warren, right, pose with friends Betty, Earl, and Ronny Dean. Cedar Ridge Trading Post closed about 1990. Nothing is left today. (Above, courtesy of Frashers Fotos Collection.)

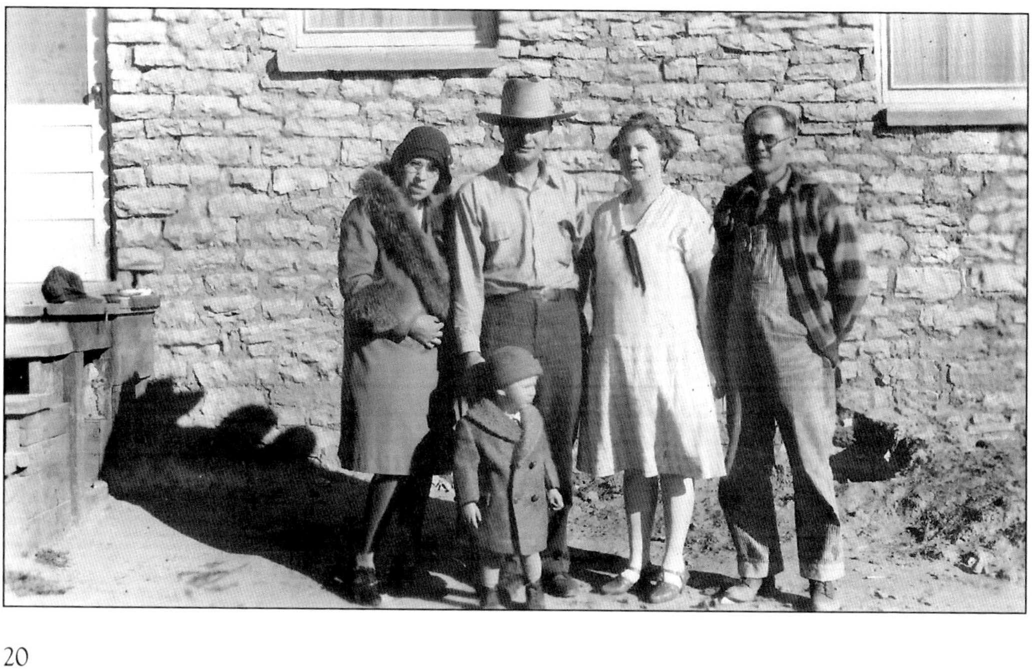

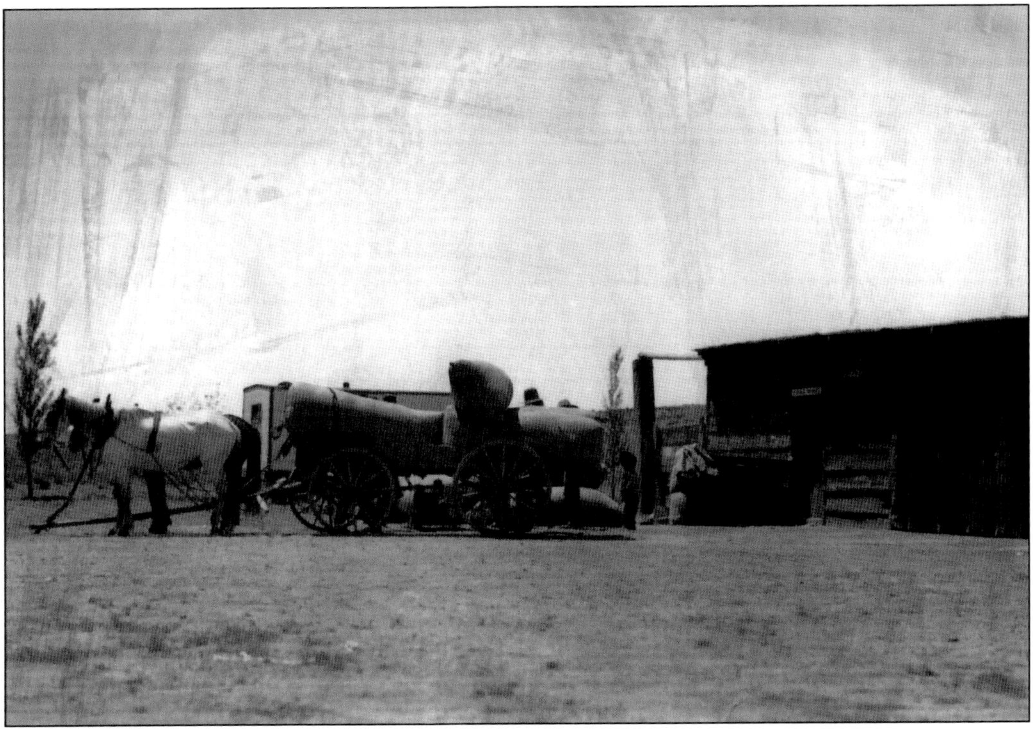

In this 1920s photograph by Harmon Percy Marble, wool bags are being loaded onto a wagon. This early photograph is of the original Cedar Ridge Trading Post that was three miles southeast of the store pictured on the previous page. The nearest railhead for shipping the wool was 90 miles to the south at Flagstaff. Below, wool bags are being loaded onto a railcar. The geometric patterns on two bags in the center foreground indicate that they are made from Navajo rug weavings or Pendleton blankets. (Below, courtesy of Tom Collins.)

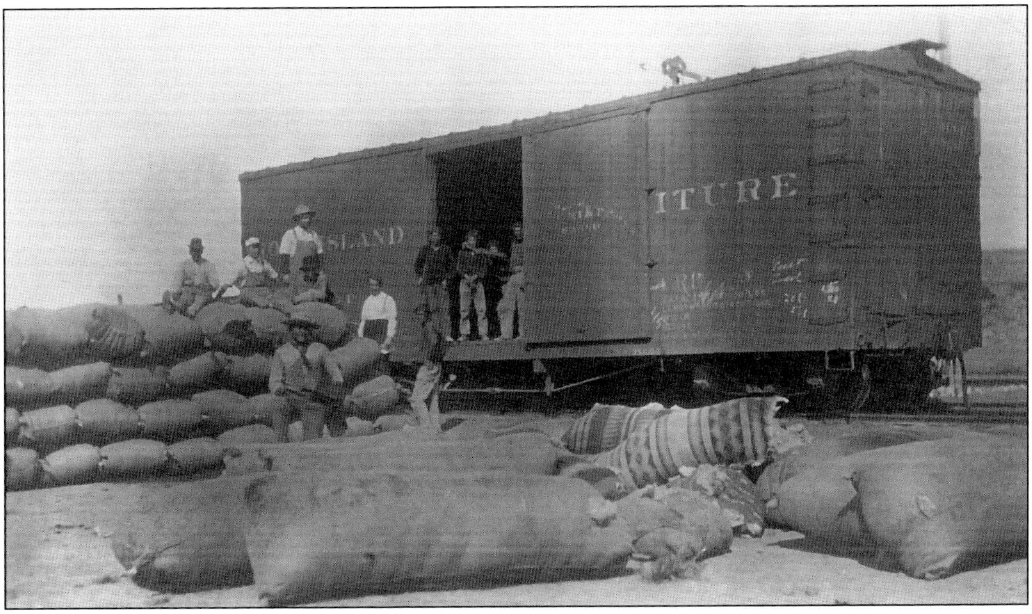

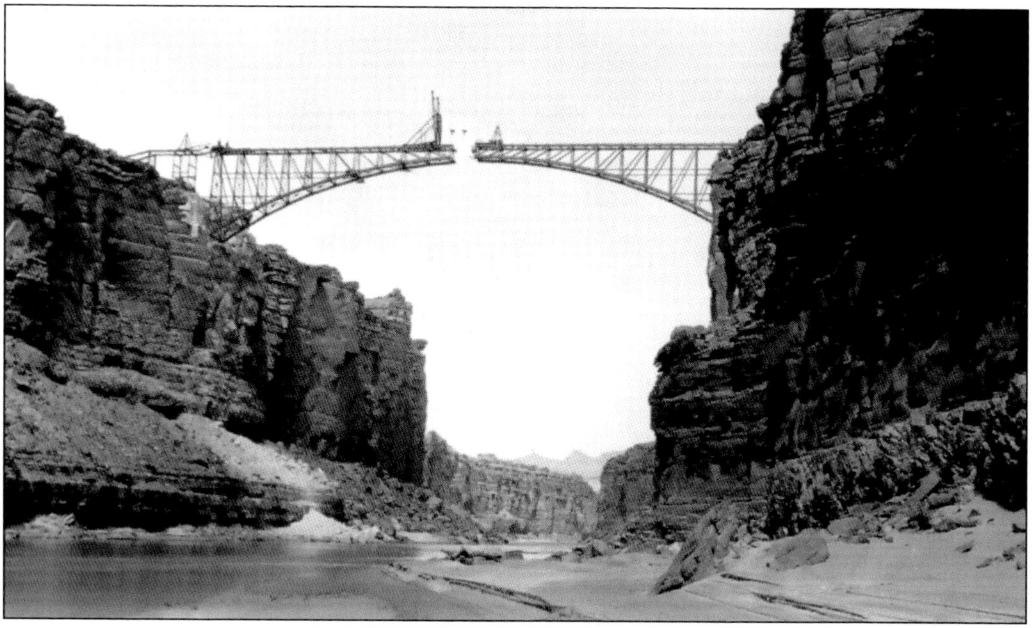

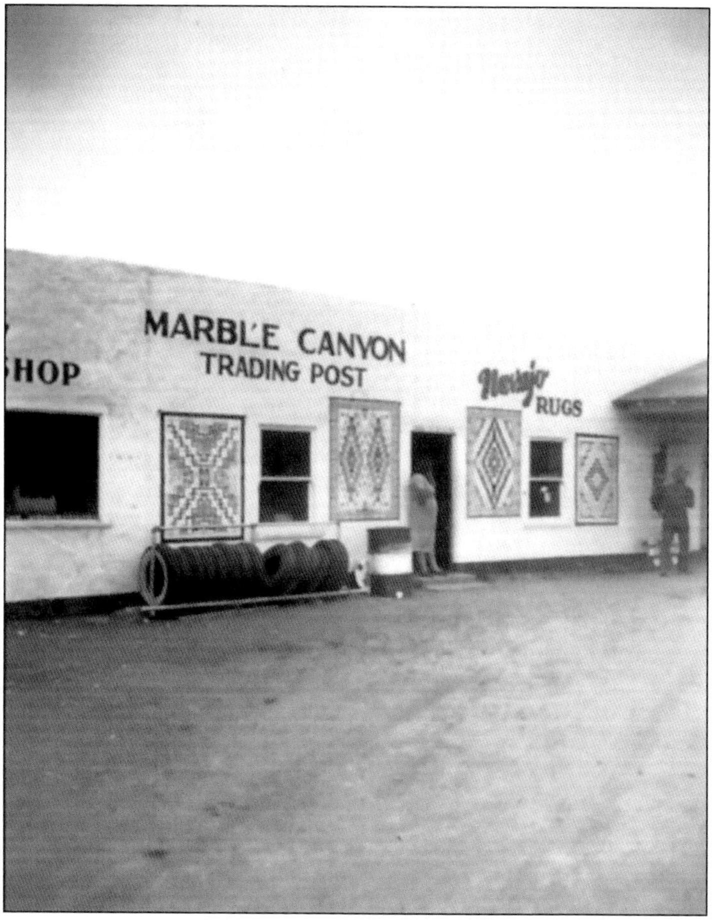

David Lowrey built Marble Canyon Trading Post in 1928 at the base of the Vermillion Cliffs on the western side of the Colorado River. Navajo Bridge, built in 1929, was the highest bridge of its type in the world. Until completion of the bridge, travelers had to make the often dangerous river crossing at Lee's Ferry, a few miles upriver. Lorenzo Hubbell Jr. acquired Marble Canyon Lodge and Trading Post in 1937. Sadly, the historic store burned in 2013. (Both, courtesy of Martin Link.)

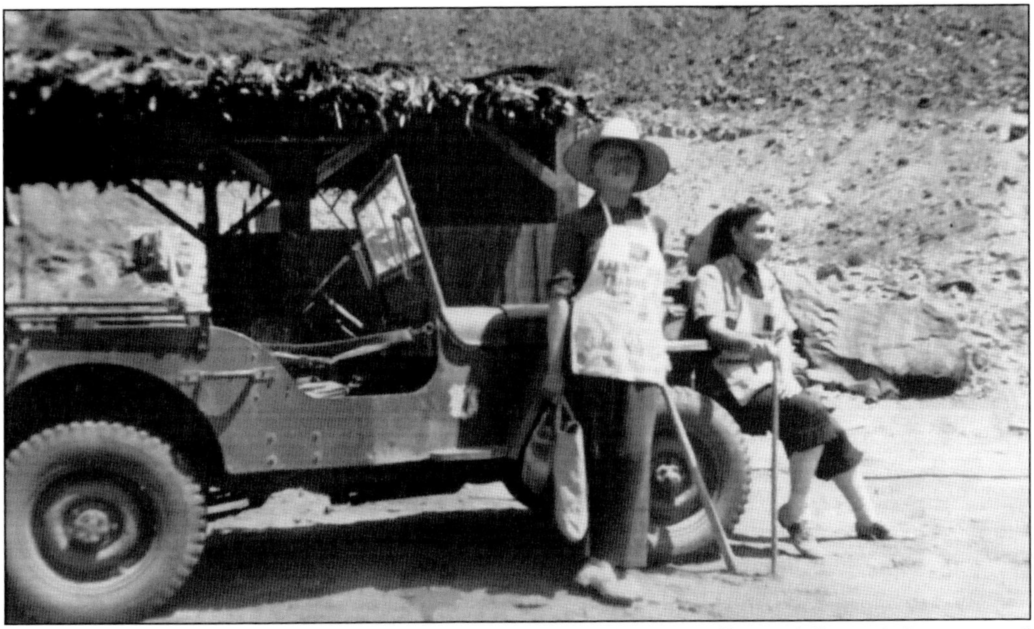

English artist Nora Cundell loved Marble Canyon and the Vermillion Cliffs, and she returned many times from her home in England. Cundell's 1940 book *Unsentimental Journey* is a tribute to the beautiful country. Nora (left) and Christina Klohr are ready to spend the day painting at Marble Canyon. After her death in 1948, Nora's ashes were scattered near Lee's Ferry. (Courtesy of Bernice Klohr.)

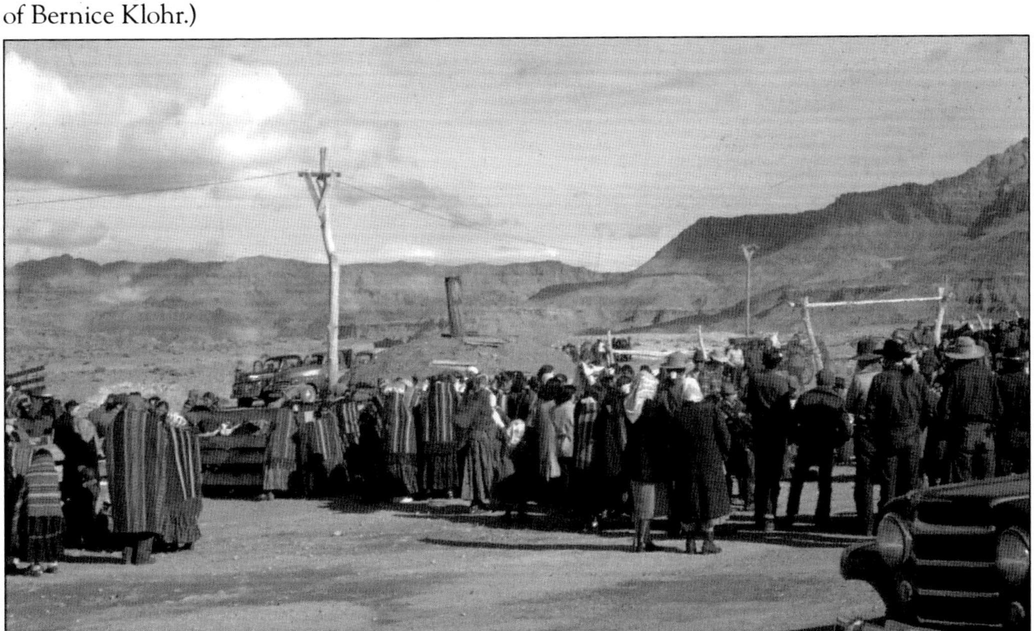

Preacher Shine Smith organized Christmas parties in various Navajo communities in the 1950s and 1960s. Solicitations for donations of money, toys, and clothing appeared in *Arizona Highways* and *Desert Magazine*, and the gifts poured in. Thousands of Navajos would gather at the appointed trading post where gifts were distributed, and everyone enjoyed a huge feast, as seen at this Christmas party near Marble Canyon Trading Post. (Courtesy of Lois McMindes.)

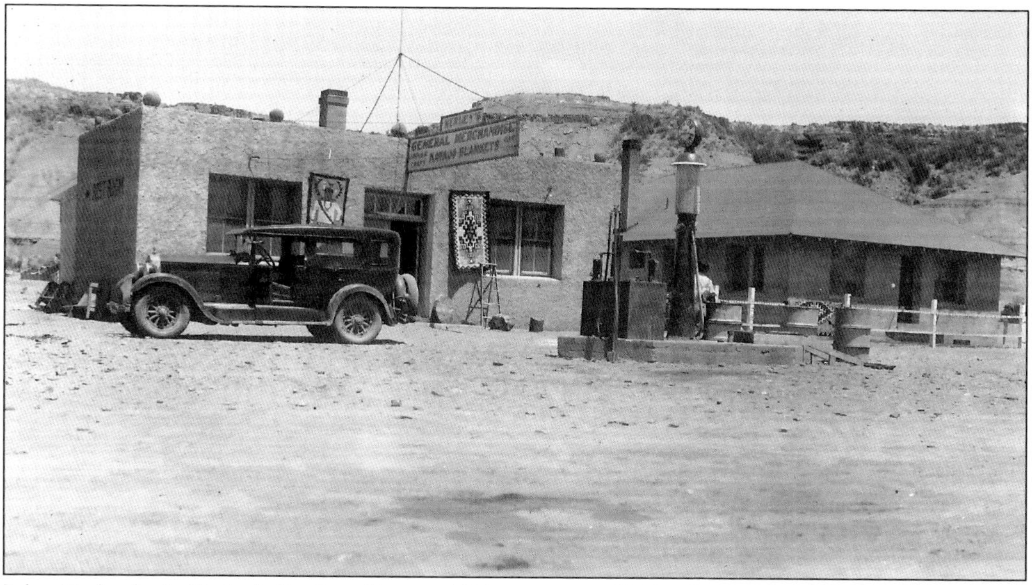

John Kerley built Kerley's Trading Post in 1921 just west of Tuba City, in an area below the mesa, known as Kerley's Valley. The old road to Tuba City veered off from Highway 89 and followed Moencopi Wash, going through Pumpkin Valley. The area was strewn with round rocks that resembled pumpkins. They are mostly all gone now, but several can be seen on the roof of Kerley's original trading post. A larger store was built in front of Kerley's and was sold in 1954 to Warner Van Keuren, who renamed it Van Trading Company. Van's still operates with a small grocery store and dry goods including wool for weavers. Van's is also one of the few stores on the reservation that takes pawn. There is a walk-in vault filled with pawn jewelry behind the counter, and several times a year, there are auctions of pawn items that have not been redeemed.

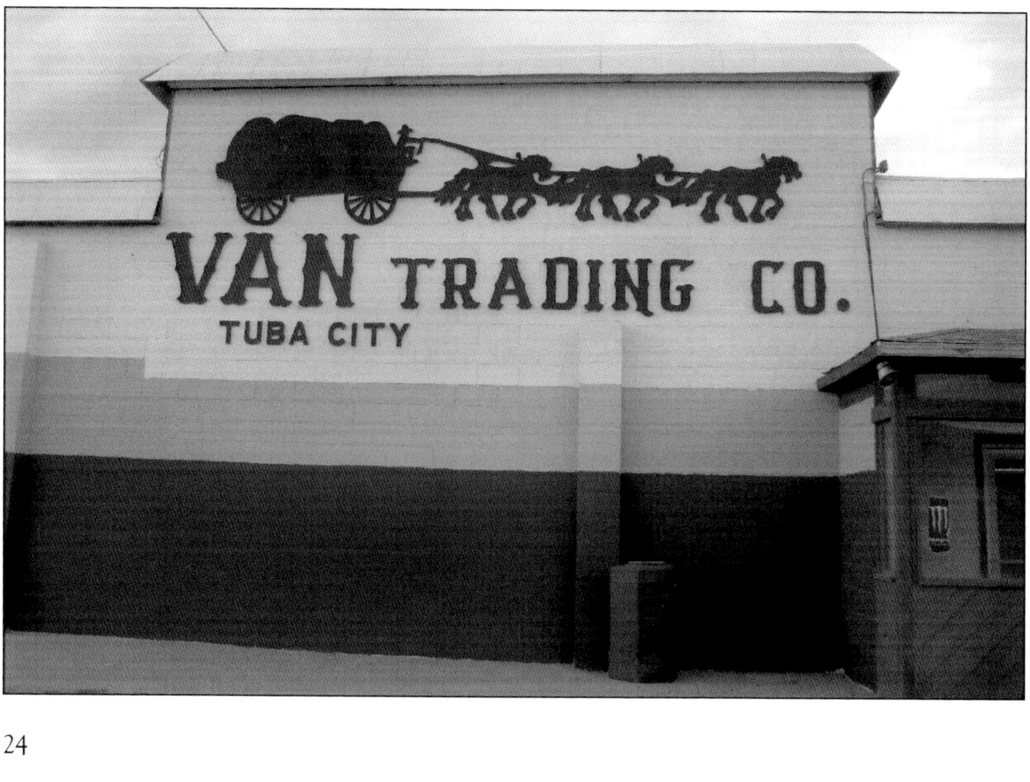

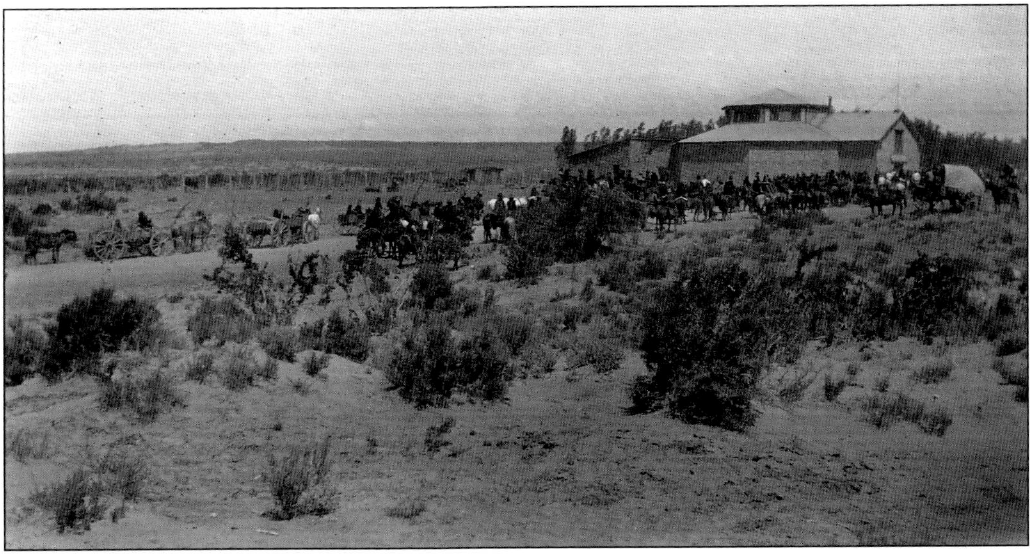

Charles H. Algert established Tuba Trading Post in 1885. The area was traditionally inhabited by Navajos as well as Hopis who farmed the area around the Moencopi Wash. As a young man working in his first job at the trading post, Carl Steckel related that one day he found a bull snake sleeping on a store shelf. Steckel killed the snake but was later rebuked by the trader who told him that snakes were useful in controlling pack rats in the store. About 1920, a two-story, hogan-shaped addition was built onto the original store using local sandstone and logs from the San Francisco Mountains. Tourists visited the post and stayed at the guest lodge. Babbitt Brothers purchased the post in 1905 and operated it until 1999, when it was sold to the Navajo Nation. Tuba Trading Post is now listed in the National Register of Historic Places.

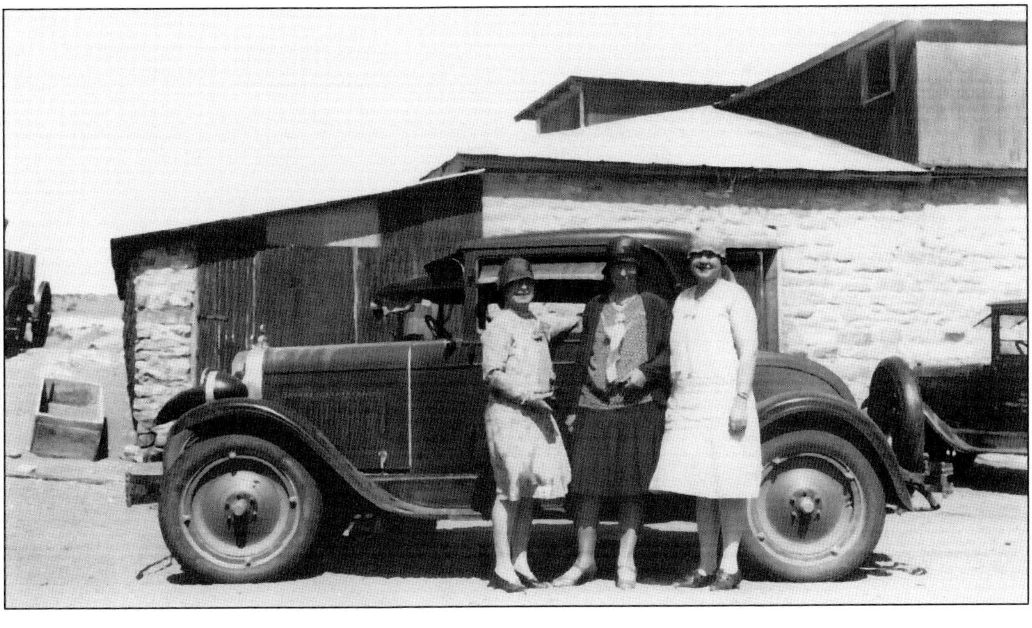

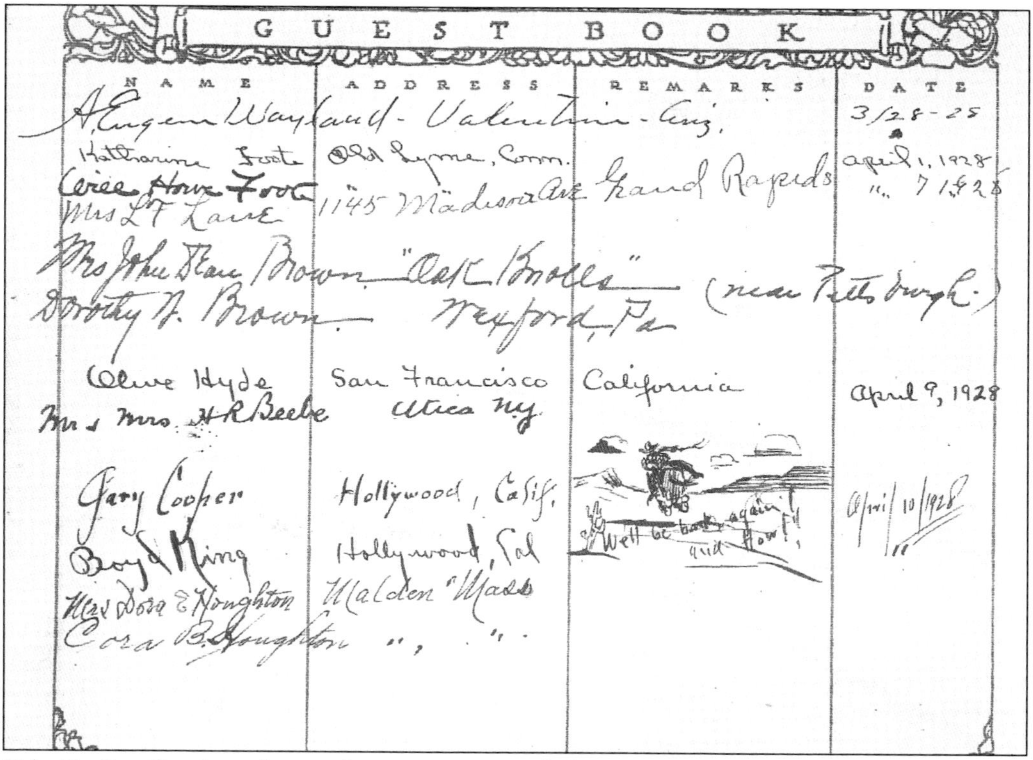

GUEST BOOK

NAME	ADDRESS	REMARKS	DATE
A. Eugene Wayland	Valentine, Ariz.		3/28-25
Katharine Foote	Old Lyme, Conn.		April 1, 1928
Mrs L. F. Lane	1145 Madison Ave	Grand Rapids	
Mrs John Dean Brown	"Oak Knolls"	(near Pittsburgh)	
Dorothy N. Brown	Wexford, Pa		
Olive Hyde	San Francisco	California	April 9, 1928
Mr & Mrs. H. R. Beebe	Utica N.Y.		
Gary Cooper	Hollywood, Calif.		April 10/1928
Boyd King	Hollywood, Cal		
Mrs Dora E. Houghton	Malden Mass		
Cora B. Houghton	" "		

Tuba Trading Post hosted many famous visitors, including Zane Grey and Theodore Roosevelt. A page from the 1928 guest book is signed and embellished by actor Gary Cooper. Arlis Cornielson operated Tuba Trading Post for Babbitt Brothers in the 1950s and 1960s. In this photograph, Cornielson (right) holds a Storm-pattern Navajo rug; the man on the left is unidentified. Storm patterns were thought to have been designed by a trader at Red Lake, located 40 miles northeast of Tuba City, around 1900. This design was patterned on a sandpainting and usually has a central rectangle with lines representing lightning radiating out to the four corners. The center is said to symbolize a hogan, emergence, or the center of the world, and the squares in each corner are the four scared mountains of Navajo mythology. (Above, courtesy of Mary May Bailey; below, courtesy of Lois McMindes.)

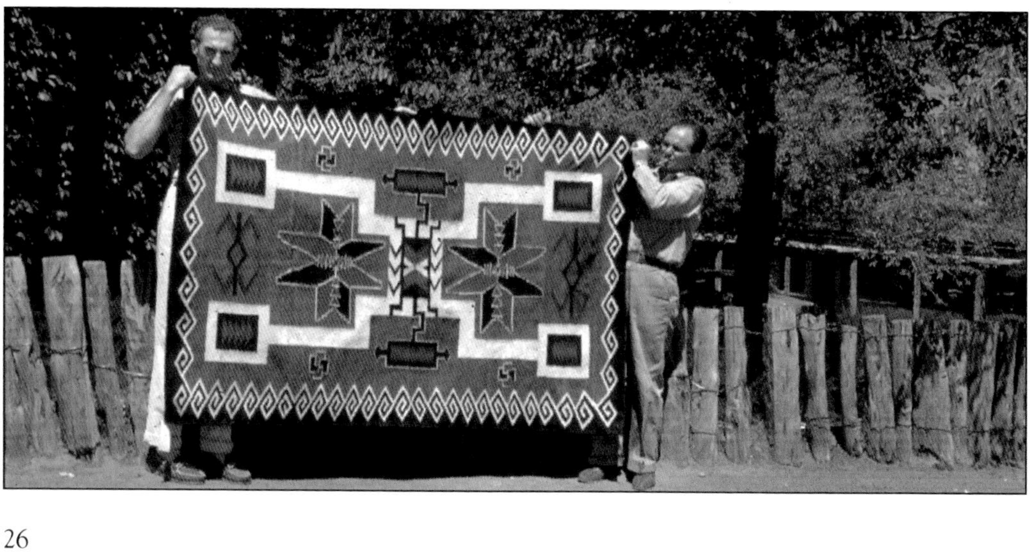

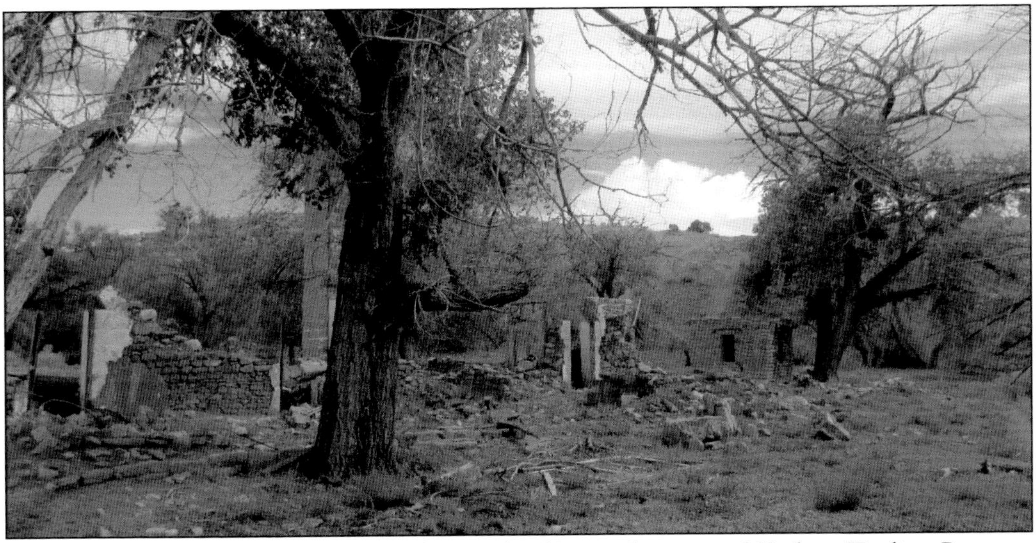

Located off of Highway 98 and 34 miles south of Page, the original Kaibito Trading Post was established by C.D. Richardson in 1914. Julia and Ralph Jones and their family operated Kaibito from 1934 to 1962. Bags of wool, below, from the 1953 spring wool season are ready to be loaded into a wagon for shipment. The original Kaibito post was abandoned when a new store was built in 1987, closer to the center of the community. Owned by Stan Patterson, the current building is a large grocery store carrying items used in a rural Navajo community, including wheelbarrows, steel buckets and tubs, tools, kerosene lamps, hand-turned corn grinders, and shelves of colorful Pendleton blankets. (Below, courtesy of Old Trails Museum.)

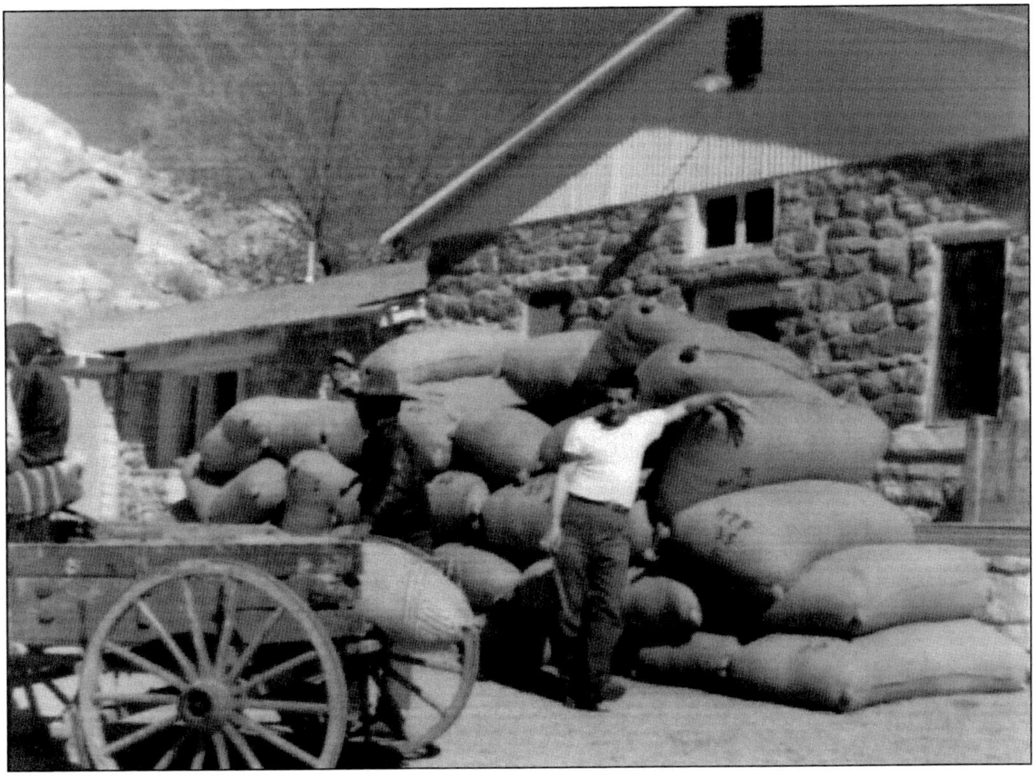

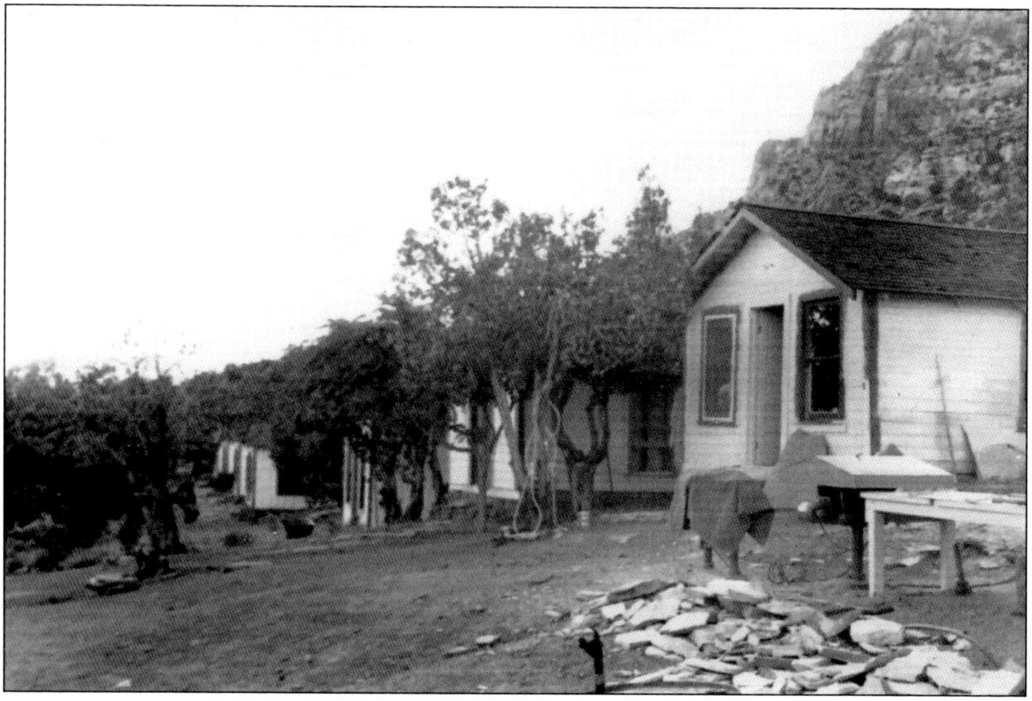

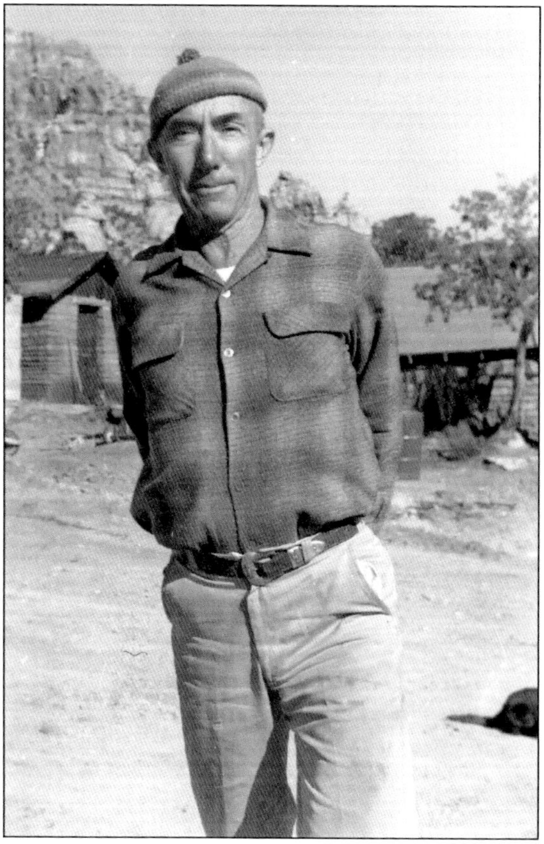

S.I. Richardson built Rainbow Lodge and Trading Post in 1924, making Rainbow Bridge accessible to tourists. The post was remote; the road from Red Lake was just a vague track. Richardson dabbed white paint on rocks as a guide for drivers. The warehouse at the store was filled with merchandise every fall. When snow came, the roads were impassible, so the trader and his family prepared for a long, solitary winter. Rainbow was part trading post and part departure point for tourists going on pack trips to Rainbow Bridge. In addition to the lodge and store, there were eight guest cabins. For many years, Barry Goldwater was a partner in the enterprise with Katherine and Bill Wilson. After their retirement, Myles Headrick, left, bought a half-interest. The business closed in 1957, and all that is left today are stone foundations. (Both, courtesy of Edythe Klopping.)

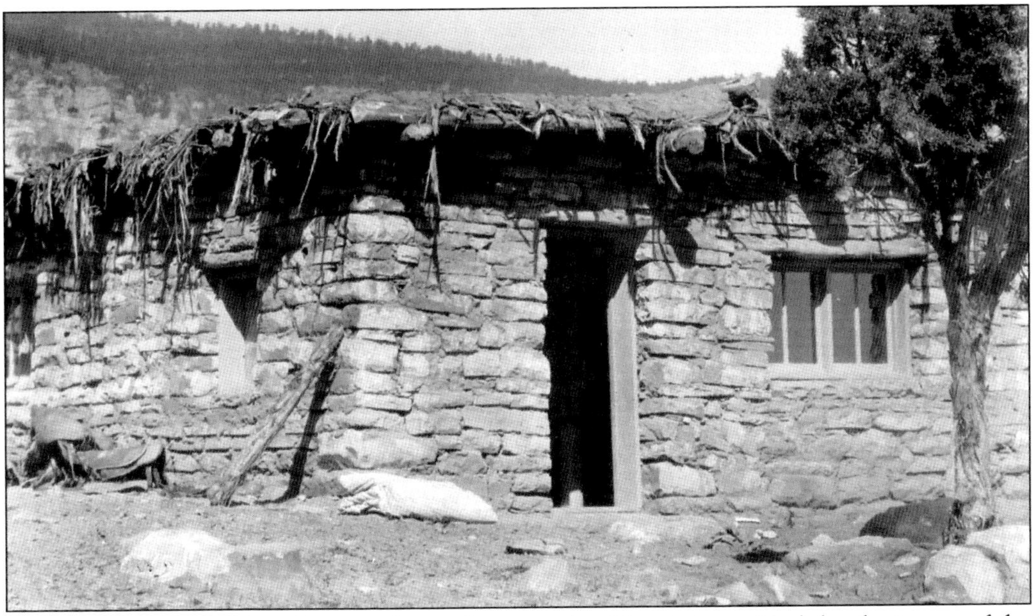

Navajo Mountain Trading Post was located just north of the Arizona-Utah border in one of the most remote corners of the Navajo Reservation. In 1928, Ben Wetherill came to this place that the Navajos call Teas-ya-toh, "Water under the Cottonwoods." The family lived in a tent with a brush shelter, and Ben constructed a stone building for the store. Below, in front of the brush structure are Louisa Wetherill (left), Myrle Wetherill, Ben's wife, and Frank Wyatt, an employee. In 1931, Ray Dunn took over the post. The store was enlarged, and living quarters were added. The Dunns were snowed in during the winters; they stocked provisions to last through the cold months, while Ray ran traplines. The Dunns left Navajo Mountain in 1937 in order to secure schooling for their children. (Both, courtesy of Harvey Leake.)

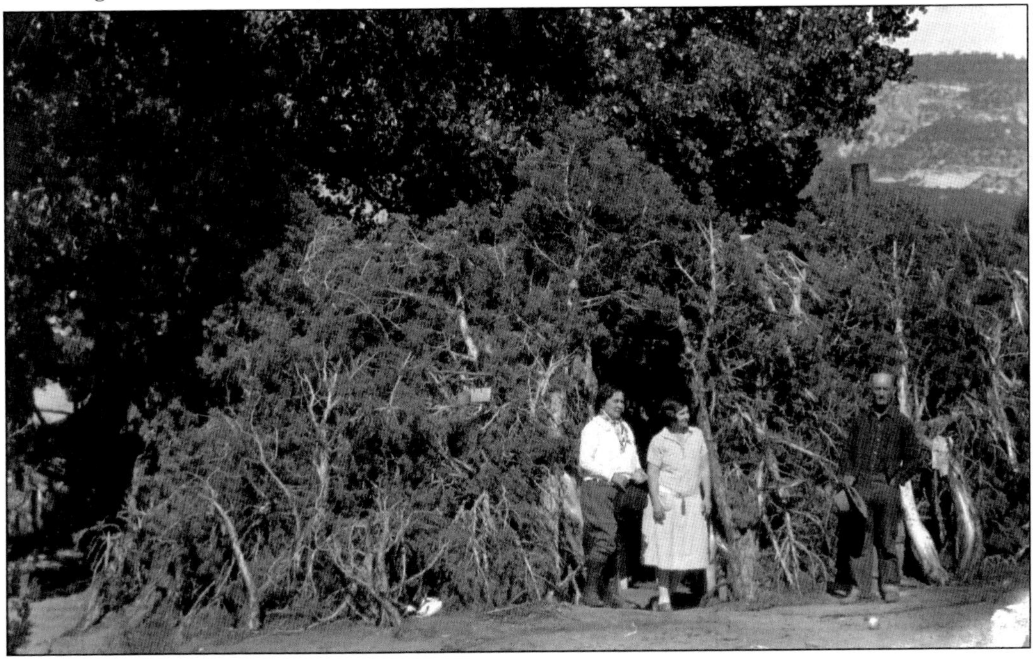

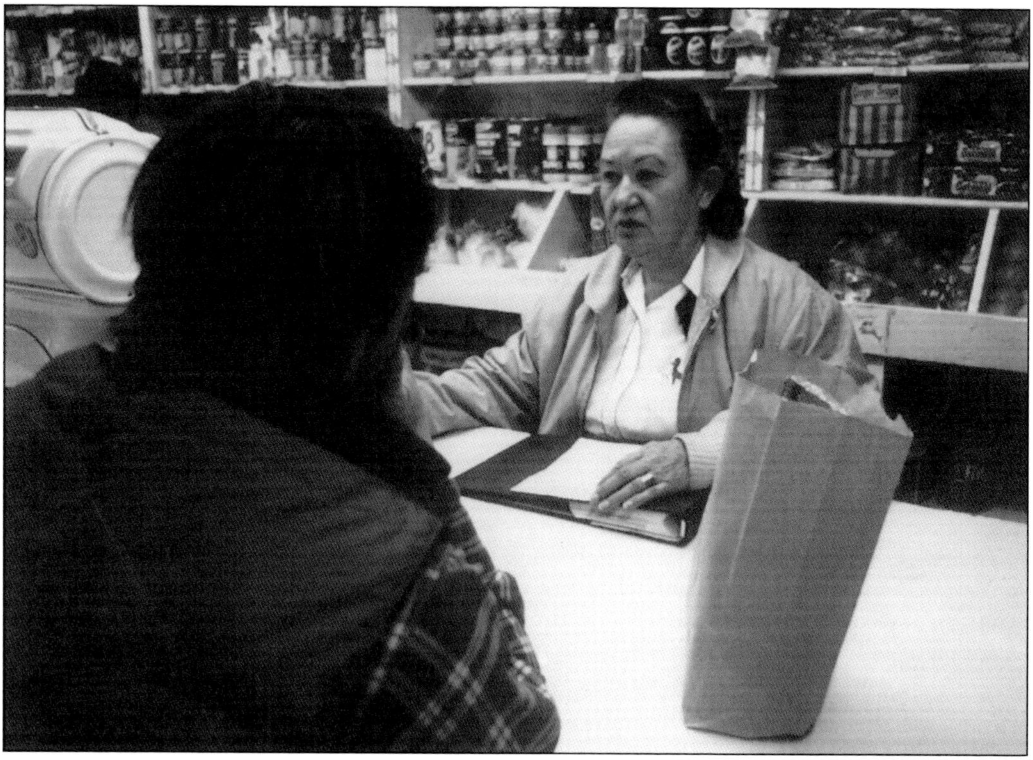

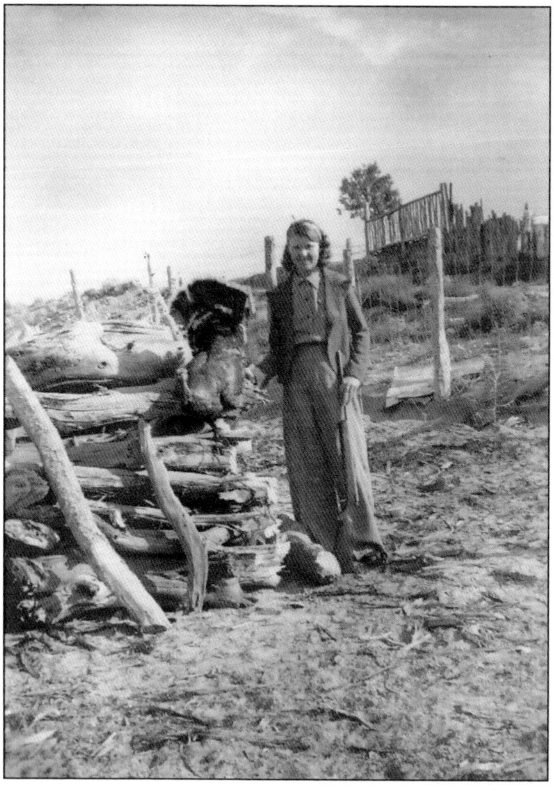

Madelene Dunn returned to Navajo Mountain in 1952 with her husband, Ralph Cameron. The post is featured in a *National Geographic* article that mentions their horseback trips to Rainbow Bridge. Madelene continued to operate the post after Ralph's death until she retired in 1979. The abandoned stone trading post at the end of a 20-mile dirt road still stands, but the small community remains isolated and remote. (Courtesy of Al and Margaret Grieve.)

Sometimes, trading posts were targets of attempted burglaries. Most stores had barred windows and heavy doors, and traders often had a rifle or handgun behind the counter to discourage any robbers. Doris Headrick, at Cow Springs in 1935, was an excellent markswoman, as seen in this photograph after a successful turkey hunt. One night at Little Red Lake, she ran off an intruder with a warning shot from her .32-caliber revolver. (Courtesy of Edythe Klopping.)

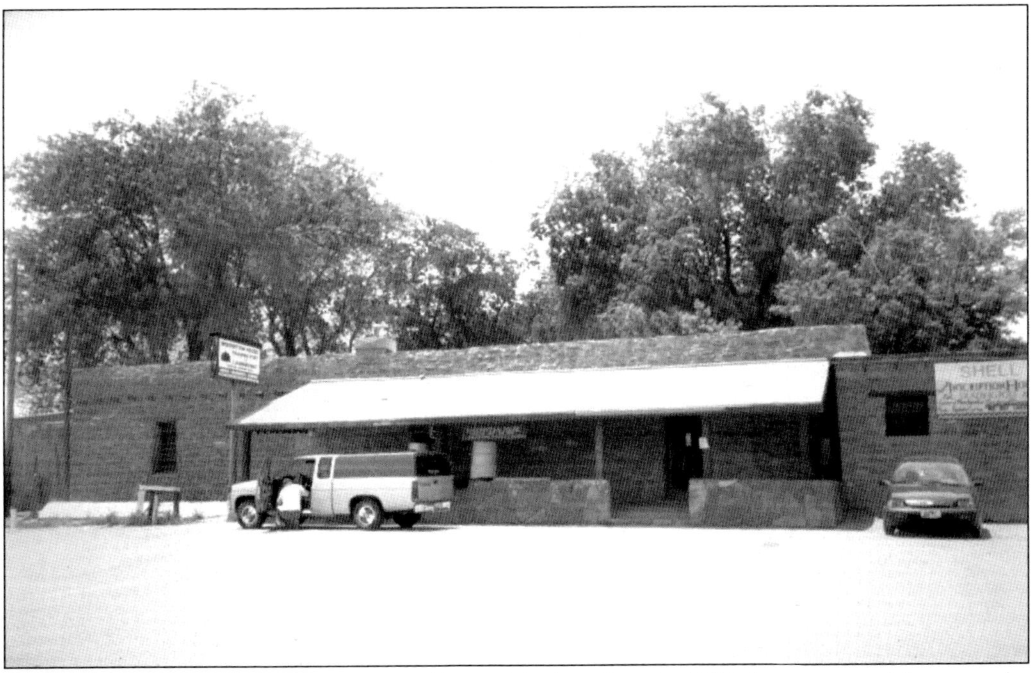

S.I. Richardson established Inscription House Trading Post in 1926. It was named for a nearby cliff dwelling, now a part of Navajo National Monument, as is Keet Seel, below. Inscription House also had guest cabins for tourists visiting Rainbow Bridge. The post is known as the home of the Navajo saddle blanket, called a "fuzzy," because these blankets were thick due to less cleaning and carding of the wool. In 1941, S.I.'s nephew Gladwell developed a more appealing blanket with a design in each corner. For those blankets, Richardson paid $2, and if there was a center design, the weaver got $2.50. He often bought 1,000 to 1,500 saddle blankets a month. After the war, rug styles at Inscription House Trading Post changed, with different breeds of sheep and wools available to weavers.

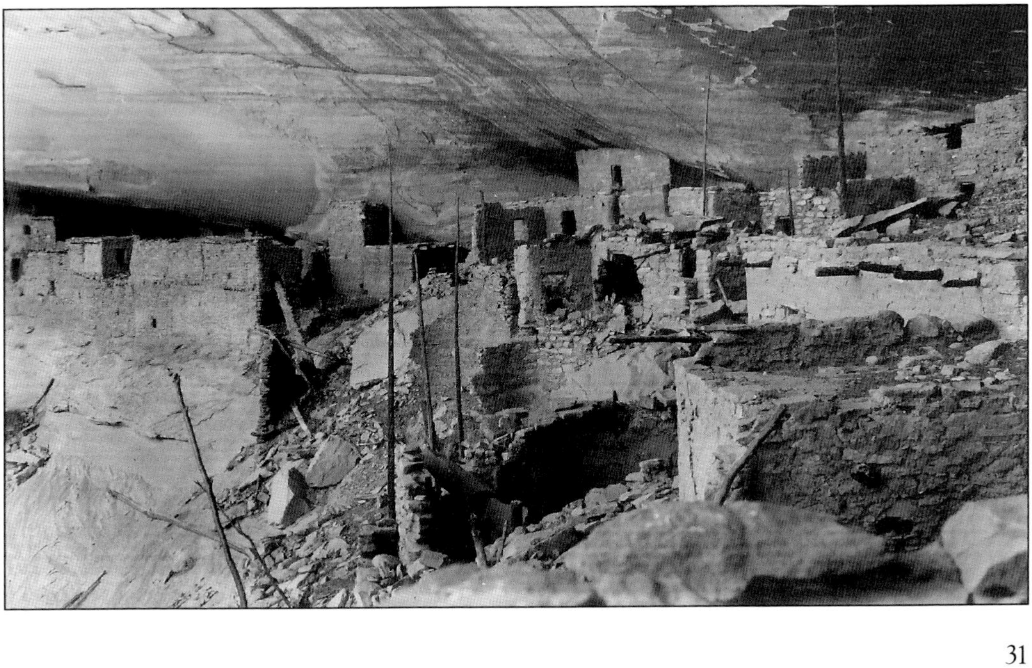

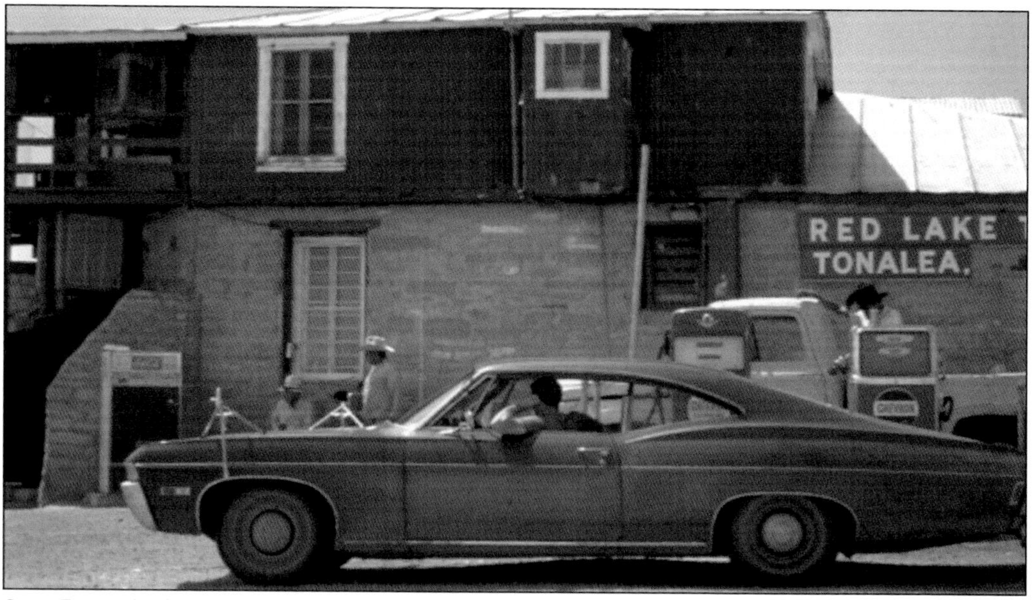

Sam Dittenhoffer bought Red Lake at Tonalea in 1888. The original log post was built in a dry lake, but shortly afterward spring flooding filled the lake so the post was moved to higher ground. Two years later, Dittenhoffer brought a lady home from Flagstaff, but shortly afterward, her admirer, who followed the couple to Red Lake, killed him in a poker game. When he died, Dittenhoffer was in debt to Babbitt Brothers, so they took over the post. This acquisition started the Babbitts in the trading post business. Floyd Boyle, a trader in the 1940s, told of a night when there was knocking at his door. A Navajo neighbor had died on the way home from Tuba City, and his family wanted Boyle to bury him. They also wanted Boyle to collect any money in his pockets. Because of Navajo fears about death, no one would touch the coins, but they took the $1.75 in trade. (Both, courtesy of Byron Hunter.)

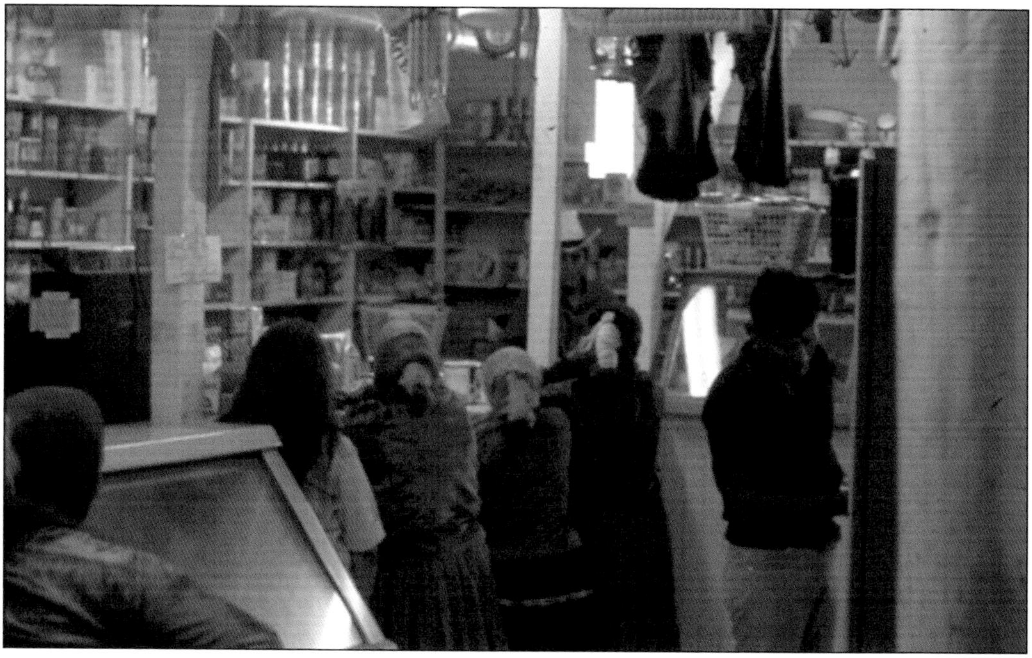

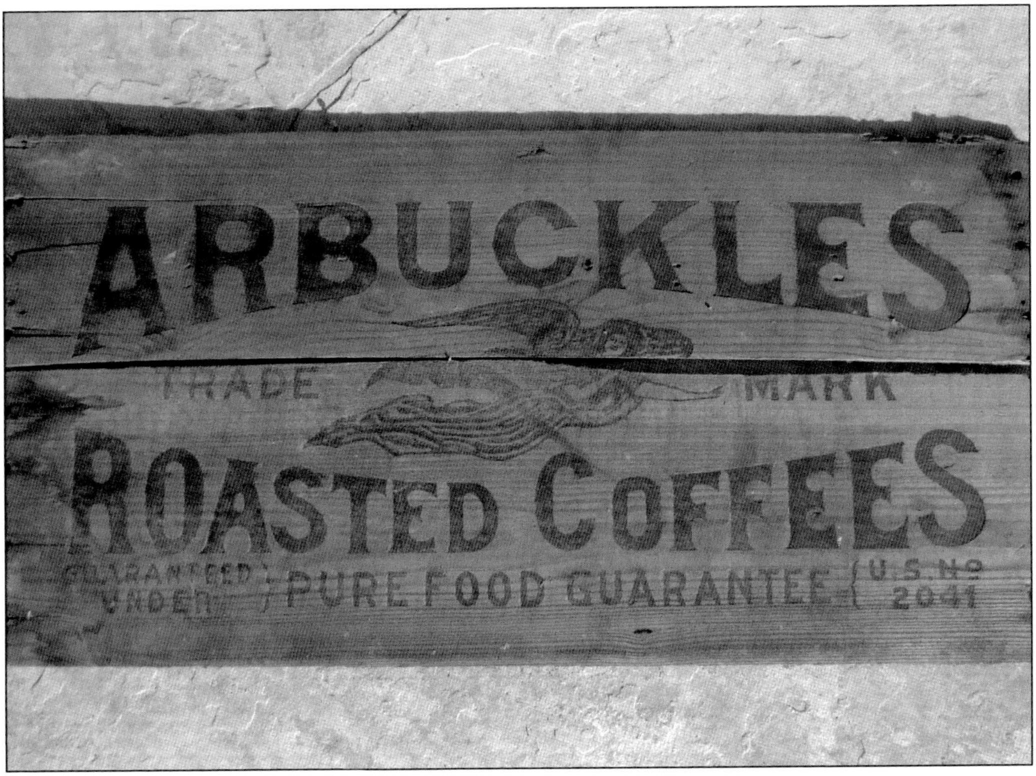

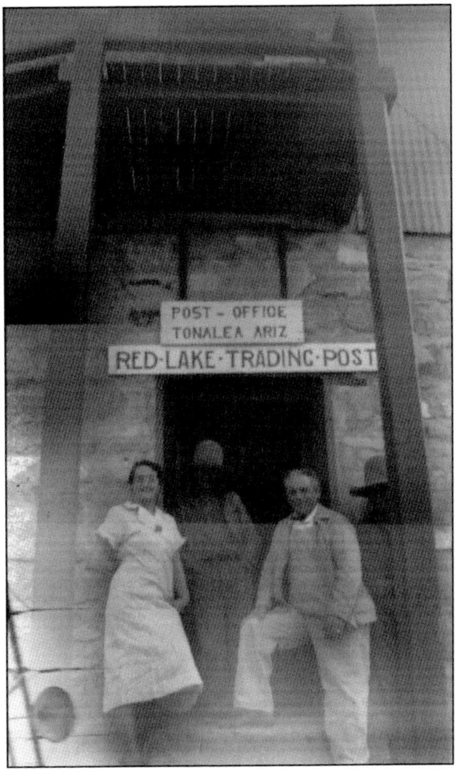

Red Lake is a two-story store. The ground level is stone, and the upper story is constructed of Arbuckles Coffee packing crates. The Arbuckles crates were used for many things, including shelving, chicken coops, cradleboards, Hopi tablitas, and coffins. Zane Grey wrote *The Rainbow Trail* while staying at Red Lake, and scenes for the movie *The Dark Wind*, based on Tony Hillerman's novel, were filmed there. Stories are told of the hundreds of rattlesnakes at Red Lake. In the summer of 1914, trader W.F. Williams killed 500 rattlesnakes. Johnny O'Farrell (right) and his wife, Cora (left), with two unidentified Navajo customers, lived at the post from 1918 to 1935. Johnny killed hordes of snakes, and Cora was known to serve "tuna" sandwiches to tourists who never guessed that the tuna was boiled rattlesnake. Cora also threaded rattlesnake vertebrate bones into unique necklaces. (Right, courtesy of Harvey Leake.)

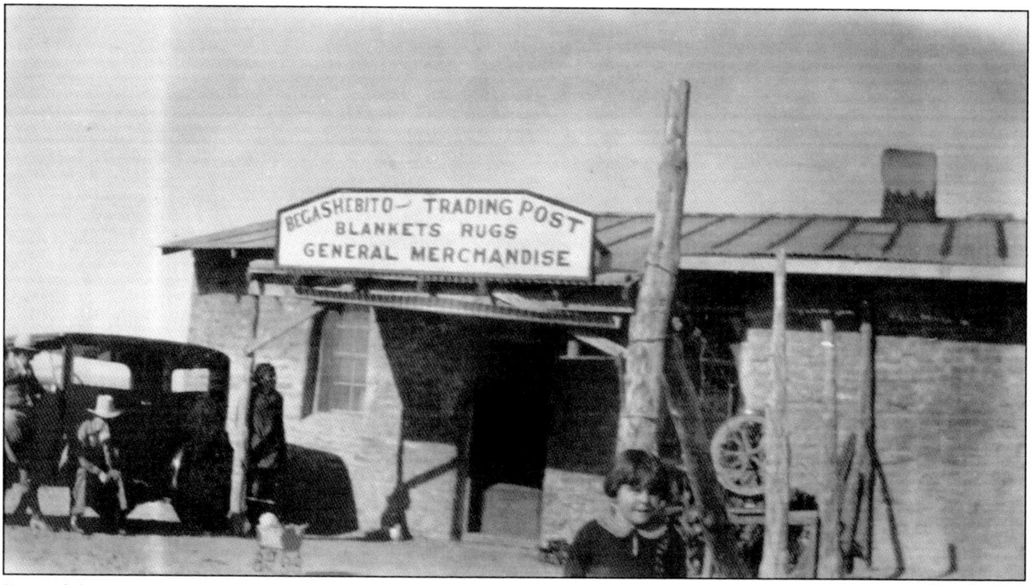

Begeshbito is a version of the Navajo word for Cow Springs. George McAdams first established the trading post in 1882 on Highway 160 about halfway between Tuba City and Kayenta. There were several stores in this area. Myles Headrick operated Cow Springs Trading Post from 1935 to 1938. The store closed in 1991, and all that is left today is rubble from the foundation and the metal skeleton of the old sign.

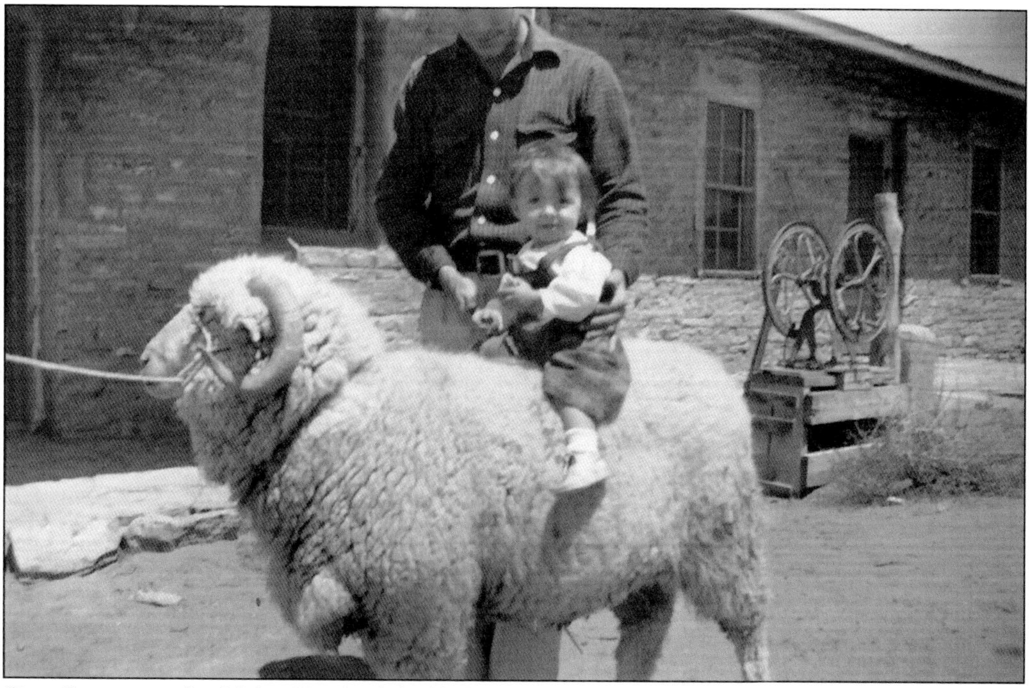

Cow Springs trader Myles Headrick holds his daughter Edythe as she sits on a Navajo ram in front of the trading post about 1938. The large corn grinder at the right was for the use of Navajo customers. (Courtesy of Edythe Klopping.)

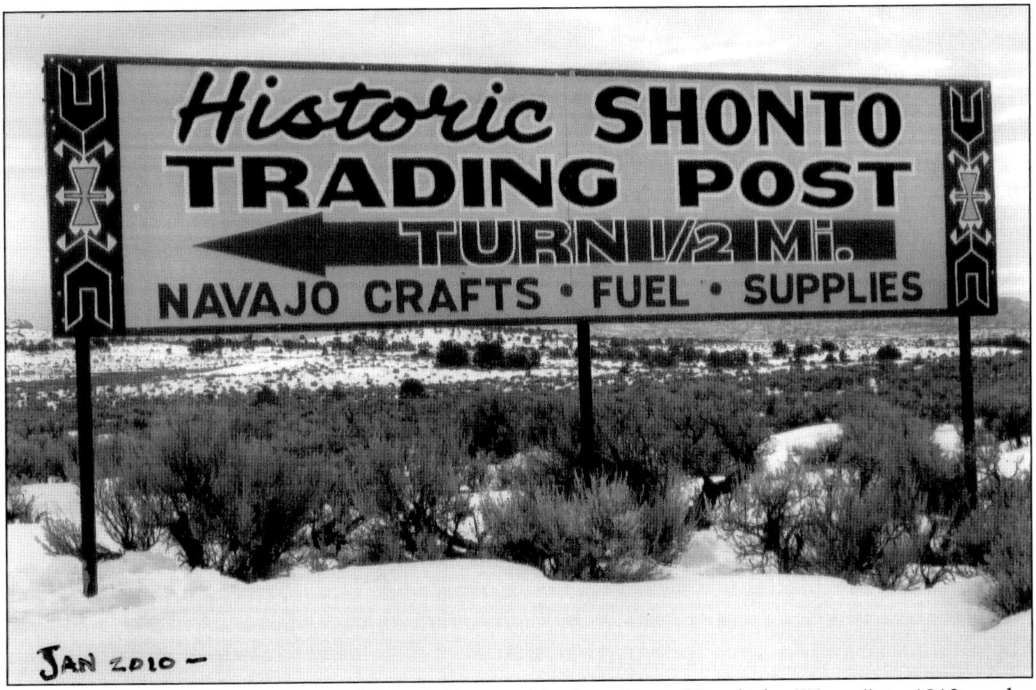

Joe Lee and John Wetherill established Shonto Trading Post, "Sunlight Water," in 1912 at the bottom of Ten Mile Canyon. The steep and treacherous route dropping into the canyon was called the "roughest damn half-mile in America." Elizabeth Hegemann and her husband, Harry Rorick, bought Shonto in 1929, and Elizabeth recorded many stories from her 15 years as a trader in her book *Navajo Trading Days*. There were sheds at the post for storing wool and bags of piñons, as well as hogans for tourists. Paper bags on a nail recorded credit accounts for the local Navajo customers. The store stocked saddles, bridles, and men's clothing. Women hand-sewed their skirts and blouses, purchasing sateen, velveteen, and Riverside Plaid cottons, along with packages of bias tape for hems. (Above, courtesy of Al and Margaret Grieve.)

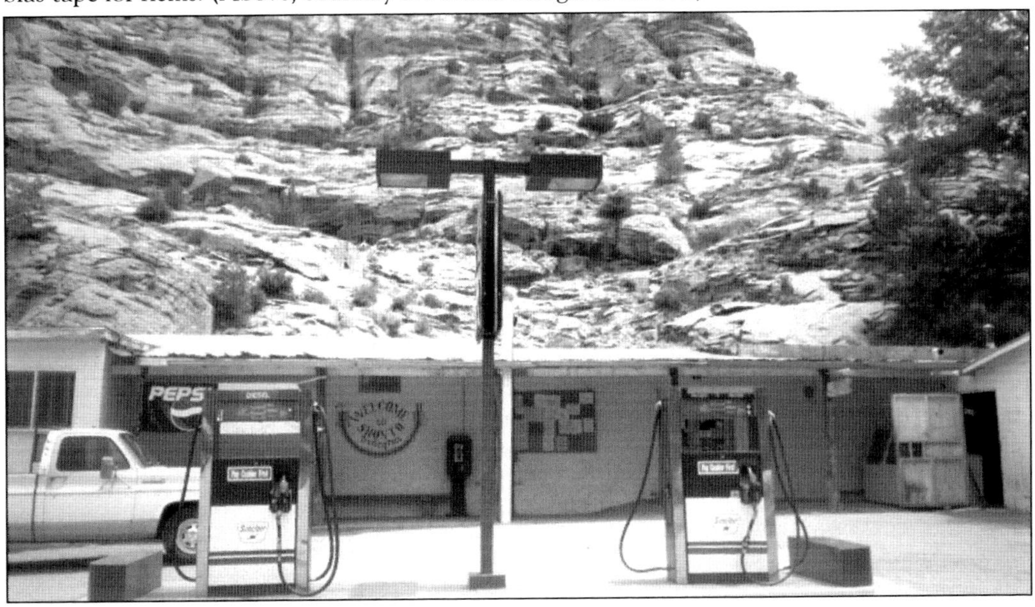

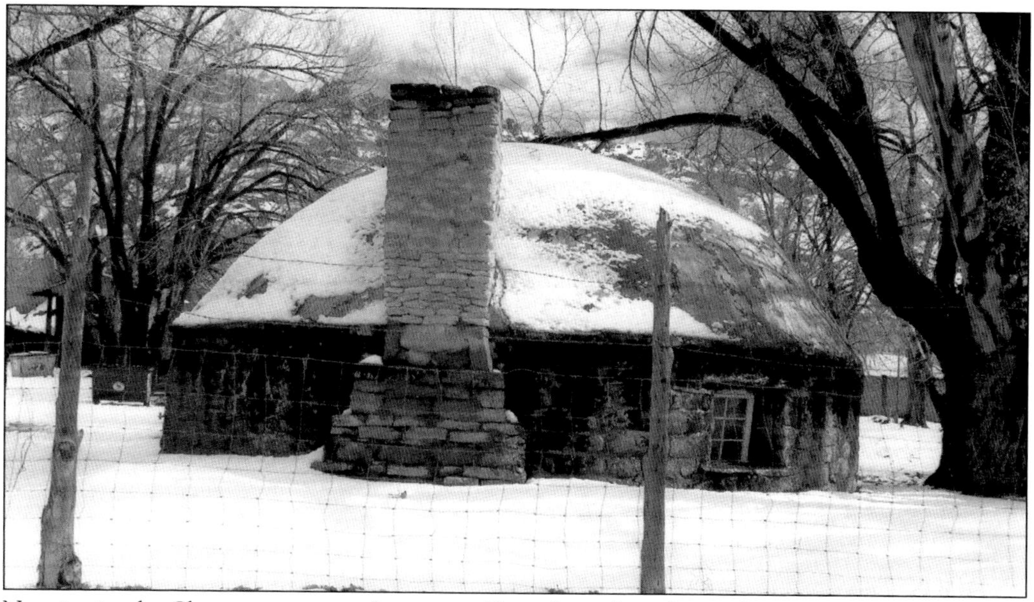

Navajos in the Shonto area were known as "long-hairs," traditional or conservative Navajos. There was a belief that a man should never look at his mother-in law, so when one couple wanted to marry, the girl's mother would not allow it because she would be left alone. The solution was for the young man to first marry the mother and, eventually, the daughter. In earlier times, it was not uncommon for a man to have two wives, so this was the solution to avoid the mother-in-law taboo.

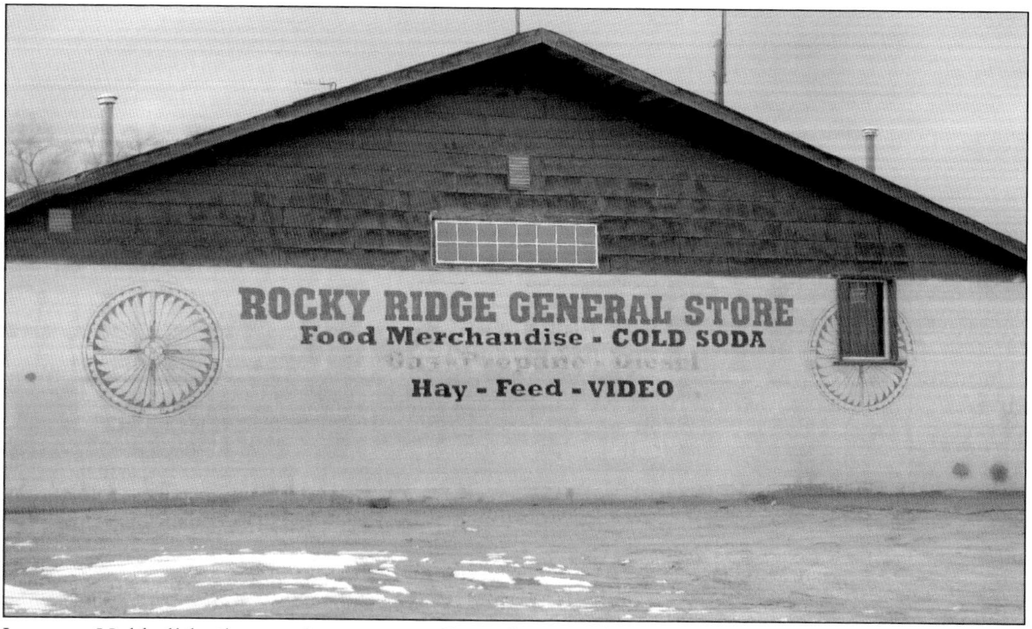

Lorenzo Hubbell built a trading post on Dinnebito Wash in 1911. The name comes from *Diné bitó*, "Navajo water," after the nearby springs. A new store was built north of Highway 264 and was later renamed Rocky Ridge General Store. At one time, there were many more people living in this area, but it was Hopi land historically. After years of legal wrangling, hundreds of Navajo families were forced to relocate to an area near Sanders, Arizona.

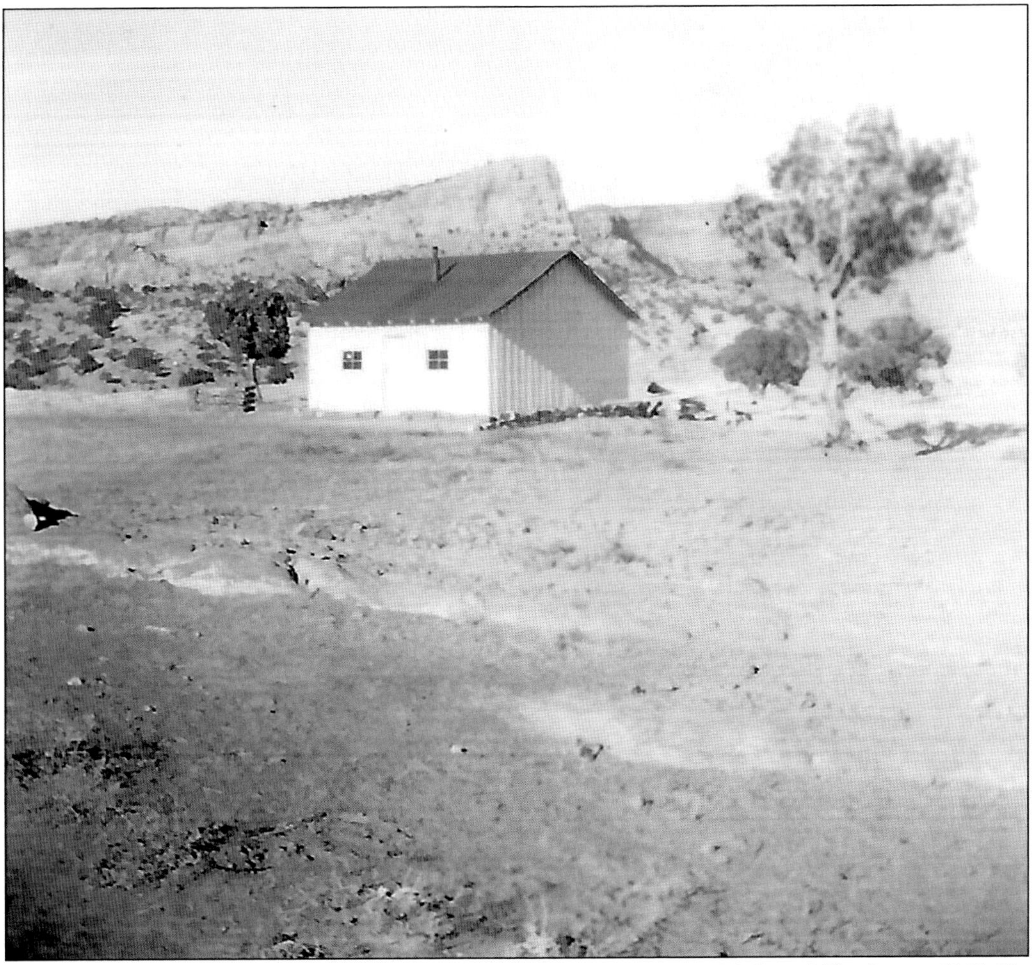

Marsh Pass Trading Post, above, was west of Kayenta. Navajo Harry T. Donald built it in 1945. He later sold it to Jim and Carol Porter, and the store was renamed Tsegi Trading Post. The Porters owned the store until their retirement in 1970. Nearby is Navajo National Monument on Shonto Plateau, overlooking Tesgi Canyon. These are the canyons where the great cliff dwellings known as Betatakin and Keet Seel are located. Marsh Pass is a narrow pass flanked by Laguna Creek. Kayenta traders John Wetherill and Clyde Colville hired workers to build a road through the pass that would ease travel to Tuba City and Flagstaff. Nothing remains of the trading post today. (Above, courtesy of Martin Link; below, courtesy of Harvey Leake.)

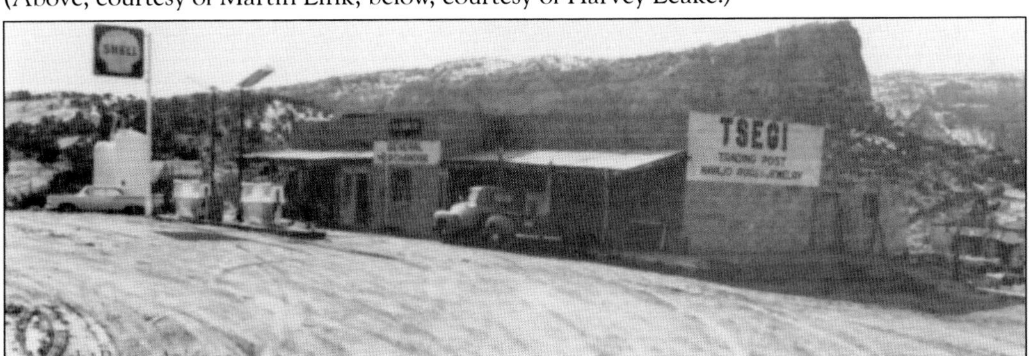

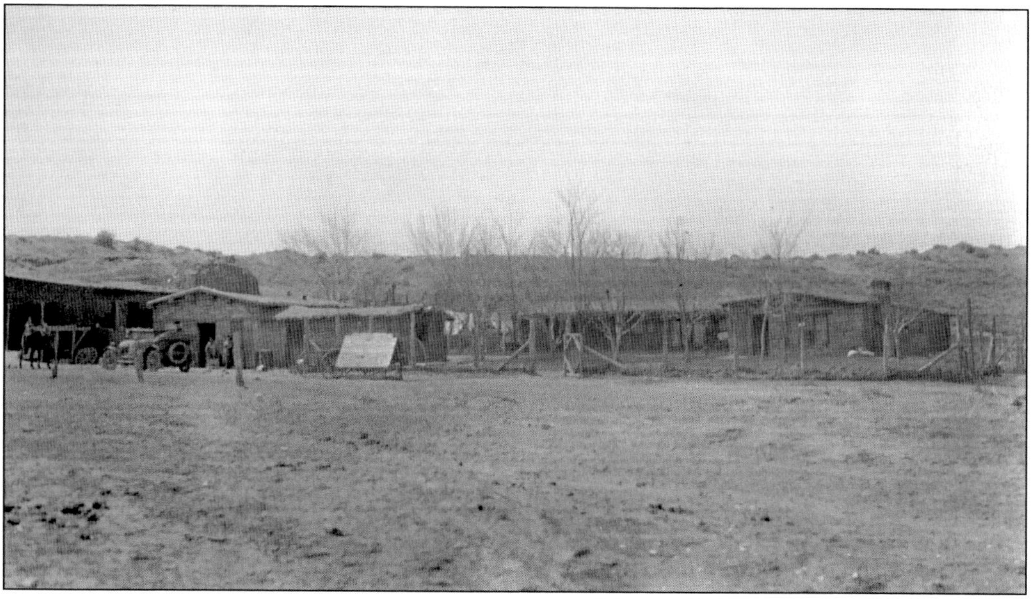

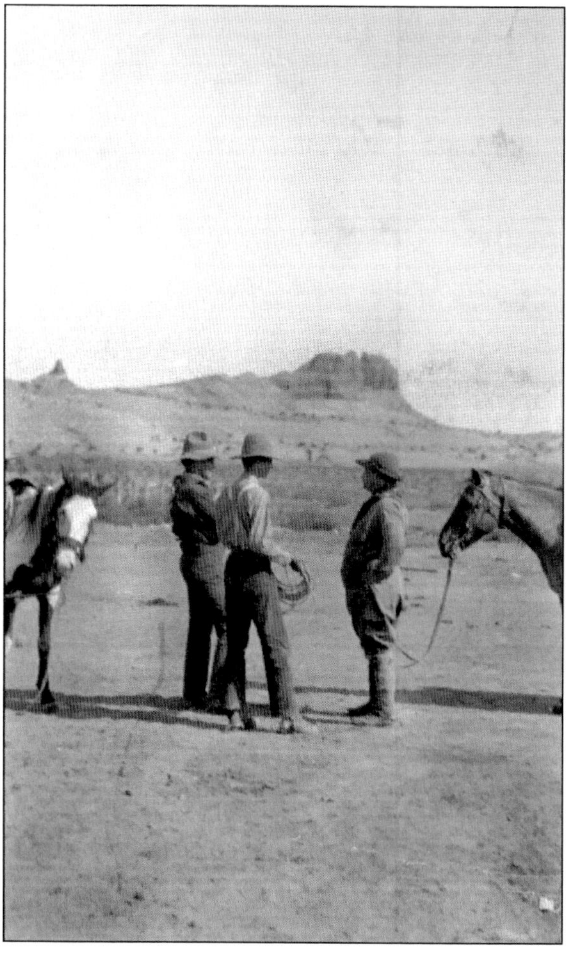

John and Louisa Wetherill moved 30 miles south from their trading post at Oljato to establish a store on the south side of Laguna Creek in 1910. That December, when they moved their trading operations, snow covered the ground. The Wetherills erected tents for living quarters and another for inventory. A wooden plank across two boxes became the store counter. Very soon, a store (at the left in the image above) was built of stone, and the house (at the right) was constructed with logs set vertically, covered with a roof of poles and brush. After the 1909 discovery of Rainbow Bridge, people made the trek to the remote trading post to embark on pack trips, led by John Wetherill, to see the stone rainbow. Theodore Roosevelt, shown at left along with his sons Quentin (left) and Archie (center), made the adventurous trip in 1913. (Both, courtesy of Harvey Leake.)

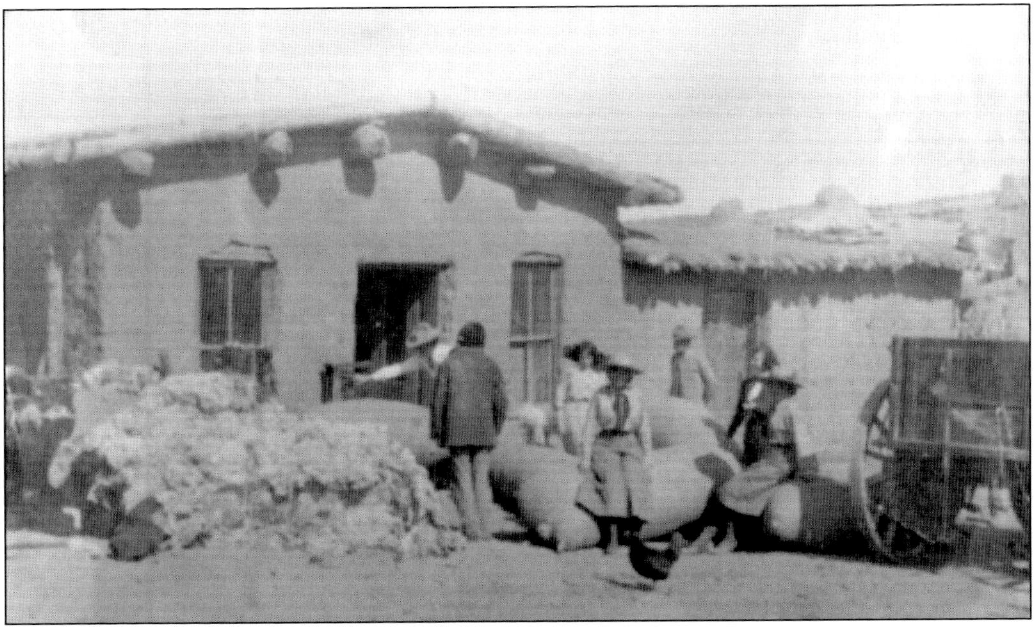

In this 1922 photograph, Kayenta Trading Post has been plastered with mud stucco. John Wetherill, at the left, is weighing wool bags, and an unidentified Navajo man stands in front of him. To the right are his daughter Georgia Ida, the artist Lillian Wilhelm Smith, an unidentified man, and Louisa Wetherill, standing just behind Mildred Smith, who is sitting on one of the huge wool bags. (Courtesy of Harvey Leake.)

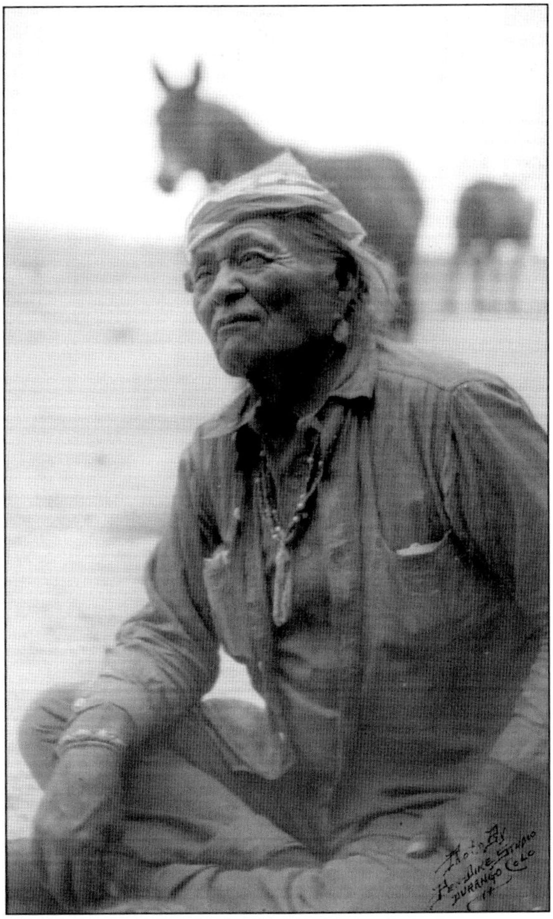

Wolfkiller was a Navajo shepherd who worked at Kayenta Trading Post. He had a vast knowledge of plants and their traditional use, which he shared with Louisa Wetherill, who was fluent in the Navajo language. Louisa recorded his ancient wisdom, and his story was published in the book *Wolfkiller: Wisdom from a Nineteenth-Century Navajo Shepherd*. (Courtesy of Harvey Leake.)

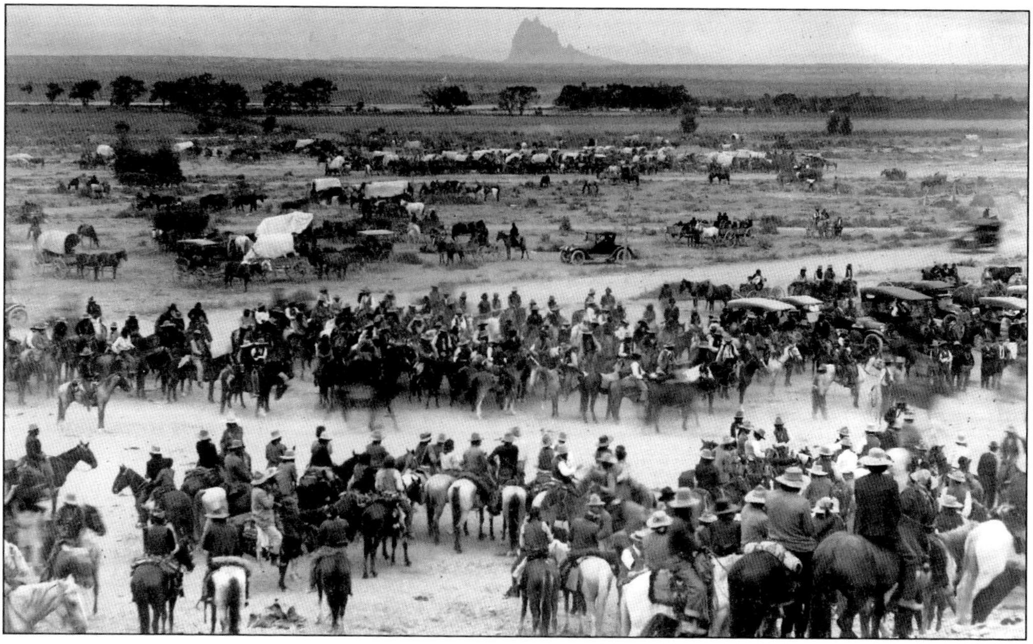

Shiprock, the jagged volcanic peak, can be seen in the distance in the image above. Known as "Rock with Wings," Shiprock holds great religious significance to the Navajo people. W.T. Shelton, first superintendent of the Shiprock Agency, organized annual fairs each October, where Navajo craftsmanship could be displayed. Over 400 weavings were exhibited at the 1912 fair. Prizes were given for rugs and silver work. (Both, courtesy of Harvey Leake.)

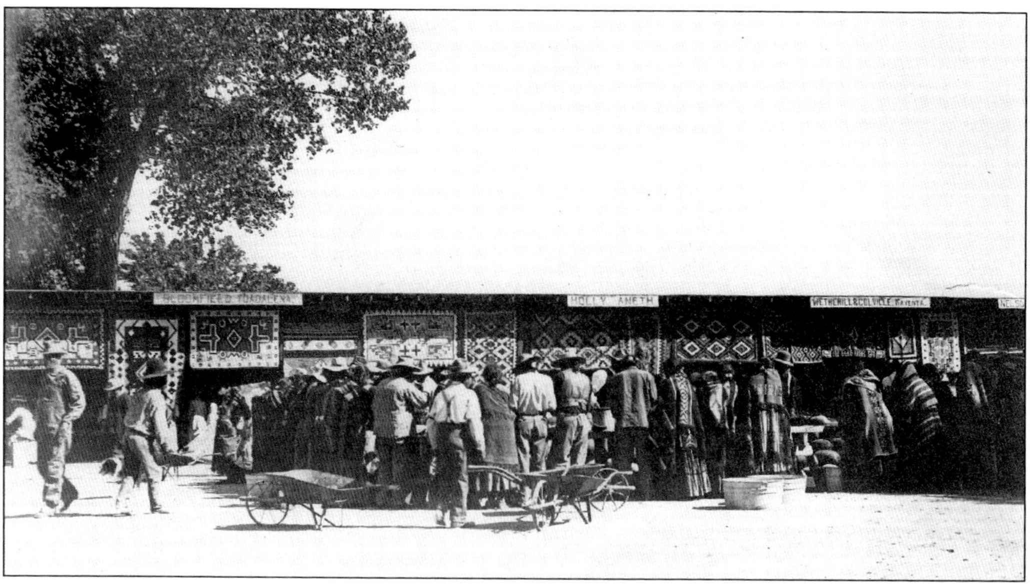

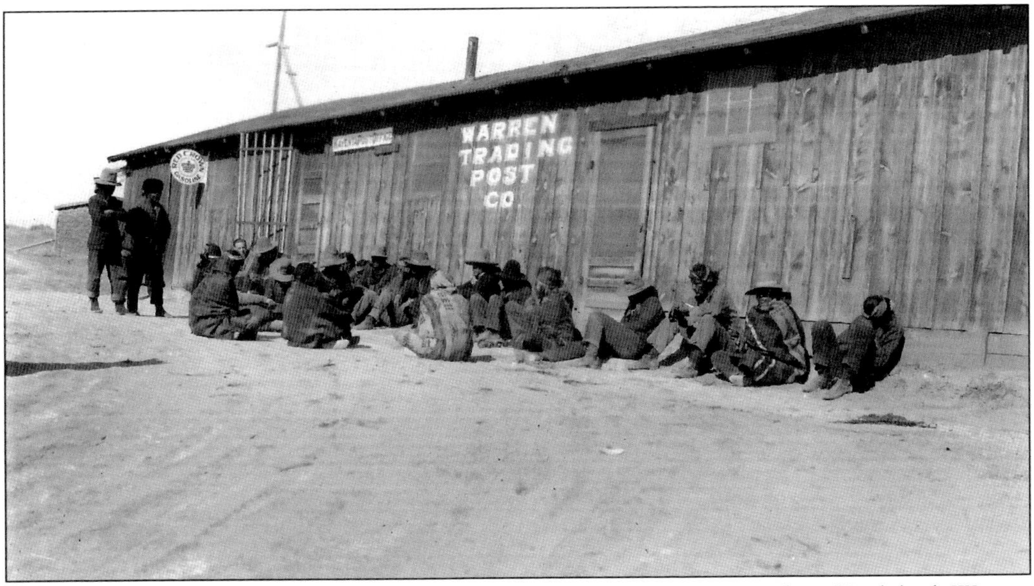

Keith Warren married Hazel Woolsey in 1925, and they went to Kayenta, where Keith built Warren Trading Post two years later. The stone step placed at the store's entrance contained dinosaur tracks. Hazel kept journals and wrote feature articles for magazines and newspapers. Many of her stories were about Navajo life. Hazel recorded that in the store frequent purchases were sodas and cookies or canned tomatoes and crackers.

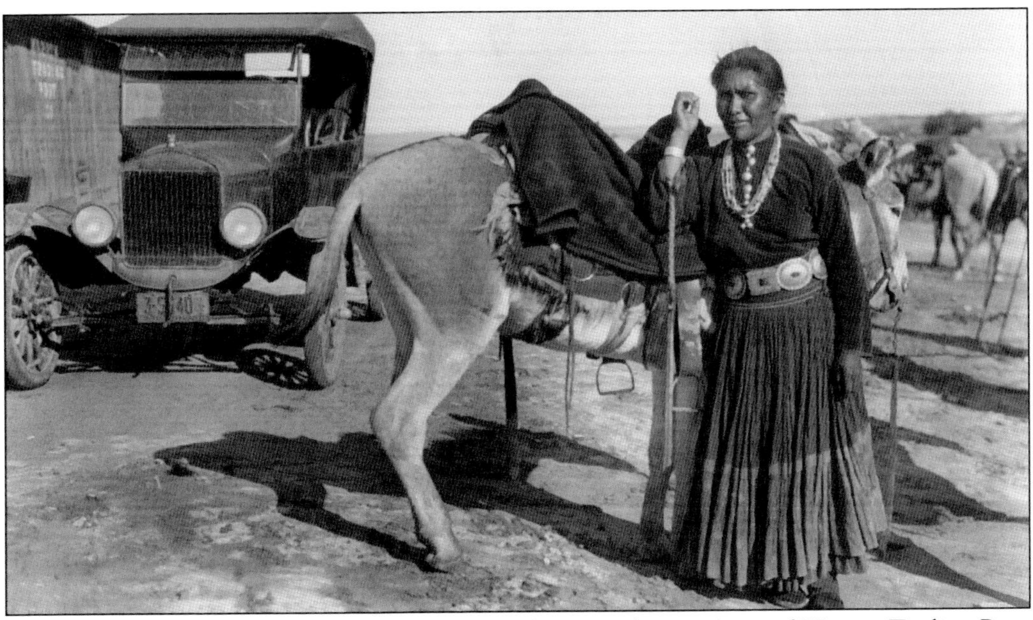

The Navajo woman in this late-1920s photograph is standing in front of Warren Trading Post. She is wearing moccasins and two skirts. In earlier times, Navajo women wore two to six skirts, partly for modesty when they rode horseback. In addition to her necklace and the silver buttons on her shirt, she is wearing a striking silver concho belt. (Courtesy of Arizona State Museum.)

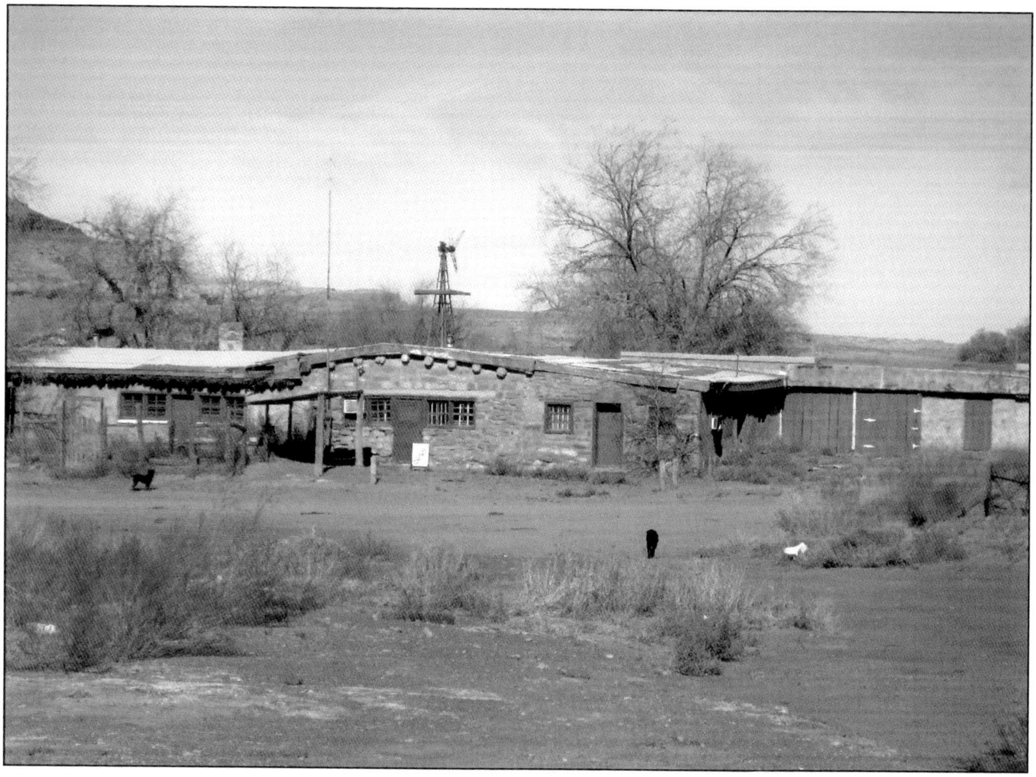

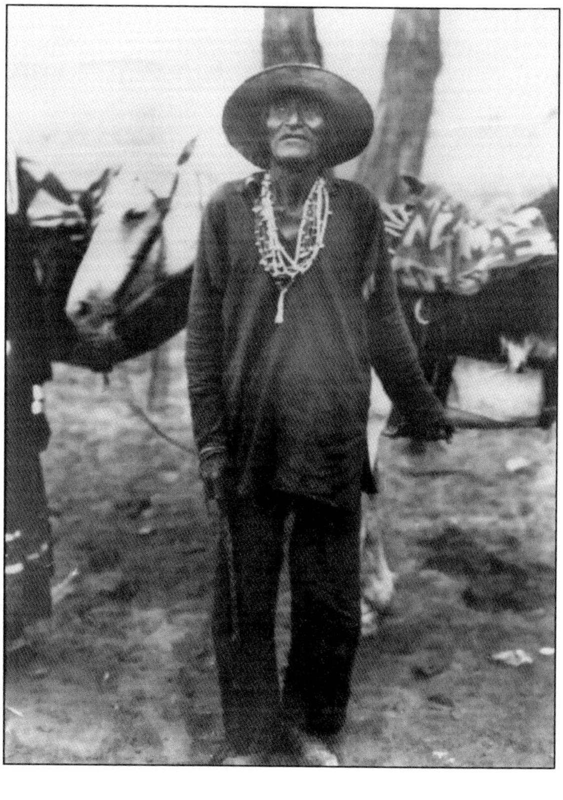

Oljato ("Moonlight Water") Trading Post is west of Monument Valley and just north of the Arizona border. John Wetherill and his trading partner Clyde Colville established the remote post in 1906. As outsiders, they were not welcome in the area. A band of Navajos, led by the famous headman Hoskininni, did not want intruders, even if they professed to be friendly. Hoskininni, seen at left, was finally persuaded to allow them to stay, and trading began with a plank laid across a pair of wooden Arbuckle Coffee crates. Wetherill and Colville built a trading post with living quarters to the side. John's wife, Louisa, soon joined them. Louisa spoke fluent Navajo and befriended Hoskininni, who adopted her and made her heir to his estate, which included his 19 Ute (slave) wives. (Left, courtesy of Harvey Leake.)

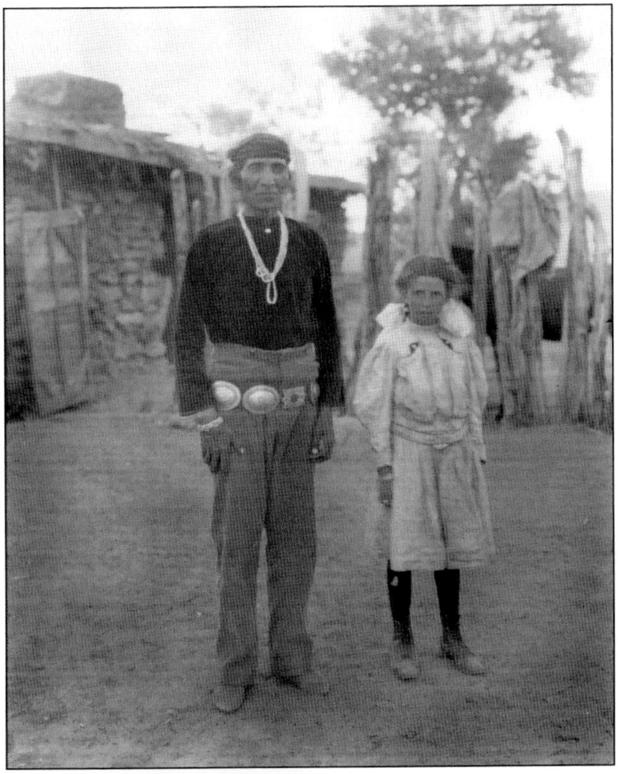

Hoskininni Begay, right, stands in front of Oljato Trading Post with 10-year-old Georgia Ida Wetherill. The Wetherills left Oljato in 1910. When Mildred and Ruben Heflin acquired the store in 1938, they paid $6,000, a fee that transferred the right to trade. The store's inventory was a separate transaction, but the land, the building, and any improvements did not transfer to the personal property of the new owners. Traders today operate under 25-year leases through the Navajo Tribe. In the 1998 photograph below, trader Evelyn Yazzie Jensen assists customer Cynthia Cobb. Oljato Trading Post is now closed. (Right, courtesy of Harvey Leake.)

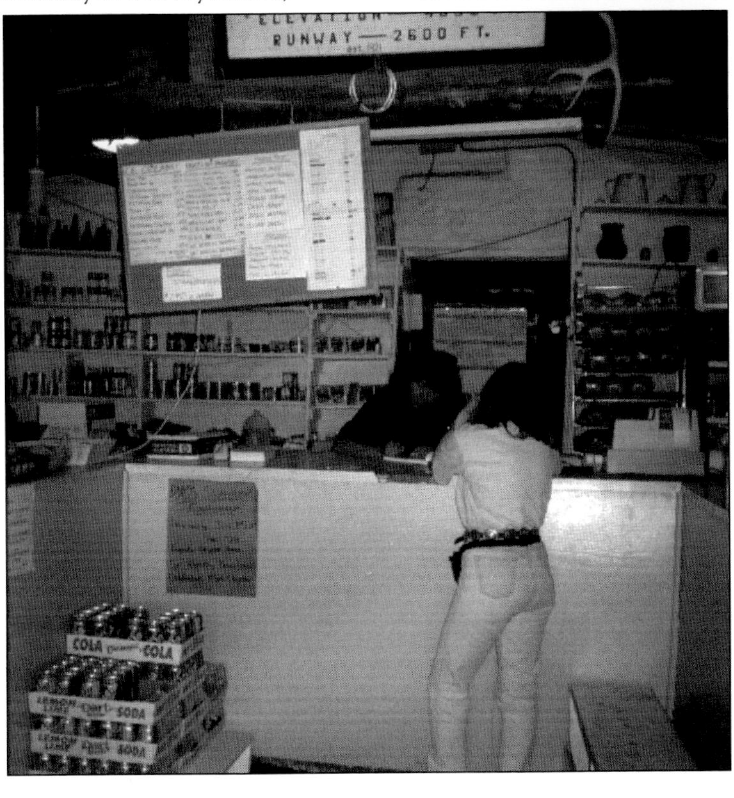

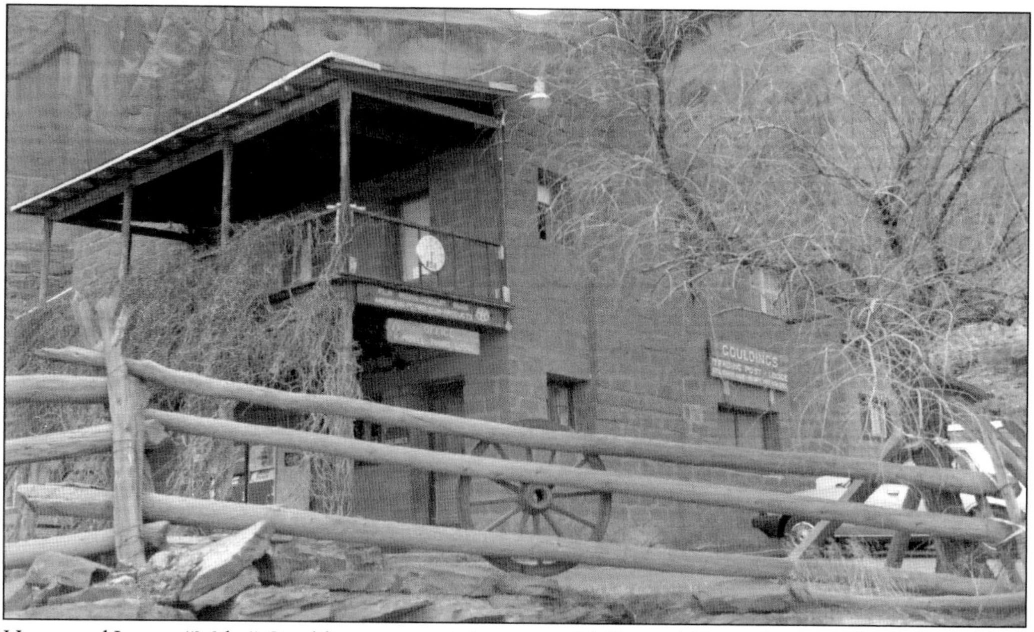

Harry and Leone "Mike" Goulding went to Monument Valley in 1923, selling goods to the Navajos from a tent. By 1928, they had built a stone trading post at the base of Big Rock Door Mesa, just over the Arizona line in Utah. Below, Goulding, standing on a raised floor behind the store counter, is talking with some Navajo customers, pulling items they wish to purchase from the shelves behind him. (Both, courtesy of Nathan LaFont and Goulding's Lodge and Trading Post.)

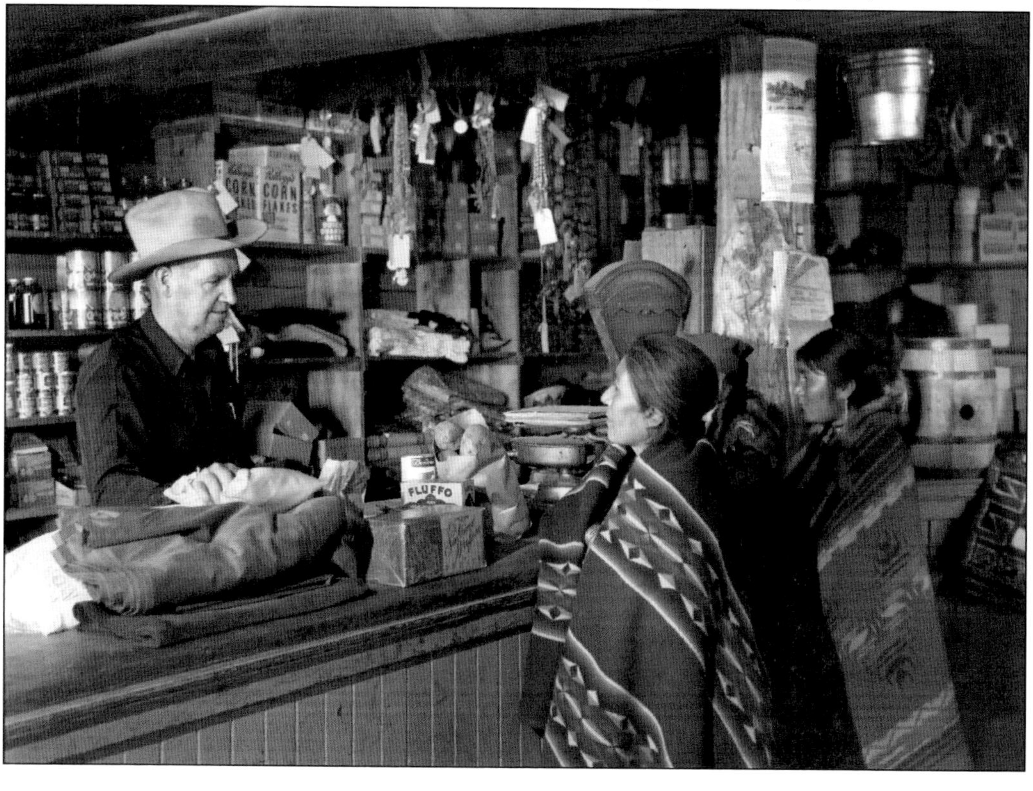

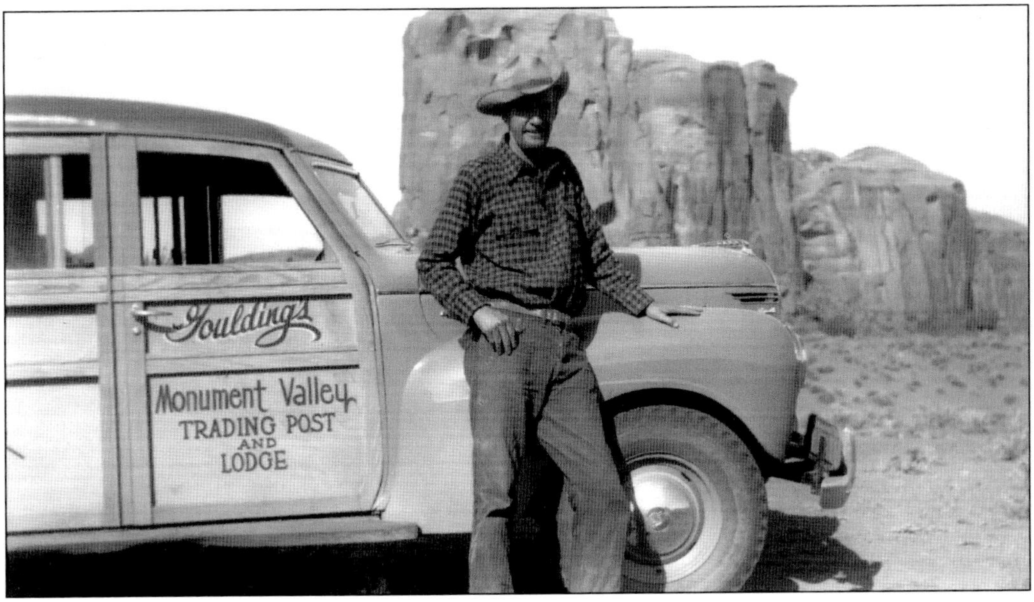

In 1938, Harry Goulding, above, went to California hoping to interest a film studio in the dramatic landscape of Monument Valley and, ultimately, to bring in work, as everyone was suffering through the Depression. Director John Ford saw the possibilities and traveled to Monument Valley in 1939 to film the movie *Stagecoach*, below. A tent city was set up near the trading post to accommodate the actors and crew. John Wayne stars in *Stagecoach* and went on to appear in many pictures filmed in Monument Valley, which he once said was where "God put the West." Not only were movies filmed in the valley, but also many television commercials, shows, and magazines have chosen that location as a backdrop. (Above, courtesy of Nathan LaFont and Goulding's Trading Post and Lodge.)

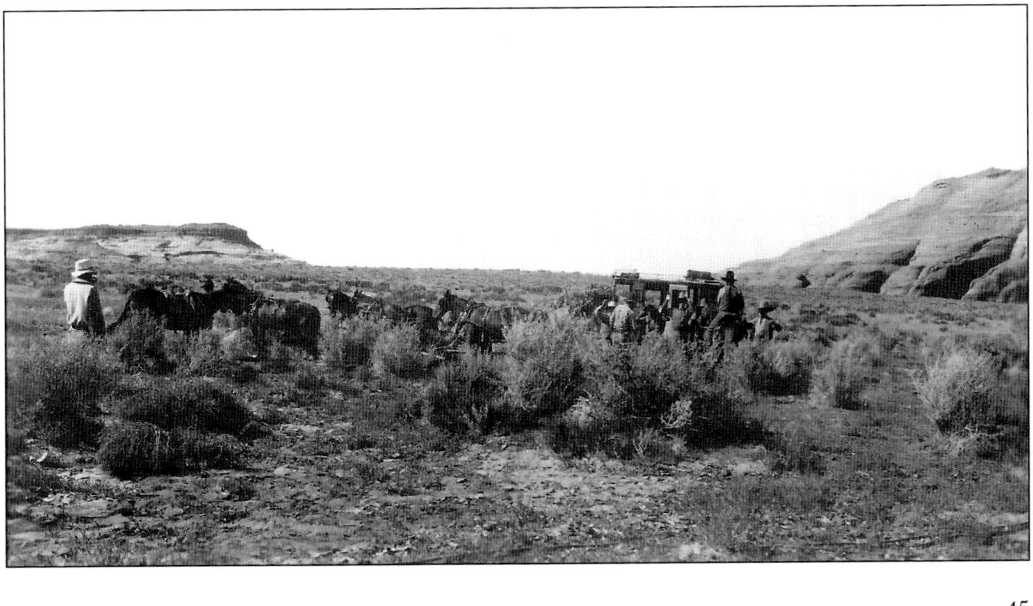

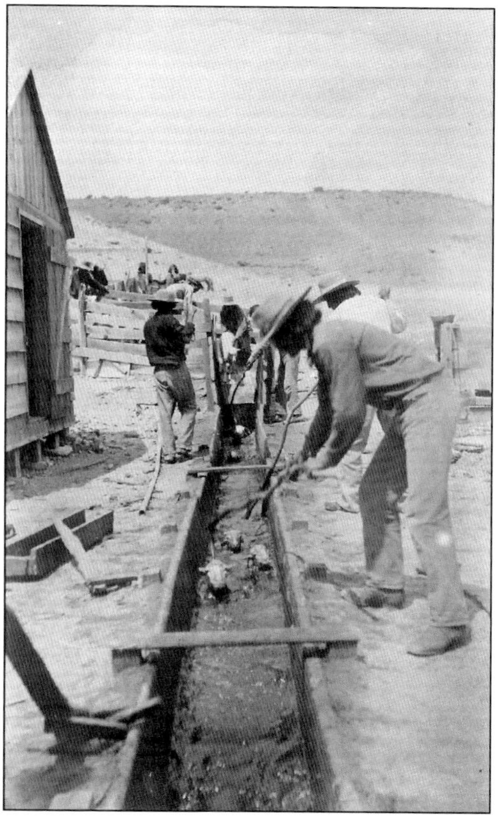

Many trading posts had dipping tanks where sheep were treated with a mixture of Black Leaf 40, a medication used to kill ticks and parasites. Long sticks were used to push the animal's heads under to completely cover the animal or to rescue a floundering sheep. Margaret Etcitty Grieve, below, shears a sheep. A steady hand was needed to clip the wool without nicking the sheep. One trader said there were two paydays in Navajo country: first, in the spring when wool was sold to the trading post when the sheep were sheared; and second, in the fall when lambs were sold. (Left, courtesy of Tom Collins; below, courtesy of Al and Margaret Grieve.)

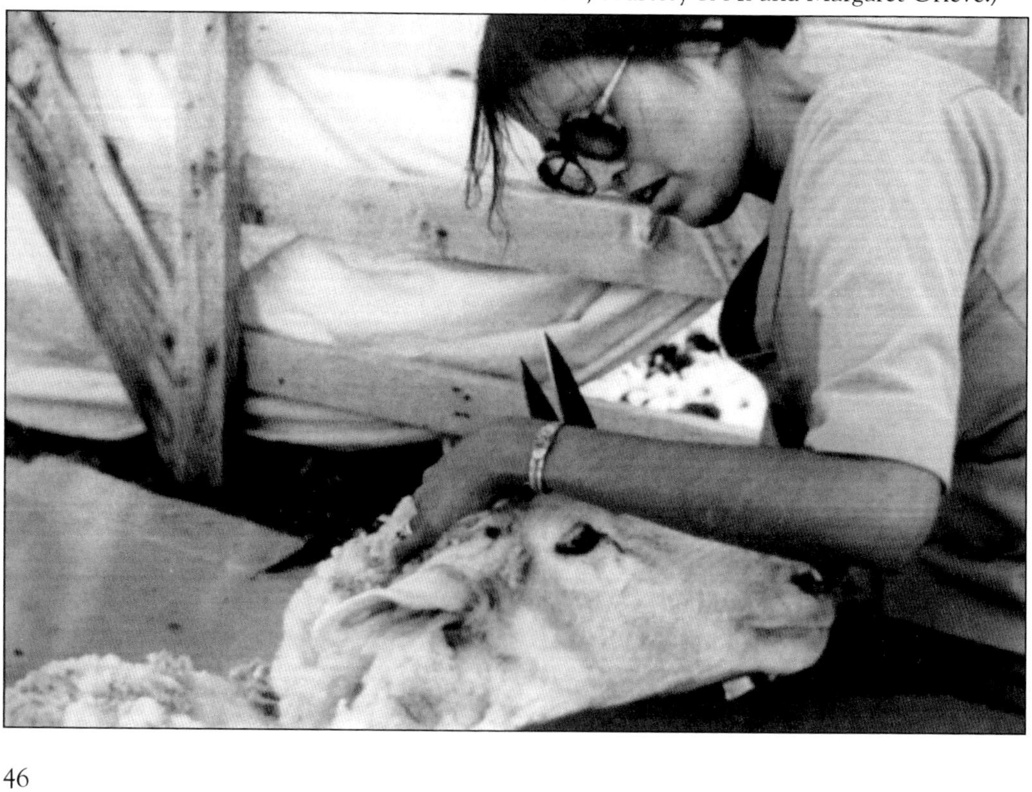

Monument Valley weaver Happy Cly has a partially completed rug on her loom. She is using tow cards to card the cleaned wool in preparation for spinning it into yarn with the spindle stick and whorl. The carding process untangles the fibers and serves as a second cleaning. After spinning, the yarn is rolled into a ball and is ready for use in weaving a rug. (Courtesy of Nathan LaFont and Goulding's Trading Post and Lodge.)

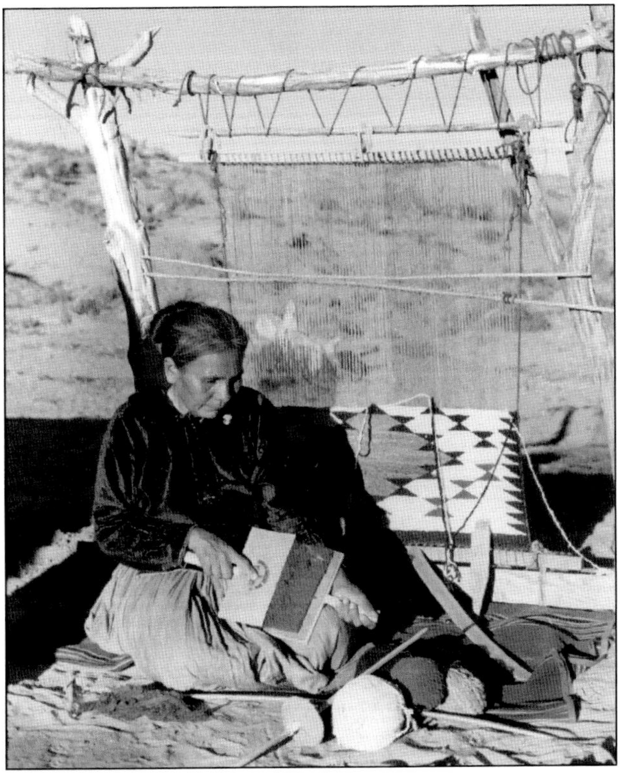

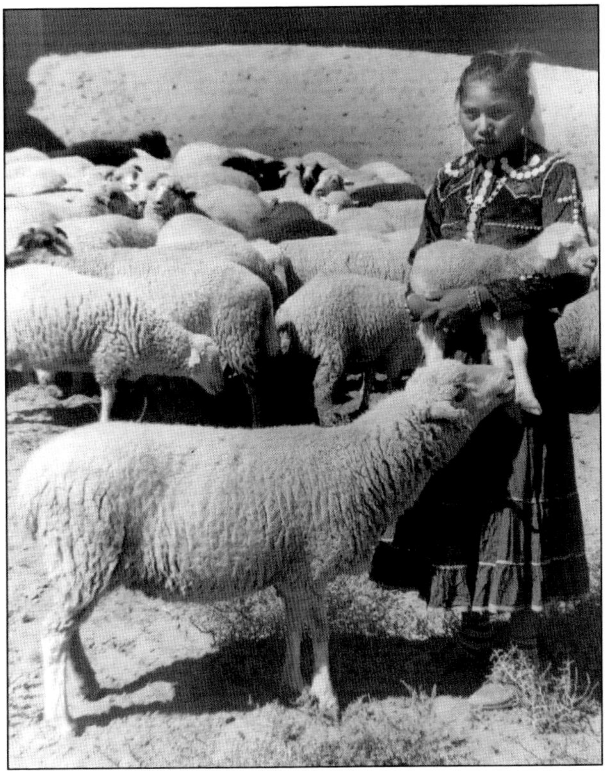

This lovely Navajo girl holds a lamb, possibly a pet. Sheep belong mostly to Navajo women, and girls are expected to help with herding and caring for the sheep. In earlier times, wealth was counted through possession of sheep, goats, and cattle. (Courtesy of Nathan LaFont and Goulding's Trading Post and Lodge.)

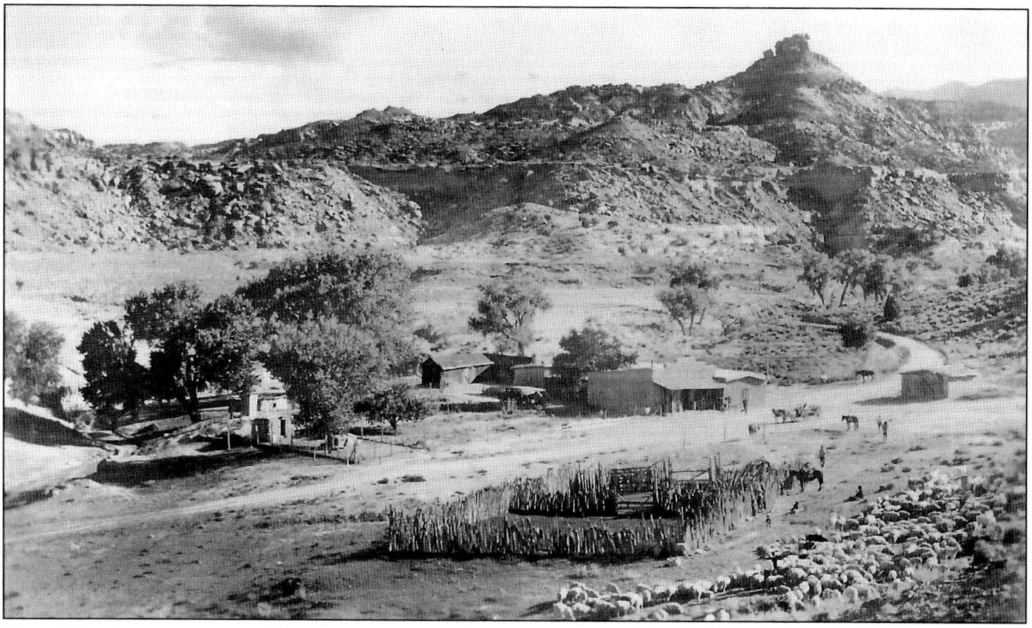

Teec Nos Pos, "Trees All Around," was the name given to Hambleton Bridger Noel's 1905 trading post. The name comes from the cottonwoods growing around the original trading post in the extreme northeastern corner of Arizona. Outsiders were not welcome, but Noel hung his Remington rifle on the back wall of the post showing that he intended to stay. About 1930, the government put a $25 corn grinder in front of the store. The trader was to charge 15¢ per 100 pounds of corn. But people were so poor that they rarely ground more than 15¢ worth of corn in a year, and it took 25 years for the grinder to be paid off. The exquisite rugs from this area are expensive and highly collectible and show a Persian influence, with wide borders enclosing diamonds, boxes, triangles, and zigzags. (Above, courtesy of Tom Collins.)

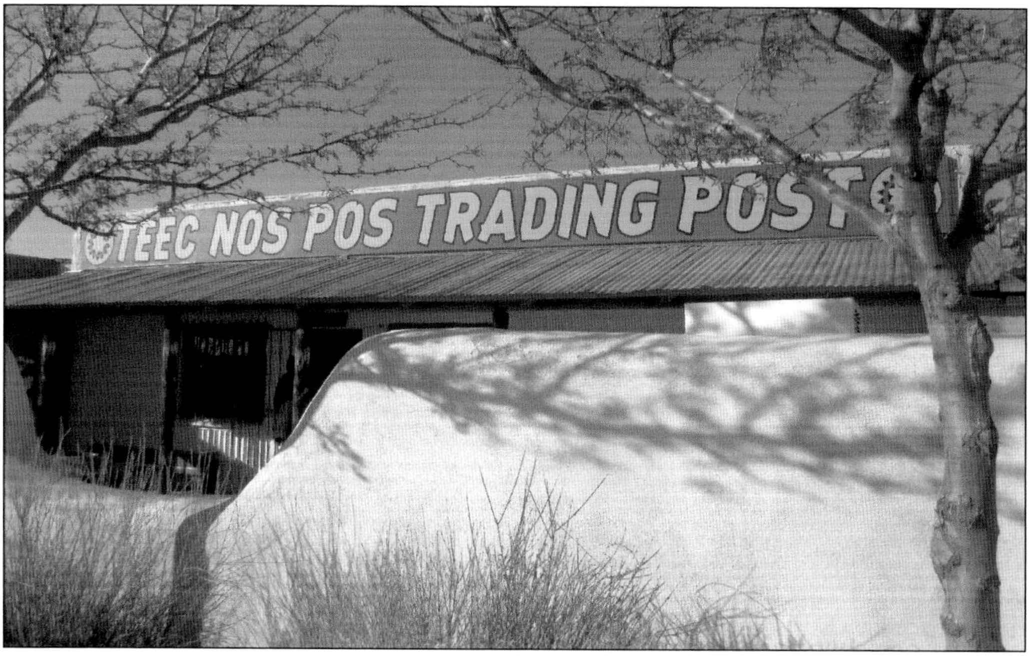

John McCulloch has been the trader at Teec Nos Pos since 1994. He is one of the few traders still buying wool, "mohair comes in first in the season, white wool is the most desirable." At the trading post, it is packed into bales and shipped to Roswell Wool. Teec Nos Pos has a large rug room, piled with collectible weavings, baskets, and wonderful Navajo folk art, such as mud figures, wood carvings, and Mamie Deschille's whimsical paintings on cardboard. Teec Nos Pos no longer has a pawn room, but McCulloch has been known to extend credit in the attached grocery store, even if the likelihood of repayment is vague. He will say that, sometimes, "that is part of operating a store." Other traders consider McCulloch to be a "real trader, he is out there buying wool, taking care of the people."

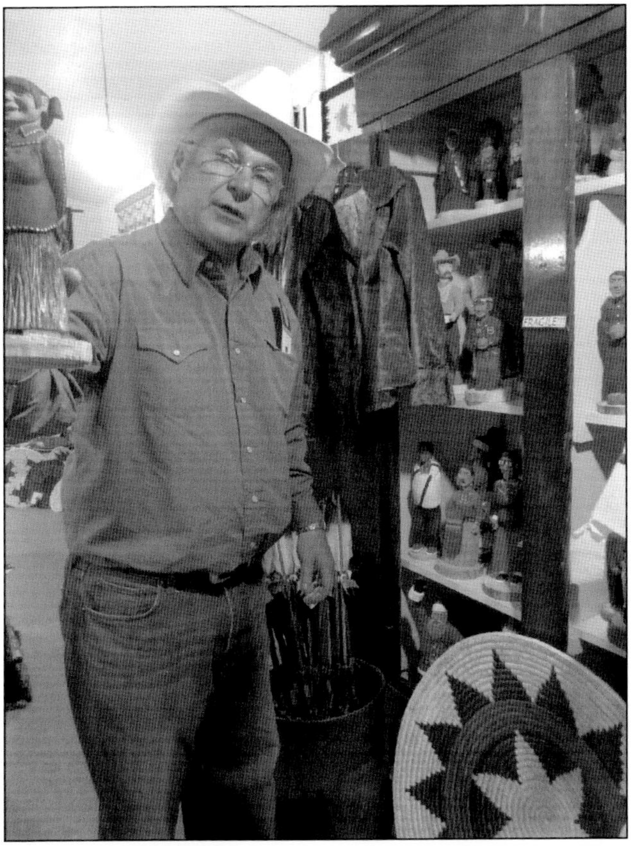

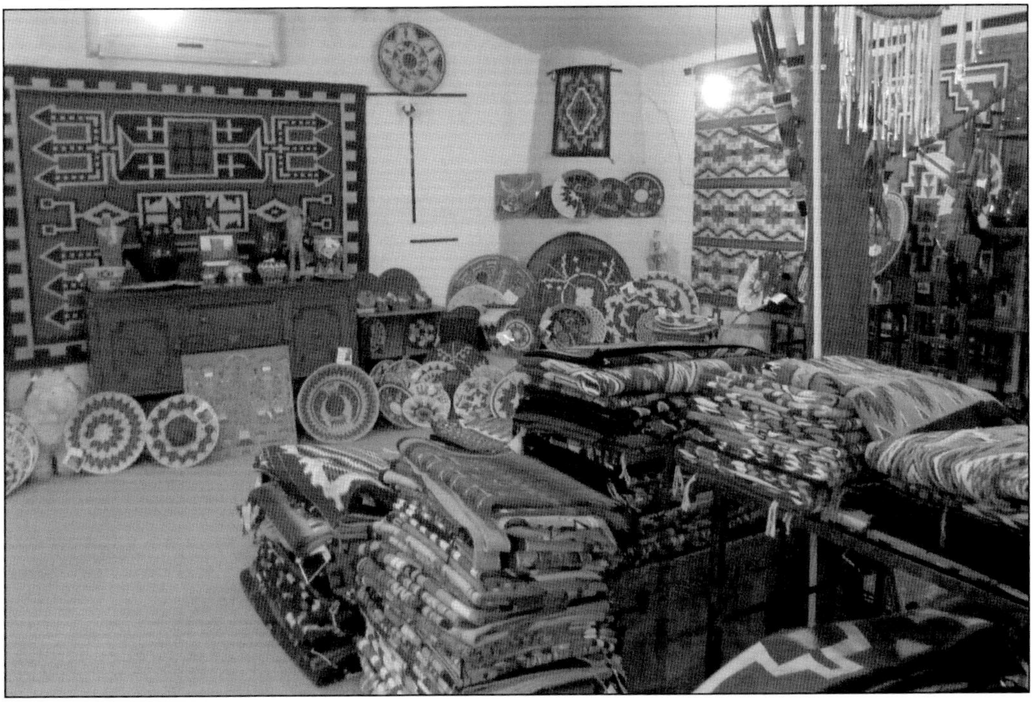

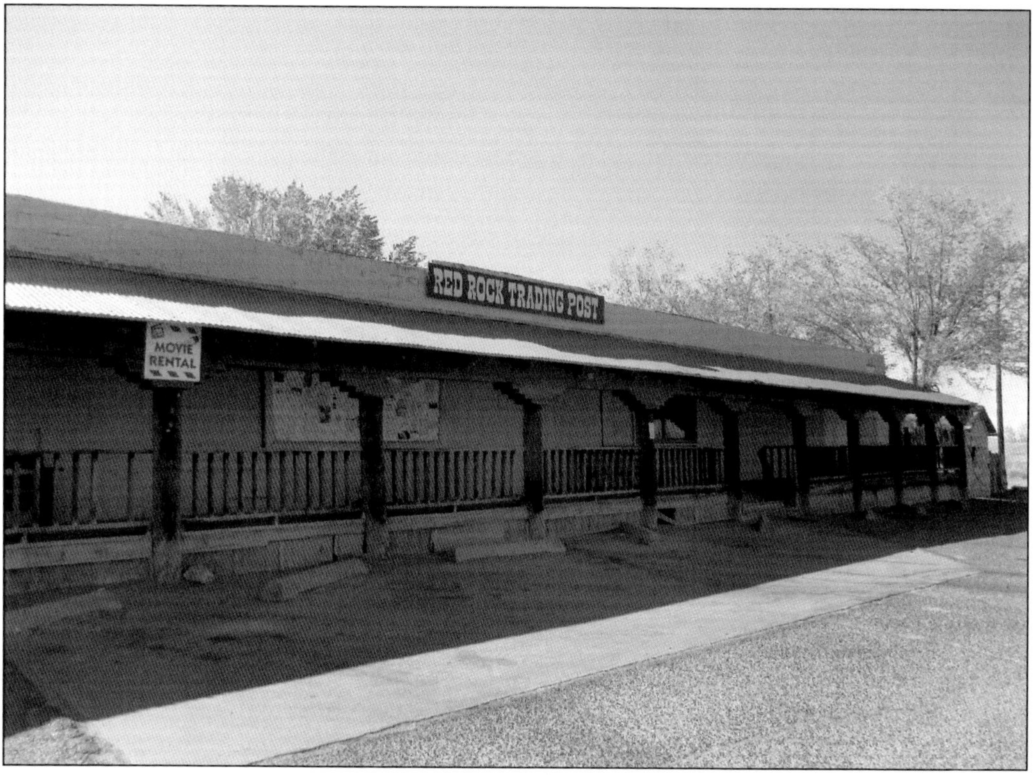

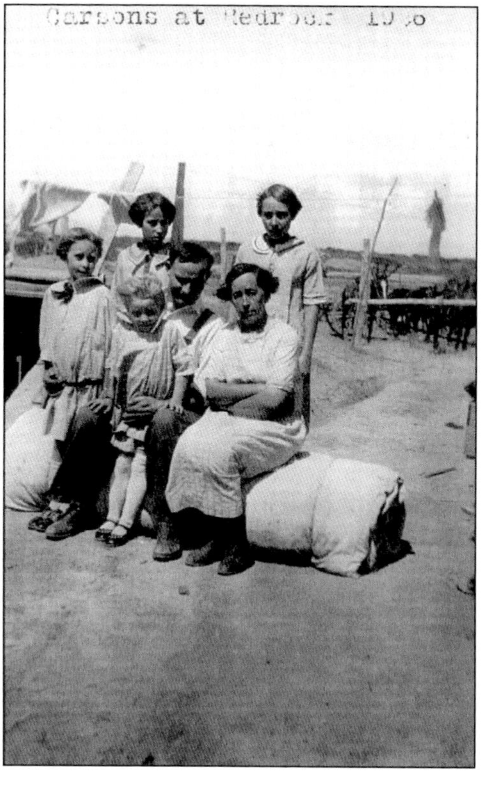

Red Rock Trading Post is less than a mile from the New Mexico border. Additions were made to the front of the original 1907 building, which is about 100 feet long with a covered porch. The legendary trader Stokes Carson managed Red Rock from 1926 to 1928. Shown here, from left to right, are (standing) Marie, Jo, and Mildred; (sitting) Chin, Stokes, and his wife, Jessie. The trading post still stands, with just a corner of the long building used to rent videos and sell groceries. Behind the store are the historic barn and the remnants of the corrals from the time when the trader bought sheep from local Navajos. When trader Franc Newcomb visited Red Rock, she noted that one shelf had expensive Pendleton shawls, while others held Levis and sheepskin-lined jackets as well as black-felt sugar-loaf hats, which were prized by Navajo men in the area. (Left, courtesy of Nina Heflin.)

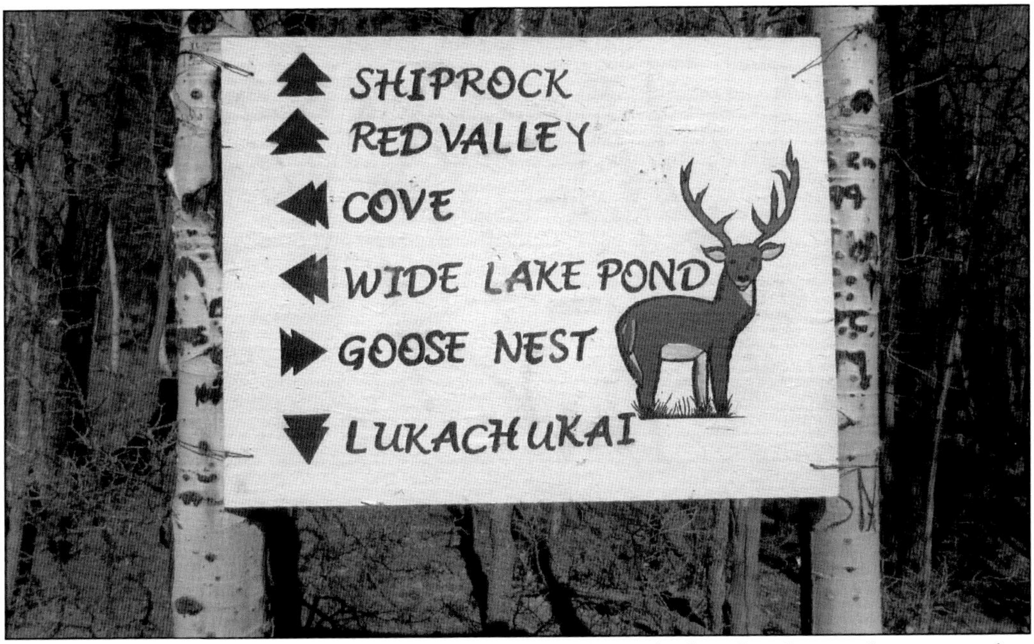

The area around Red Rock is remote and nearly roadless. The handmade sign directs travelers over Buffalo Pass in the Lukachukai Mountains. To the north is high-desert country that dissolves into a maze of washes and rough dirt roads. Totsoh trader Hank Blair, in giving directions, offered the advice that anyone traveling north would need "two rosaries and a shovel" to safely navigate that way.

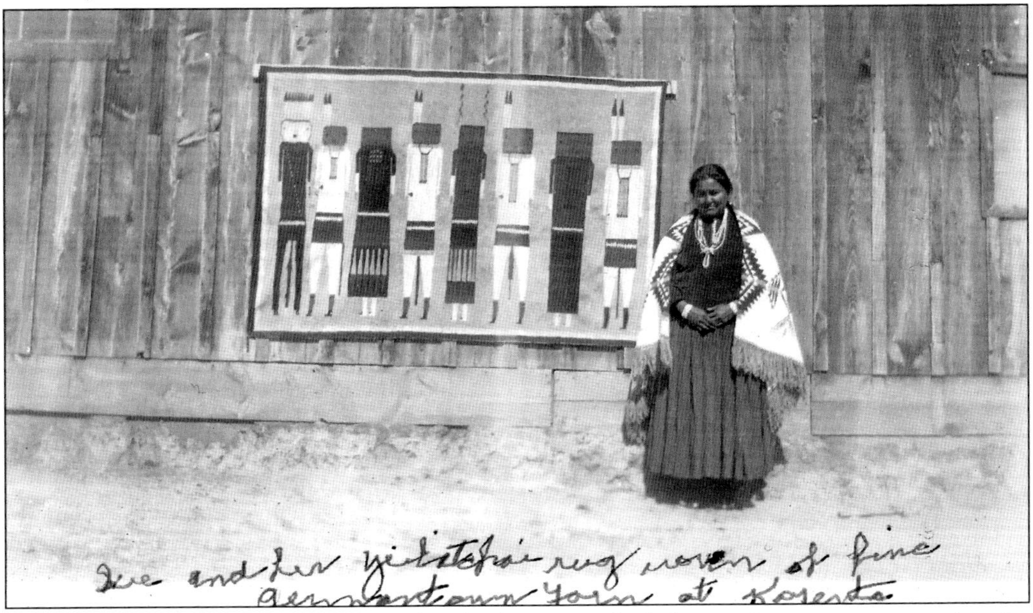

Yei rugs depicting the Holy People, and Yeibechai rugs, which feature dancers impersonating the Yei, were developed in the Red Rock and nearby Shiprock area. Early rugs depicted one figure, but then developed into a line of front-facing Yeis. This style of rug was developed from Navajo sandpaintings after World War I by trader Will Evans. Around 1930, Sue Bradley, a weaver from Kayenta, stands in front of her beautiful Yei rug woven with Germantown yarns.

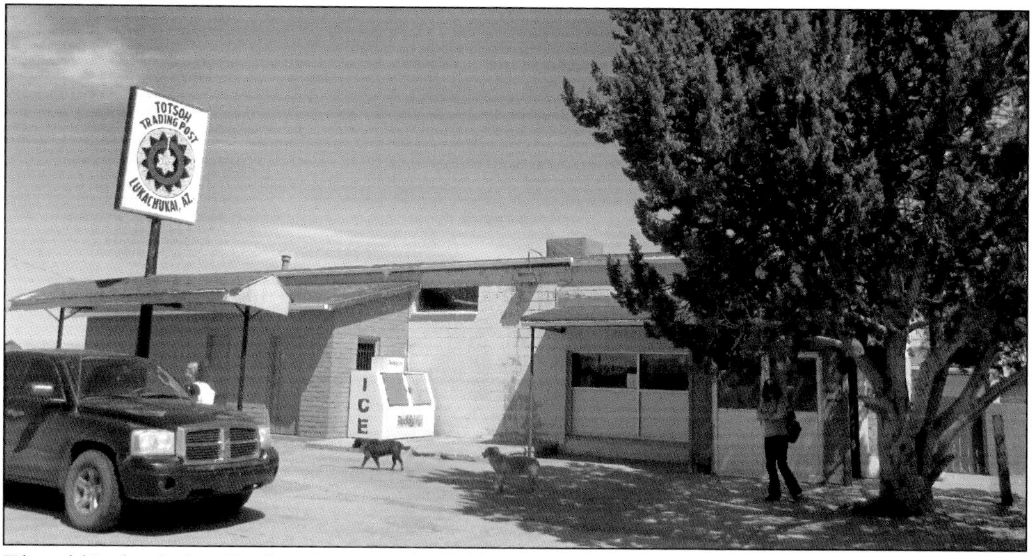

The old Lukachukai Trading Post on the hill about a mile away from Totsoh was closed in 1979 and then was vandalized because of rumors that money was hidden in the walls. Nothing remains today. Vernon Jack built Totsoh Trading Post at Lukachukai in 1962. Hank and Victoria Blair bought Totsoh in 1984. Hank was raised at Red Mesa Trading Post and, later, Kayenta. Victoria is Navajo, from Kayenta. She told the story that her great-great-grandmother was captured by Comanches, and when she was found at a pueblo, Navajos traded a basket of fruit to get her back. When Hank and Victoria went into the trading business, they realized they would go broke if they stayed in Kayenta because of the Navajo tradition that families must share everything. So they moved to Lukachukai.

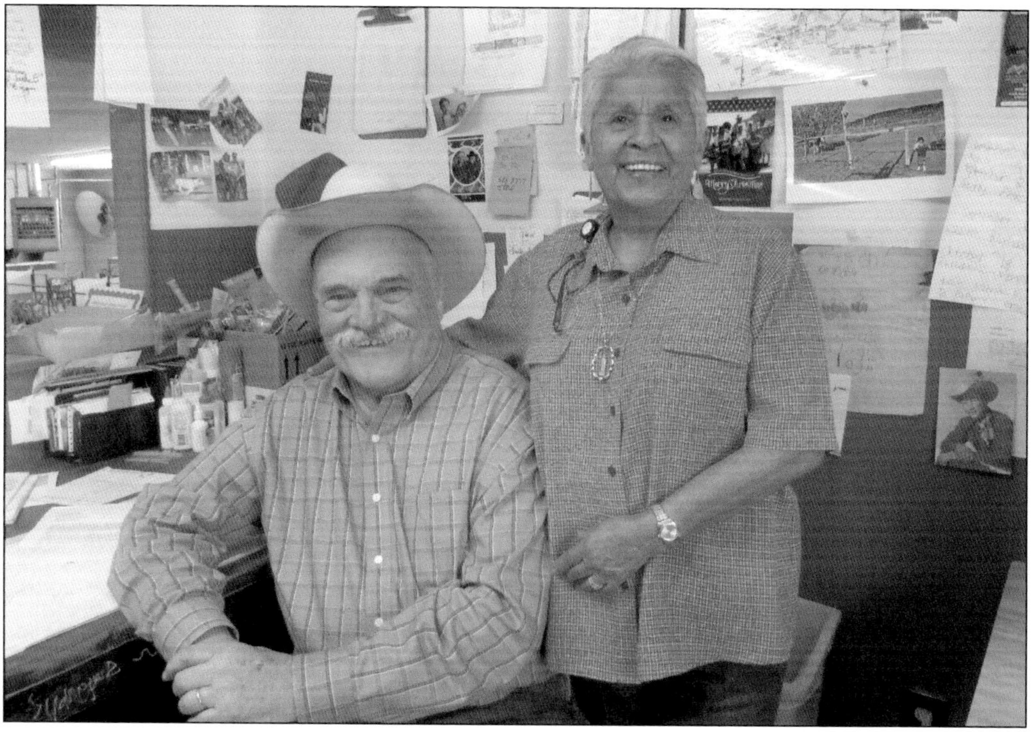

Totsoh Trading Post sells groceries, baskets, deer hides, and cradleboards. Hank Blair remarked that the store is the center of the community, and as a trader, "you can make enough money to live, but you cannot make enough to leave." Like most of the remaining traders, Hank and Victoria Blair are an integral part of their community; they have chosen to stay.

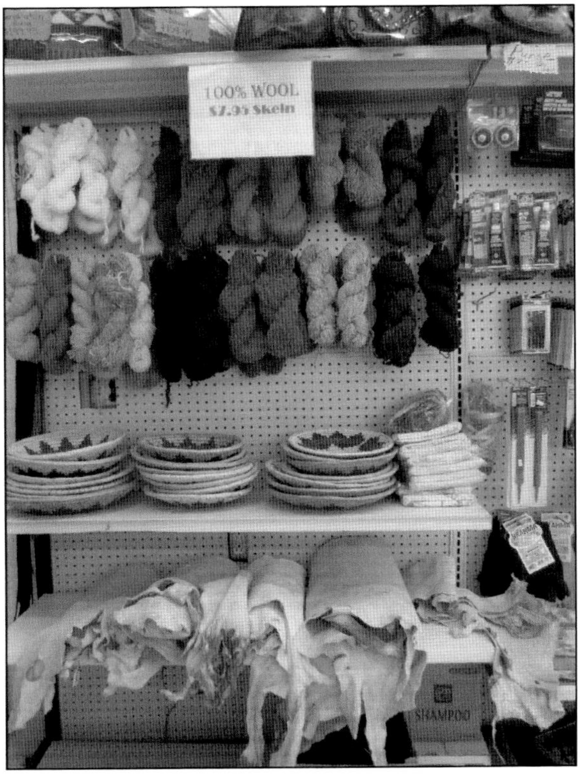

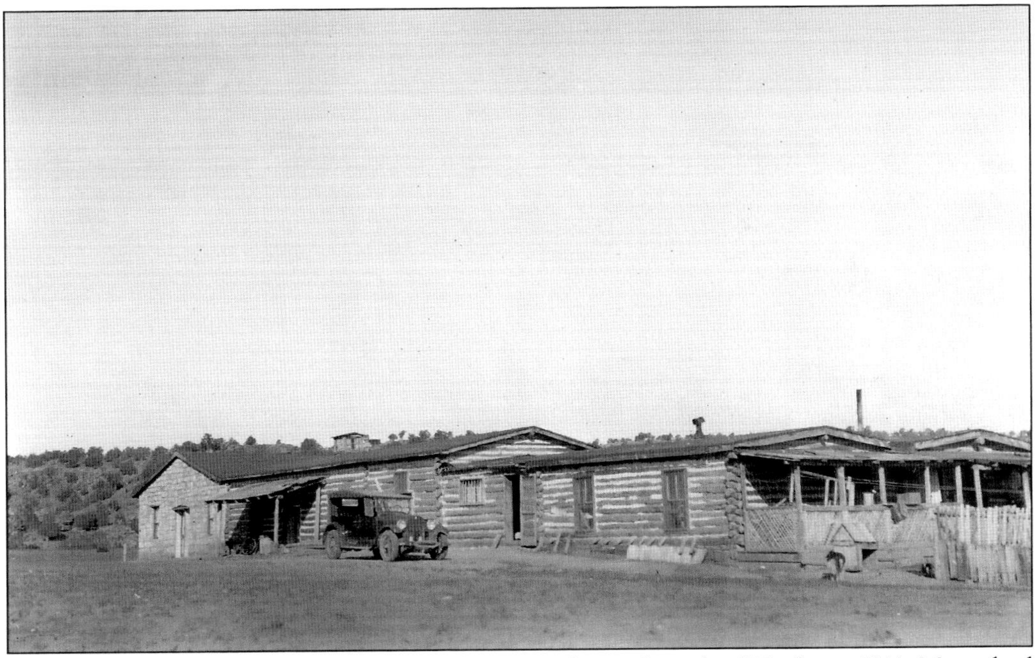

Oscar Marty built upper Greasewood Trading Post, located north of Tsaile, in 1911. Marty had a dispute with a Navajo over a 10¢ claim, and he refused to pay the dime to his customer. The Navajo returned to the post and fired his rifle through the store window. The shot hit the store clerk and grazed Marty's son's head. Soon after the shooting, Marty sold out and left the area.

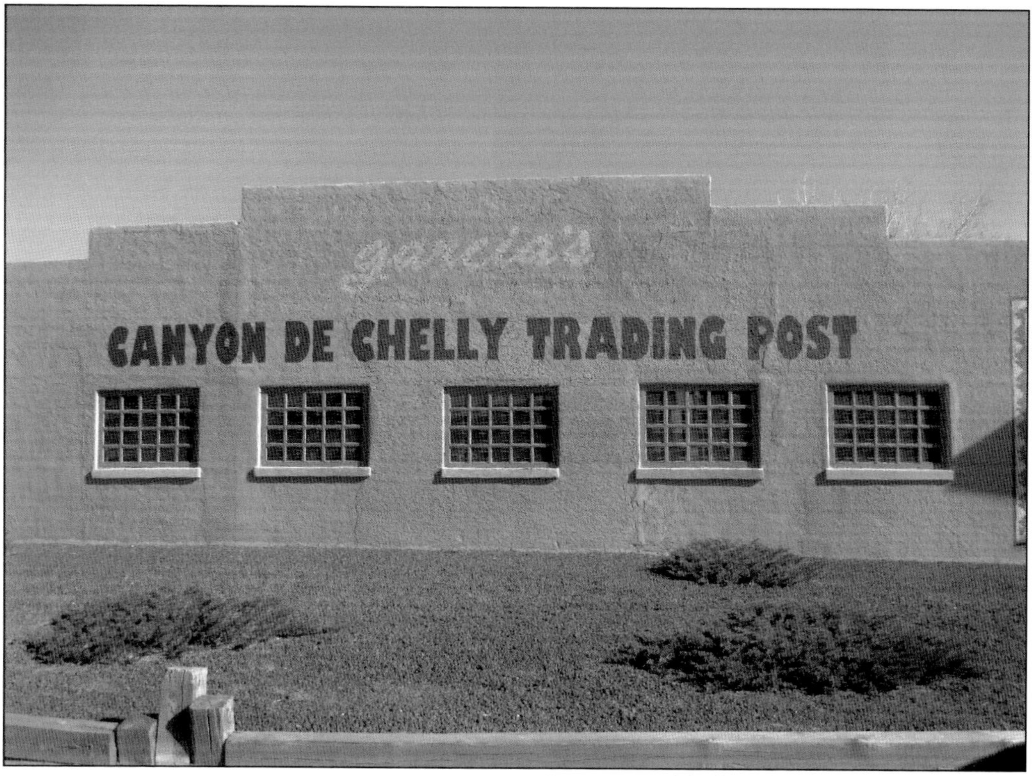

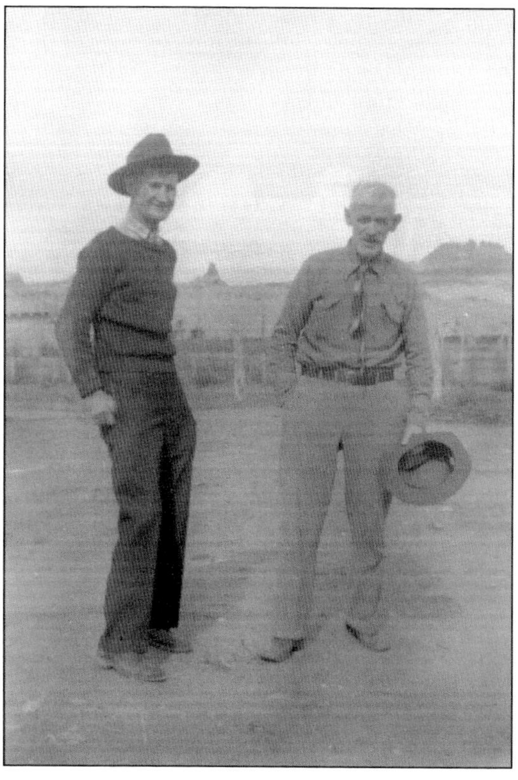

Lorenzo Hubbell and C.N. Cotton started a trading post in an abandoned hogan west of the entrance to Canyon de Chelly in 1885. Hubbell later sold out to Cotton, who sold the store to Camille Garcia, Cozy McSparron, and Hartley Seymour. Garcia bought out his partners and named his store Canyon de Chelly Trading Post. In 1992, a hotel was added that hosts thousands of tourists who visit the canyon.

Sam Day (left), shown here in a vintage photograph with Kayenta trader John Wetherill, built a log store near the entrance to Canyon de Chelly in 1902. Photographer Edward Curtis stayed with Sam Day in 1904 and photographed in the canyon. Day sold out three years later but went on to operate other trading posts and also served in the Arizona Legislature. (Courtesy of Harvey Leake.)

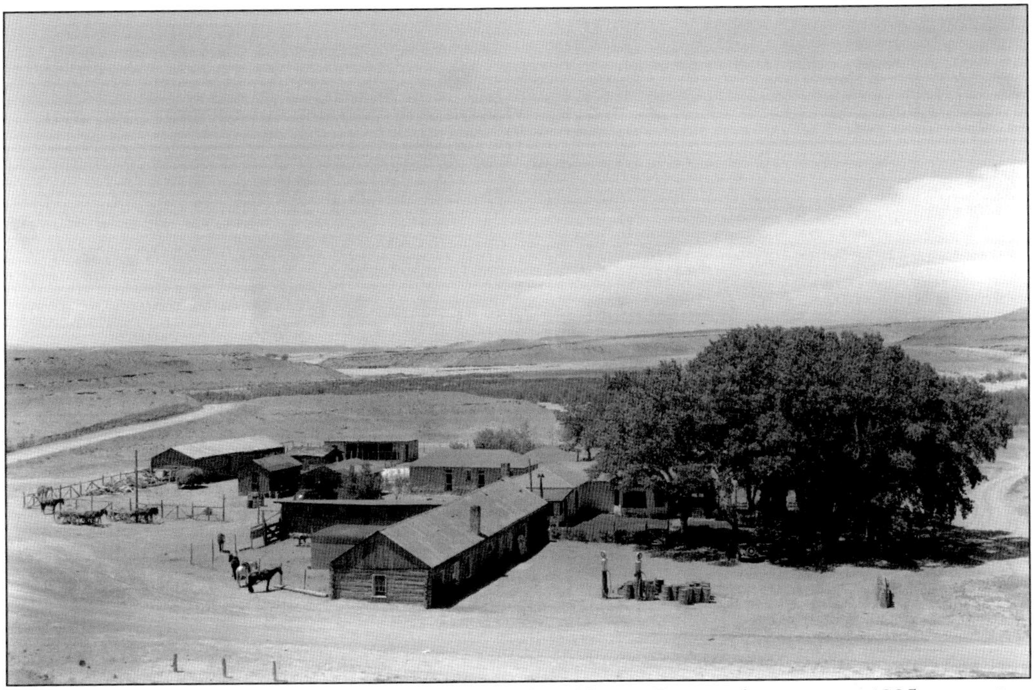

Leon "Cozy" McSparron acquired ownership of the old Sam Day trading post in 1925, renaming it Thunderbird Lodge and operating it as a trading post and dude ranch for the next 30 years. Thunderbird was a destination for the Fred Harvey Motor Tours, along with artists, writers, and movie stars. Douglas Fairbanks filmed a movie in the area. The story is told that Cozy was at Thunderbird for so long that he lost count of the years, so every New Year's Eve he shot an arrow into the ceiling of the lodge to help him keep track of the time. Cozy's arrows are still visible in the photograph below. He retired and sold out in 1954. (Above, courtesy of WACC; below, courtesy of Frashers Fotos Collection.)

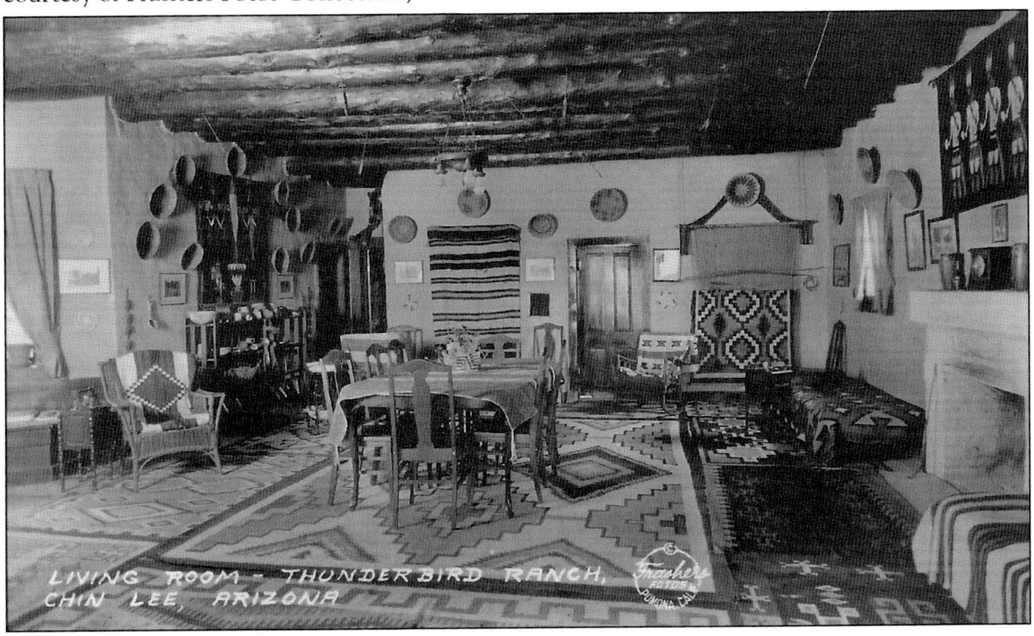

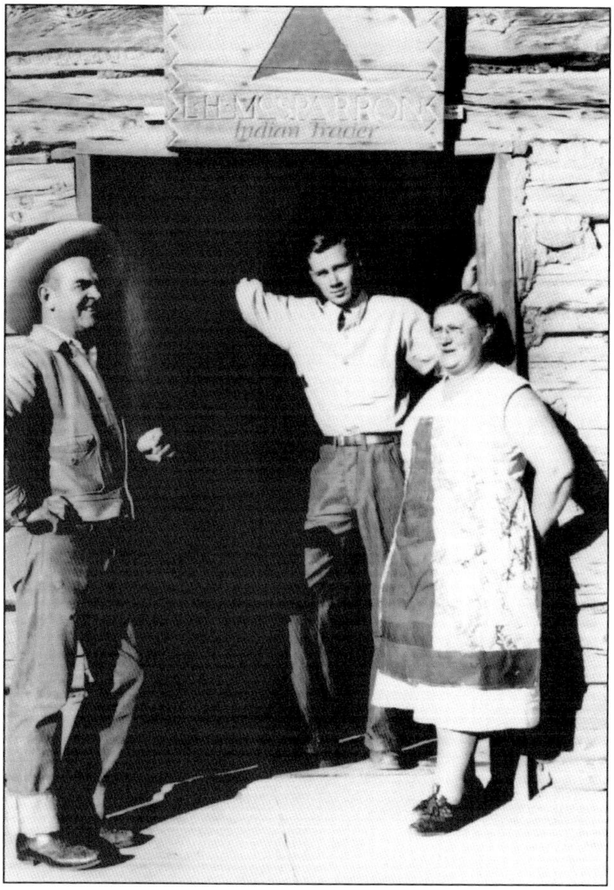

In this 1930s photograph, Cozy McSparron (left) is standing at the door of Thunderbird Trading Post. Bill Cousins clerked at the store, and Tugboat Annie was the cook. Dama Margaret Smith, who wrote under the name Mrs. White Mountain Smith, visited Thunderbird in 1938 and recalled that Cozy got the news that the daughter of a Navajo friend had died the night before. Cozy took a red calico dress, shoes, a blue ribbon, and beads from the store, and he and Mrs. Smith went into the canyon and dressed and buried the young girl. Because traditional Navajos had an aversion to death, traders were often called to perform burials in earlier times. If a Navajo died inside of a hogan, a wall was broken out for the spirit to escape, and the hogan was abandoned. The hogan below is a seasonal Navajo home in the canyon. (Left, courtesy of Mary Engels.)

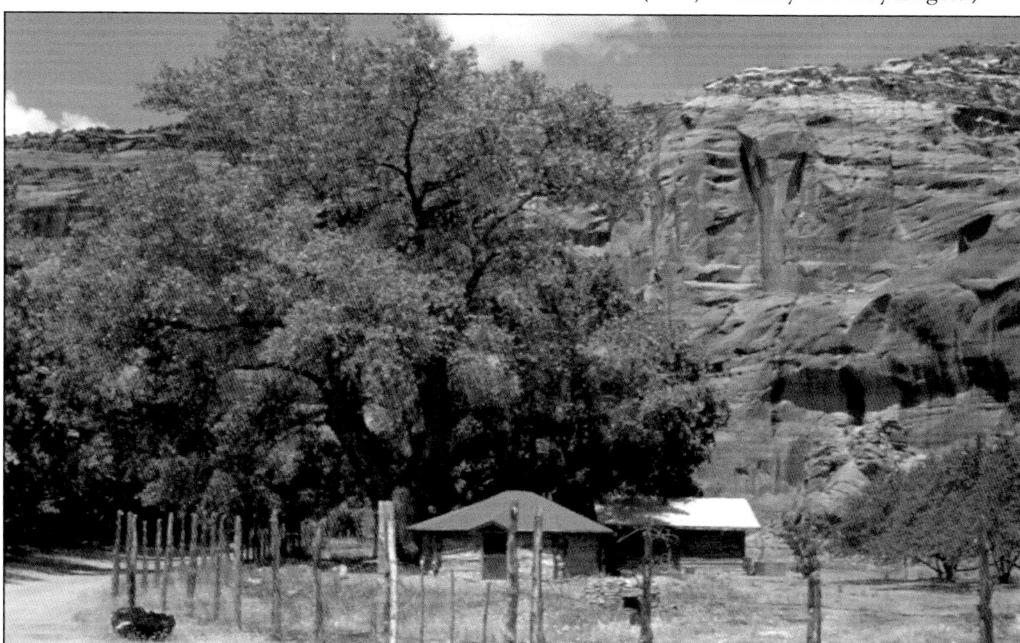

Pres. Herbert Hoover declared Canyon de Chelly a national monument in 1931, and Cozy McSparron served as the first superintendent. In this 1930 photograph by T. Cronyn, a Navajo couple in a wagon takes bales of hay to their hogan in the canyon. (Courtesy of WACC.)

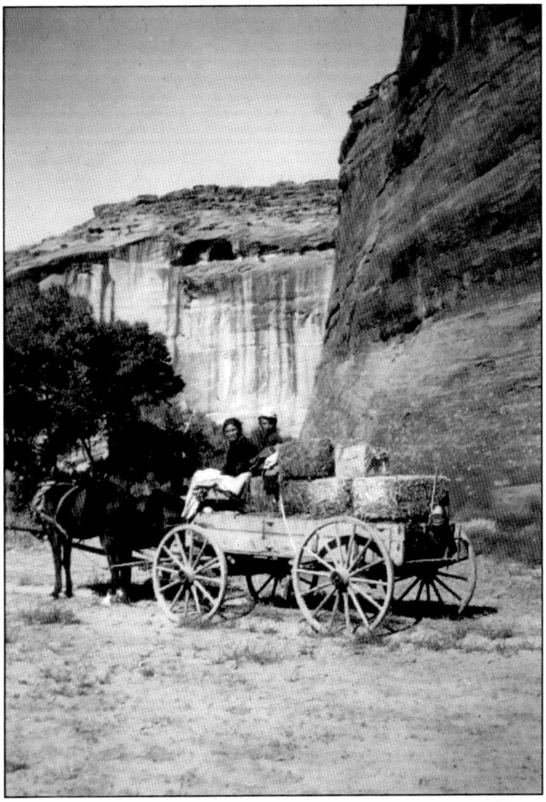

Myles and Doris Headrick managed Thunderbird Trading Post and Lodge in the mid-1950s. As more tourists came to Canyon de Chelly, the lodge expanded. Doris cooked, and the three Headrick children served meals. Doris was an avid collector of Fiestaware dishes. Breakfast was served on yellow and gray dishes, lunch was placed on rose and turquoise dishes, and dinner was displayed on chartreuse and forest-green dishes. The family still has those treasured dishes. (Courtesy of Edythe Klopping.)

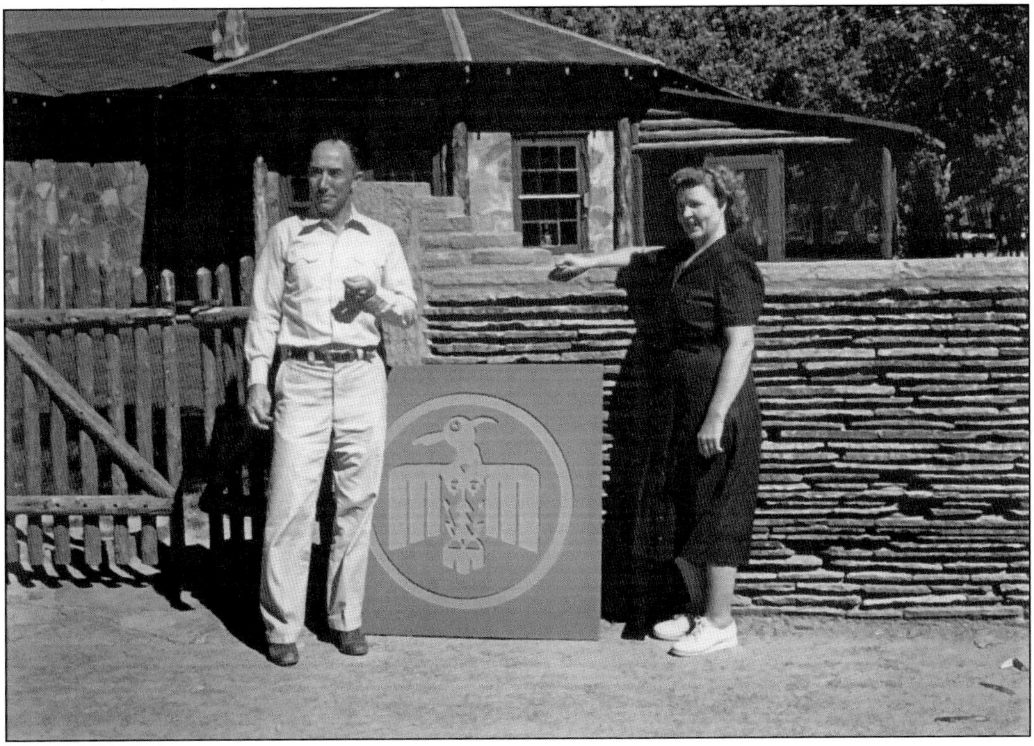

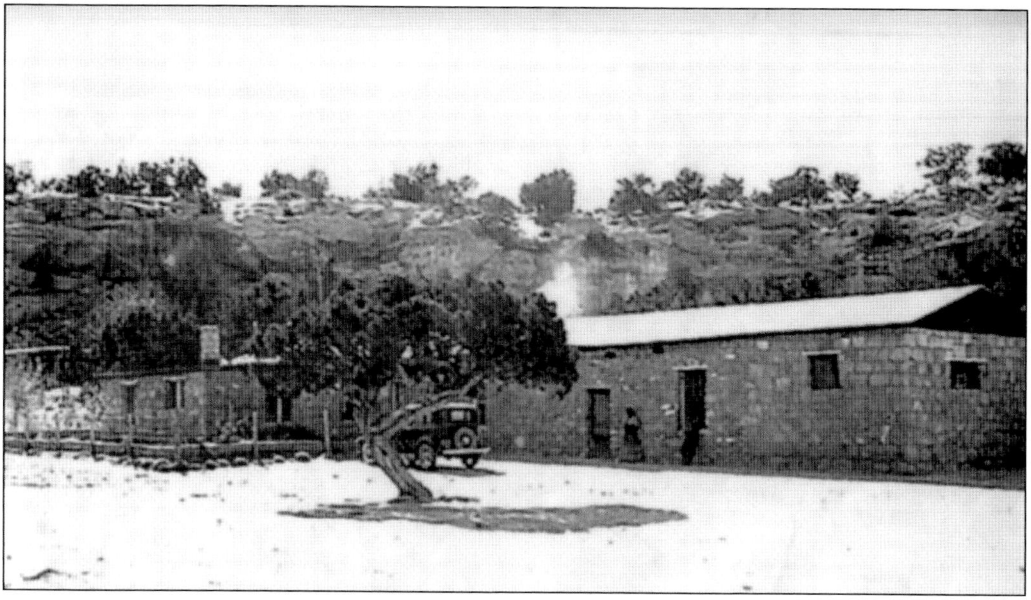

Located 30 miles northwest of Chinle, Rough Rock Trading Post was built about 1897 by Navajo mason Clitso Dedman. Rough Rock, Tsch'izhi, was named for the granular sandstone at a nearby spring. The post was remote, and supply trips to Gallup took two days—and two weeks to return with the heavily laden wagons. Con Shillingburg owned the post from 1919 to 1946. He had been a baker at Hubbell Trading Post and was called Hosteen Din Chu, "Mr. Yeast." In the Tony Hillerman mystery series, Navajo police sergeant Jim Chee is said to have grown up at Rough Rock. The current trader, Al Grieve, below, stands in front of the original stone post on Trading Post Wash. A newer, L-shaped store, with attached living quarters, was constructed in front of the building in the 1930s. (Above, courtesy of Al and Margaret Grieve.)

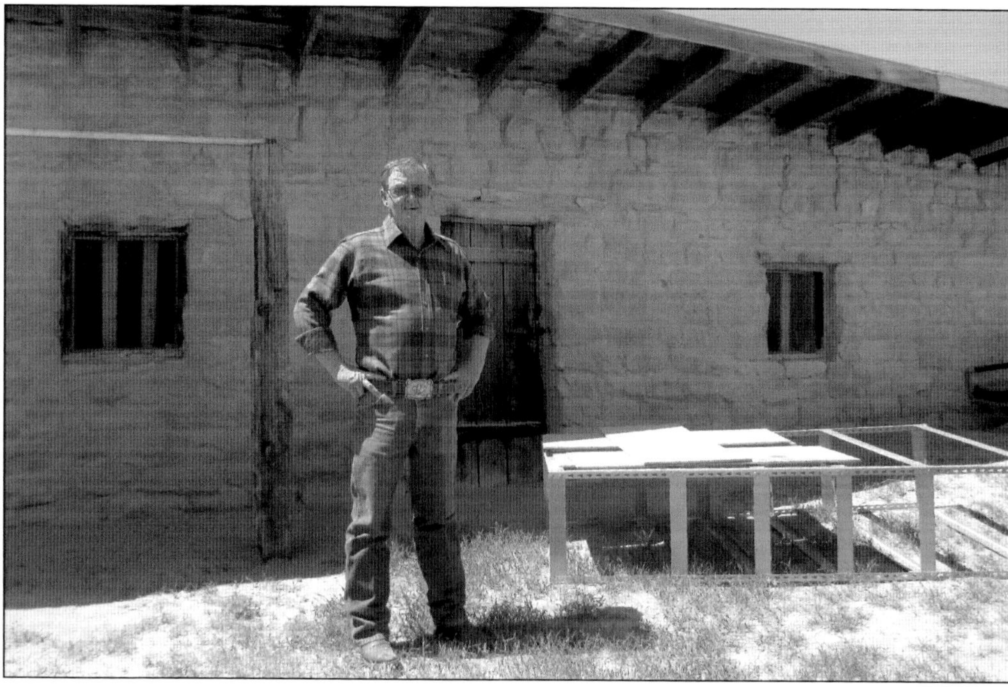

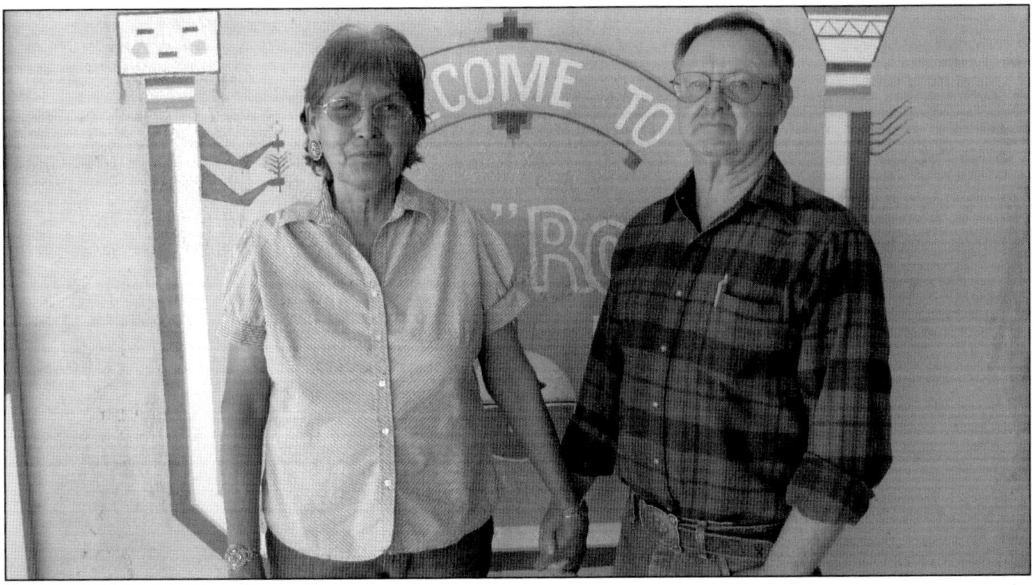

Over the years, Al and Margaret Grieve managed several trading posts, including Rough Rock. Margaret was often at the stores alone when Al was away buying cattle or selling rugs. She had a loom in a front room where she could weave and wait on customers when they came to the post. Margaret has won many blue ribbons for her rugs. If customers wanted to sell sheep, she would lock the store and go out to the back where a hand scale hung from a beam. She would tie a rope around the belly of the sheep and attach it to the scale. Sometimes, there were hundreds of sheep to weigh. Below, a customer shops for a pair of shoes. Shoes were a recent addition to the store's inventory, as handmade moccasins were standard wear early on. (Below, courtesy of Al and Margaret Grieve.)

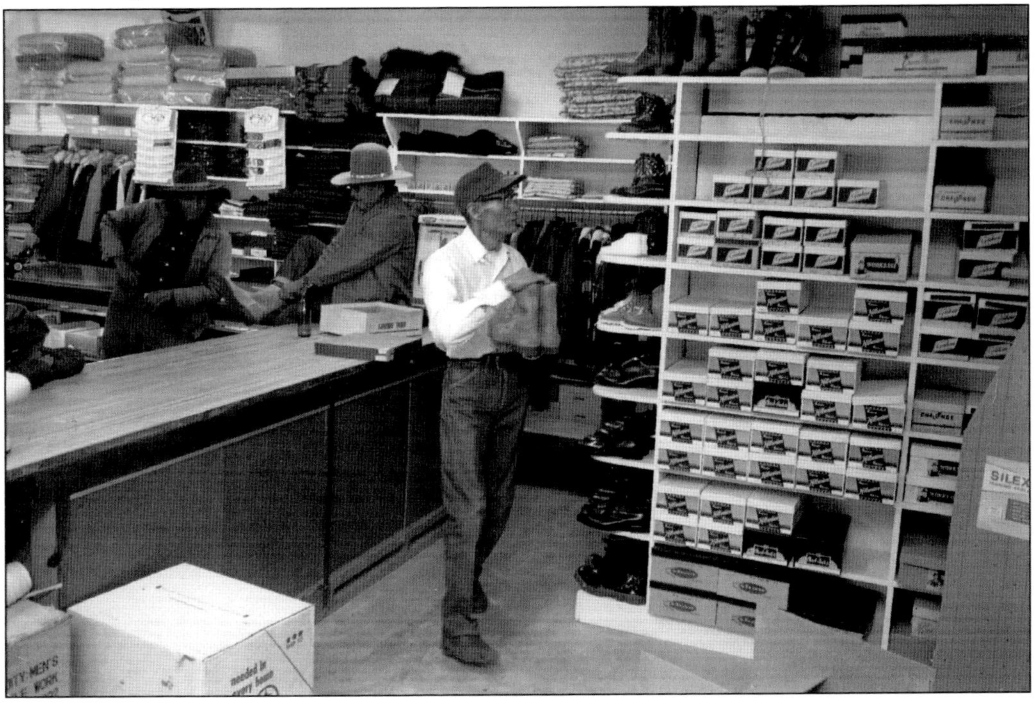

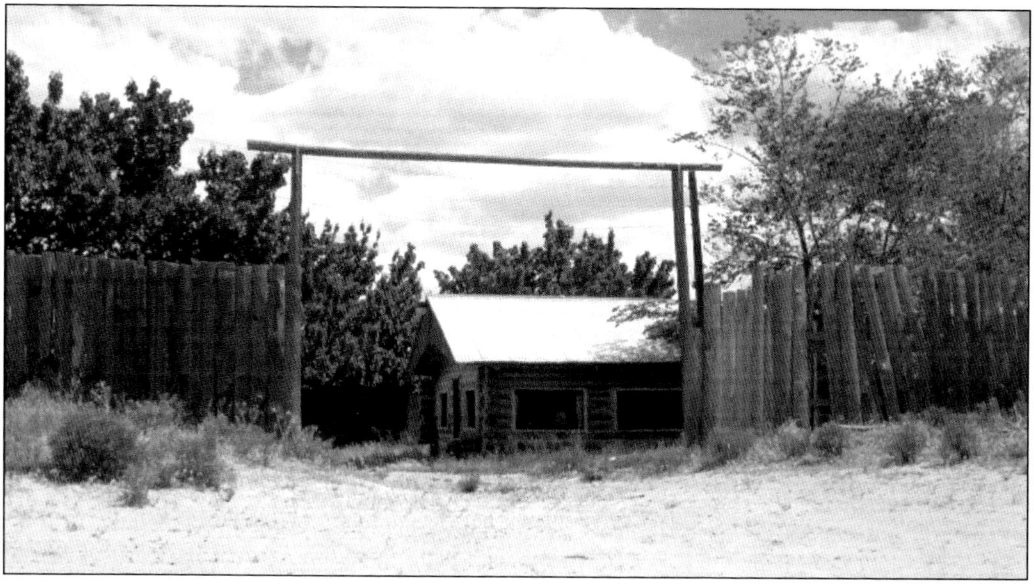

George and Mary Kennedy established Salina Springs Trading Post in 1913. Supplies were freighted in from Gallup, 100 miles southeast, which was a 13-day-long trip that could take twice that long in the winter. According to Mary, Navajo women wore skirts that required 12 yards of fabric, and it was customary for them to wear several skirts at the same time. Cracker Jacks and strawberry soda, called *toh-le-chee* ("red water"), were popular items. Owner Dave Murray's son was shot and killed at the post in 1987. Soon after, the Navajo Tribe took over and closed the post in 1995. Below, trade tokens were used at many posts. This "tin money" could only be used at the trading post where it was issued, and eventually, the government banned the use of tin money.

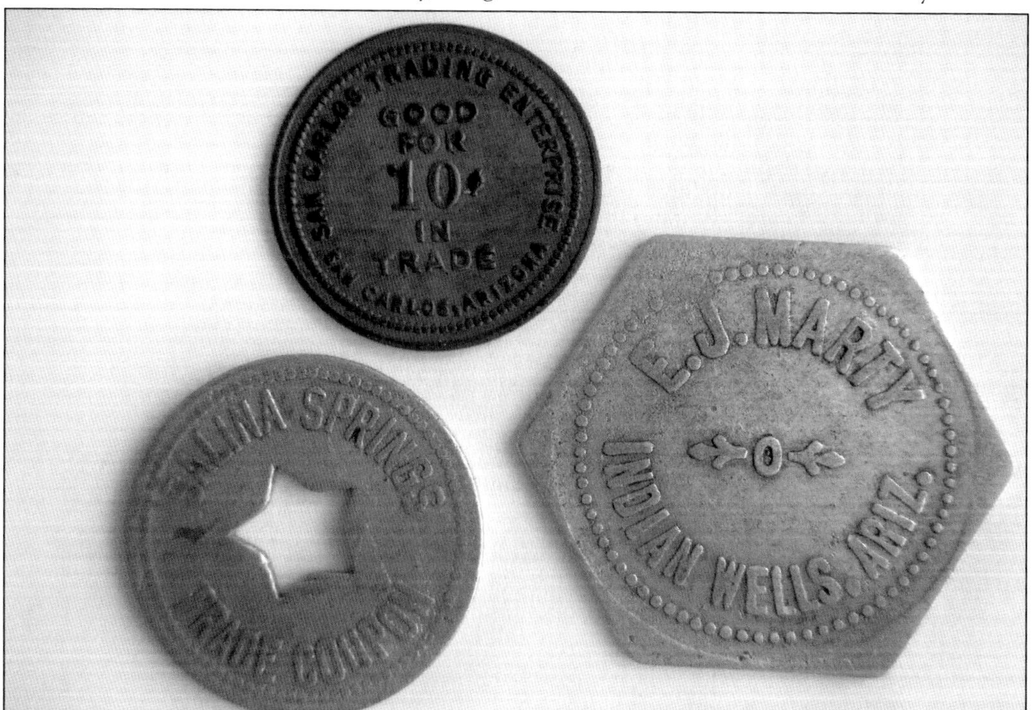

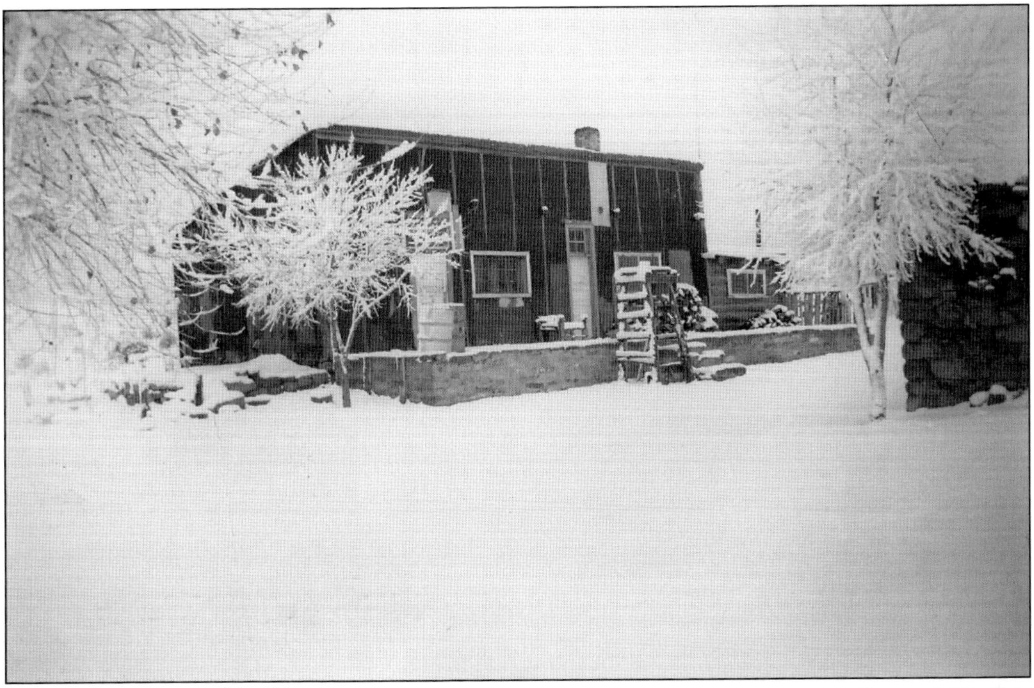

In 1914, Lorenzo Hubbell built Black Mountain Trading Post, located west of Chinle, and then sold to other traders. Myles Headrick managed the store from 1938 to 1940. With his wife, Doris, and two young children, Edythe and Miles "Bob," he lived in a large hogan next to the trading post. There was a fireplace for heat and Navajo rugs on the floor as well as on the walls. The store burned down in 1975. (Both, courtesy of Edythe Klopping.)

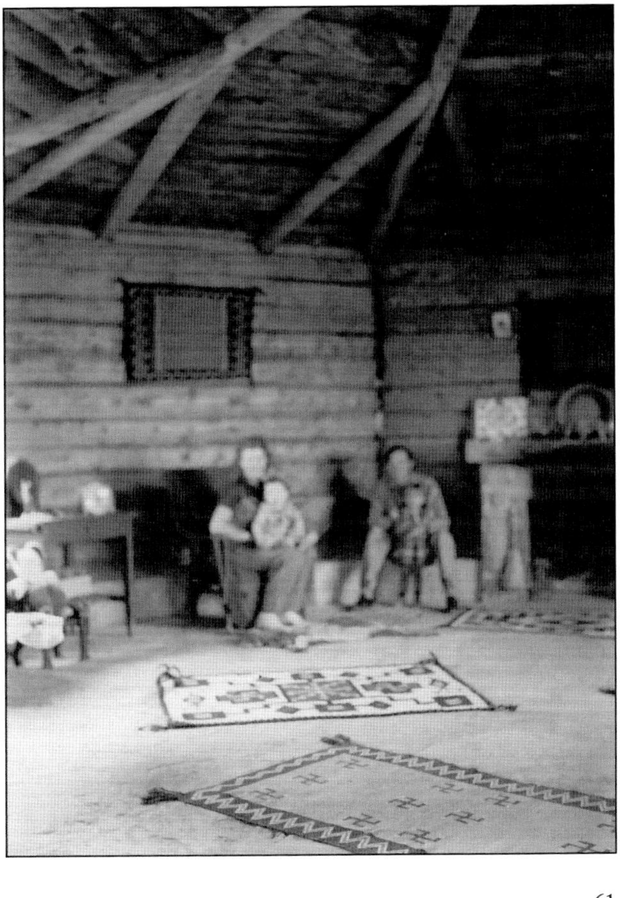

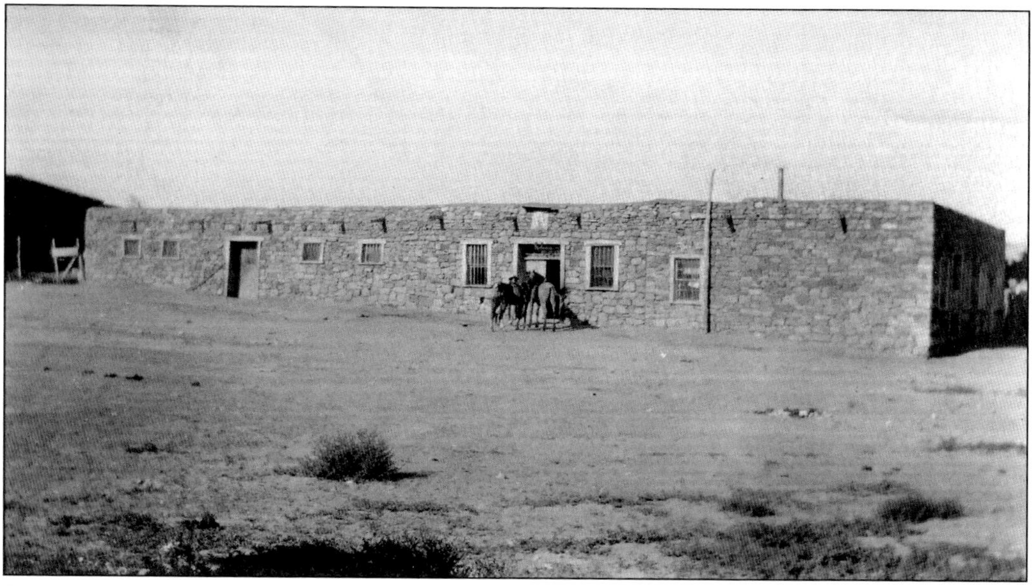

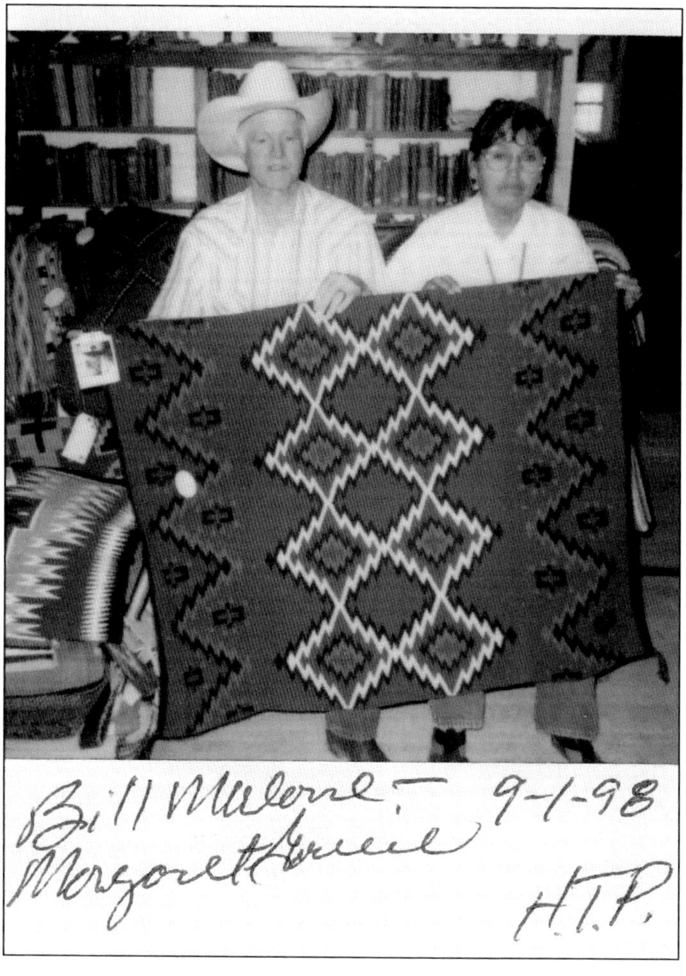

Charles Crary started the original trading post at Ganado in 1871. Lorenzo Hubbell bought the store in 1878 and built a large stone building, which is still in use today. Hubbell built a huge trading community and owned 24 other posts and two wholesale stores. He died in 1930, but his family continued to manage his enterprises for nearly 40 more years. Today, Hubbell Trading Post is a National Historical Site. Hubbell's adjacent home is filled with paintings from the many artists who were his guests. A distinctive rug design, with a red background and a cross or diamond in the middle, was developed in this region, and was named "Ganado Red" for Hubbell's Navajo friend, Ganado Mucho. Weaver Margaret Grieve poses with her rug that was purchased by Hubbell trader Billy Malone in 1998. (Above, courtesy of Harvey Leake; left, courtesy of Margaret Grieve.)

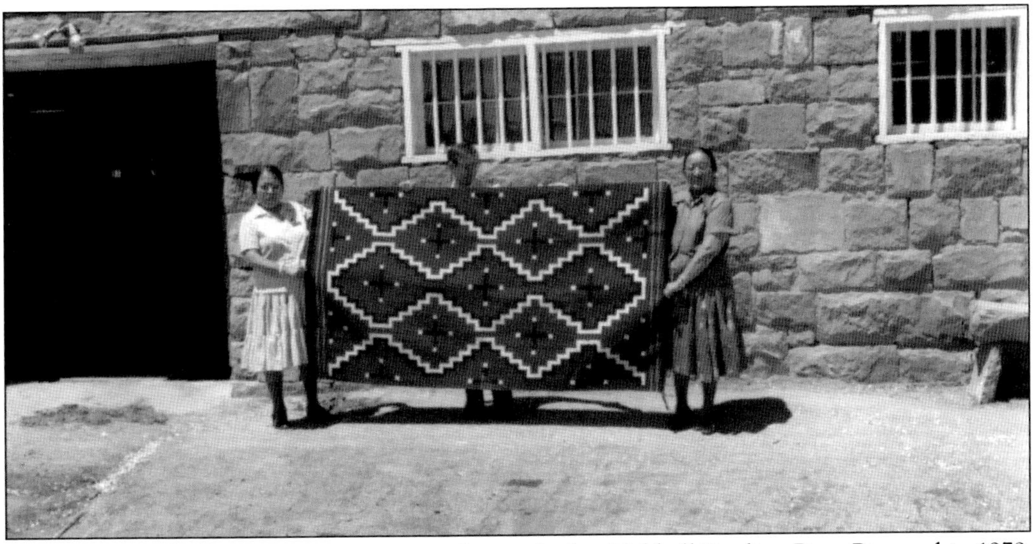

Evelyn Curley (left) was a master weaver who worked at Hubbell Trading Post. Pictured in 1979, she is in front of the trading post with her large rug. This rug features the distinctive Ganado red coloring and crosses and diamonds. To achieve the deep-red color, weavers at Hubbell used a double portion of red aniline dye. These commercial dyes had become popular during the last quarter of the 19th century, replacing the traditional use of vegetal dyes. Al Grieve (center) was the Hubbell trader from 1979 to 1982; the woman at the right is unidentified. Below, Grieve fills seven-foot-long wool sacks weighing 200 to 250 pounds each. The tops of the wool sacks were stitched together when full. (Both, courtesy of Al and Margaret Grieve.)

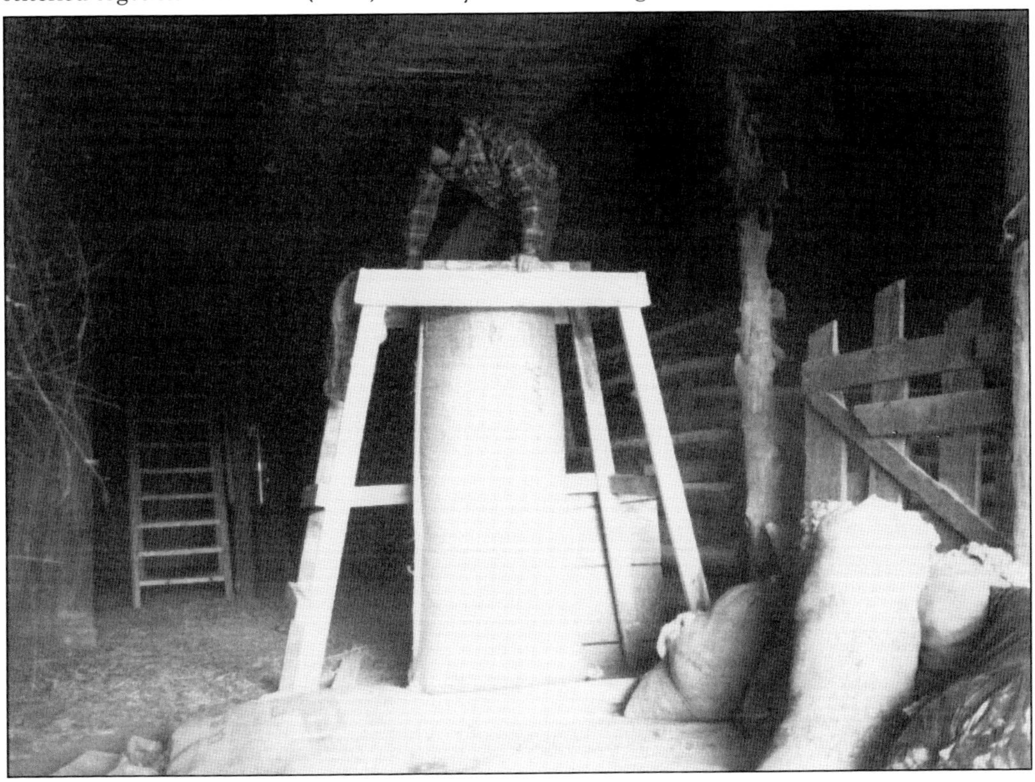

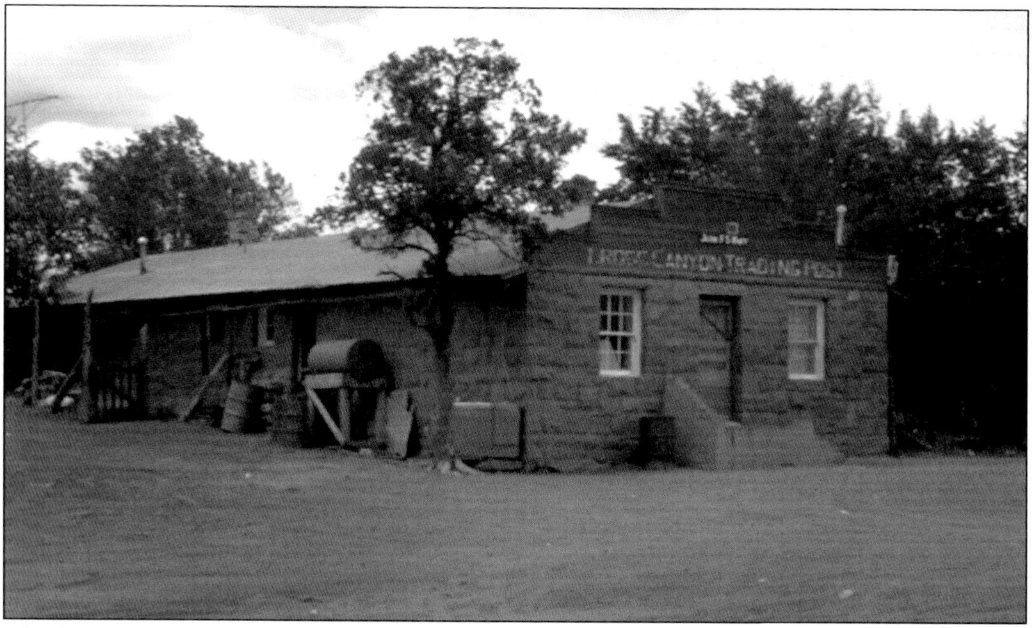

Charles Manning built Cross Canyon, located eight miles east of Ganado, in the early 1900s. The site was named for an old Navajo trail that crossed through the canyon. In 1922, the store was robbed by a group of Navajos after the trader Frank Dugan received a large shipment of goods. After Dugan was killed, the post was looted and then burned to the ground. Dugan's frozen body was found in the spring. Navajo deputy and US marshal Sam Day followed wagon tracks leaving the post and eventually apprehended the culprits, but none were ever convicted. A new trading post was built a few miles north of the original store. Cross Canyon Trading Post was closed in 1987 and has now fallen into ruins. (Above, courtesy of Byron Hunter.)

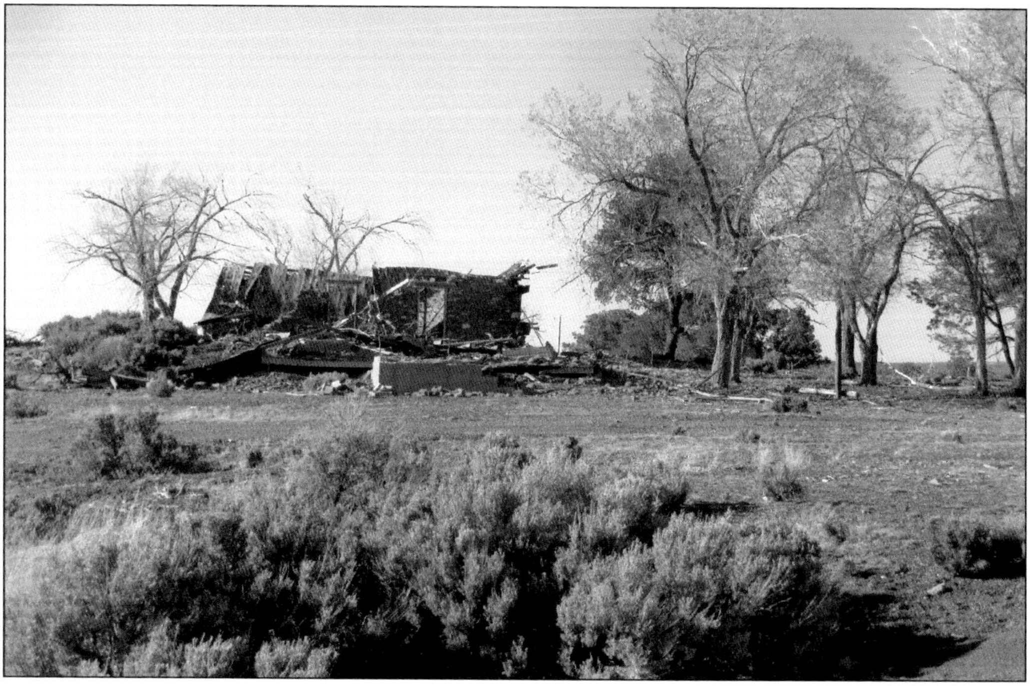

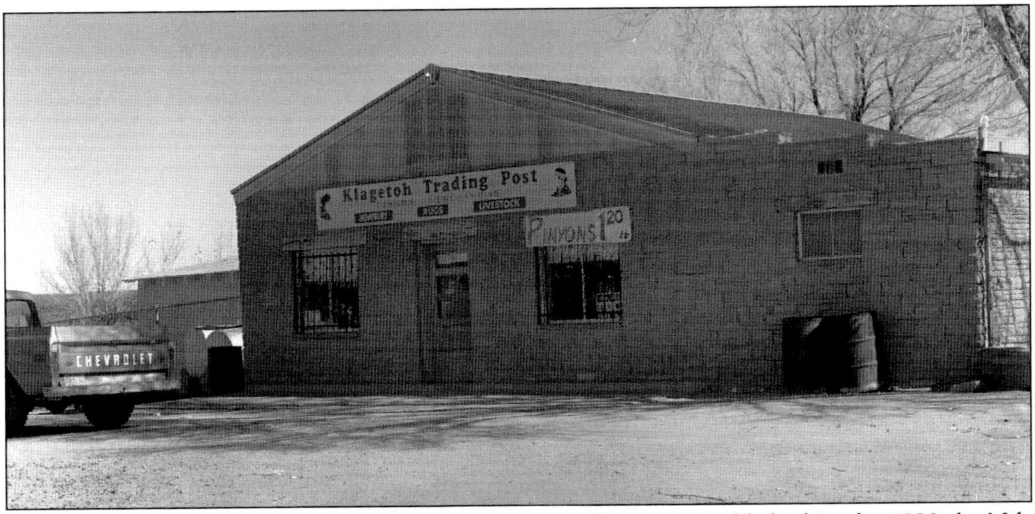

Located 15 miles south of Ganado, Klagetoh Trading Post was established in the 1920s by Nils Hogner. Earlier, a Navajo known as "Yellow Policeman" had run a small trading operation. In her book *Native Roads*, Fran Kosik tells of a 1935 incident when Winnie Balcomb, the Wide Ruins trader, came into the Klagetoh store and shot up the place with her .45-caliber pistols. Balcomb had heard that Klagetoh was selling flour for 10¢ less than Wide Ruins. When she learned that was not true, Balcomb holstered her guns and apologized. Kosik also notes that Bluebird Flour from the Cortez Milling Company was popular with Navajos and Hopis because it has a higher gluten content than other flours and was better for making fry bread. Helga Teiwes took the 1976 photograph above. (Above, courtesy of Arizona State Museum.)

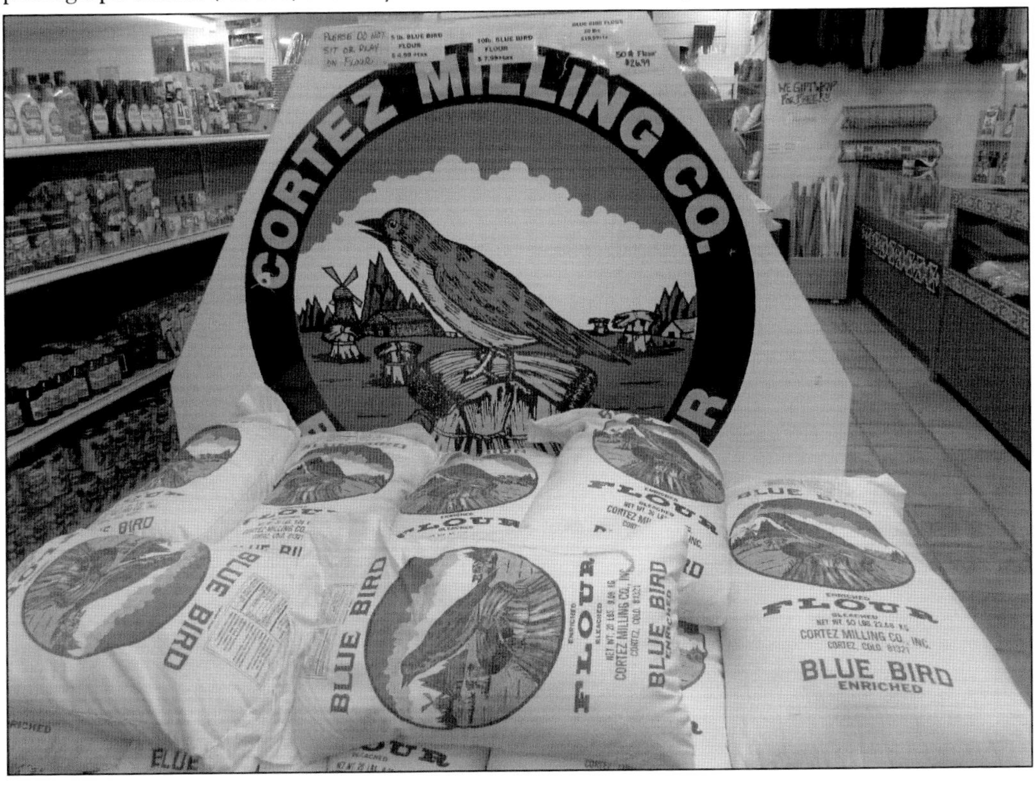

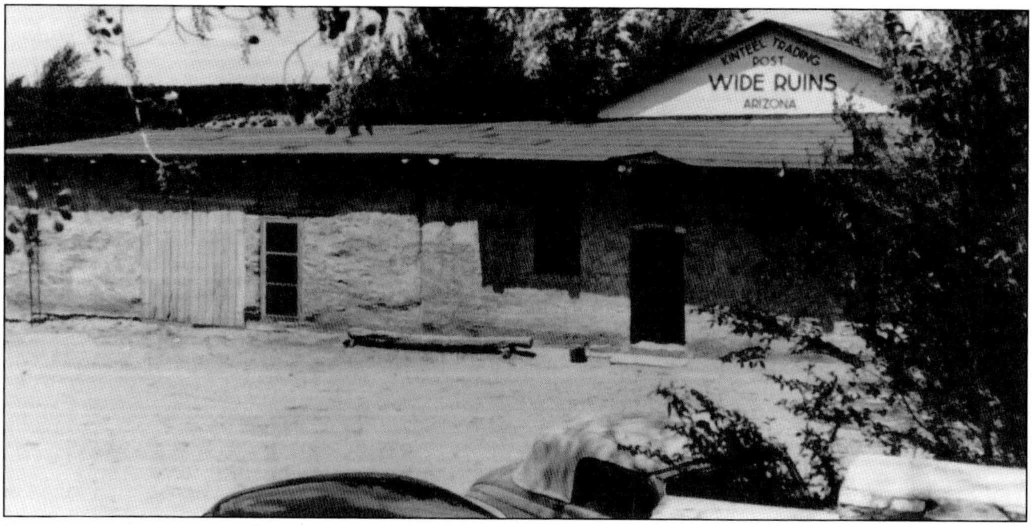

Spencer and Winnie Balcomb established Kinteel Trading Post in 1902. Shown here in the 1940s, the Kinteel "broad house" was named for the Anasazi ruins and was the site of a prehistoric trading center. A wall constructed of vertical logs enclosed the store compound. When Bill and Sallie Lippincott took over Kinteel in 1938, they renamed it Wide Ruins. The Lippincotts are credited with bringing back the use of vegetal dyes in the local Navajo weavings, replacing the commercial aniline dyes. Wide Ruins–style rugs with their horizontal stripes and bands are still popular and collectible. Bill and Jean Cousins also lived at Wide Ruins and managed the store. Pictured behind the counter are, from left to right, Bill Cousins, Bill Lippincott, and J.B. Fordyce, with unidentified Navajo customers in front. (Both, courtesy of Mary Tate Engels.)

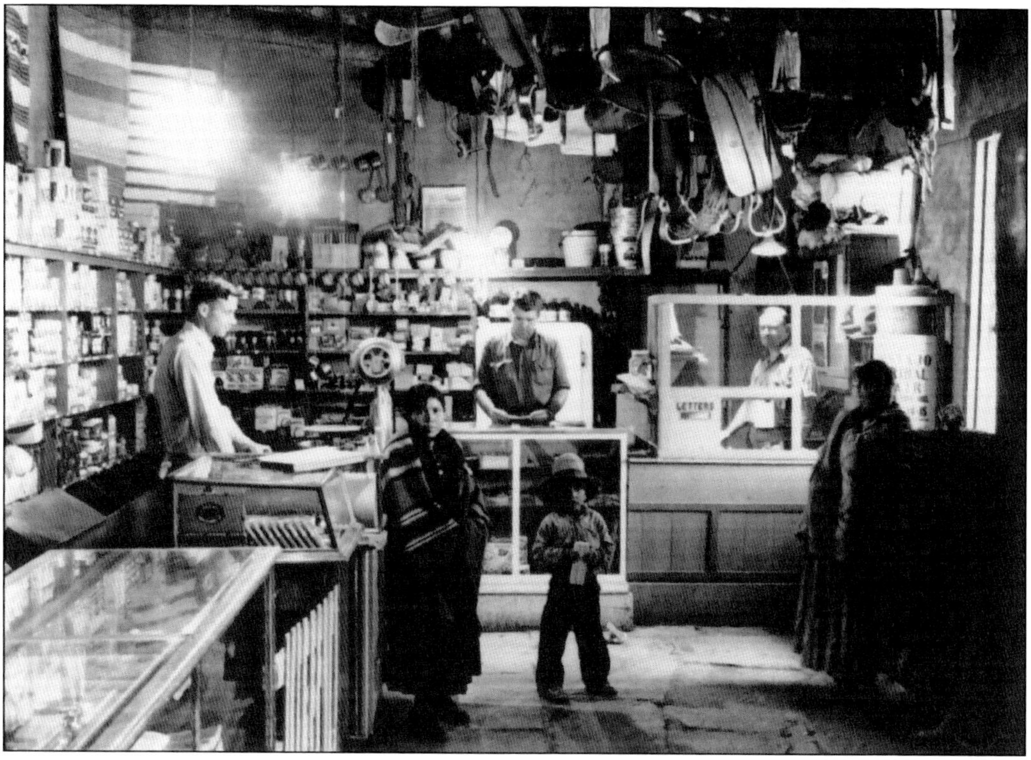

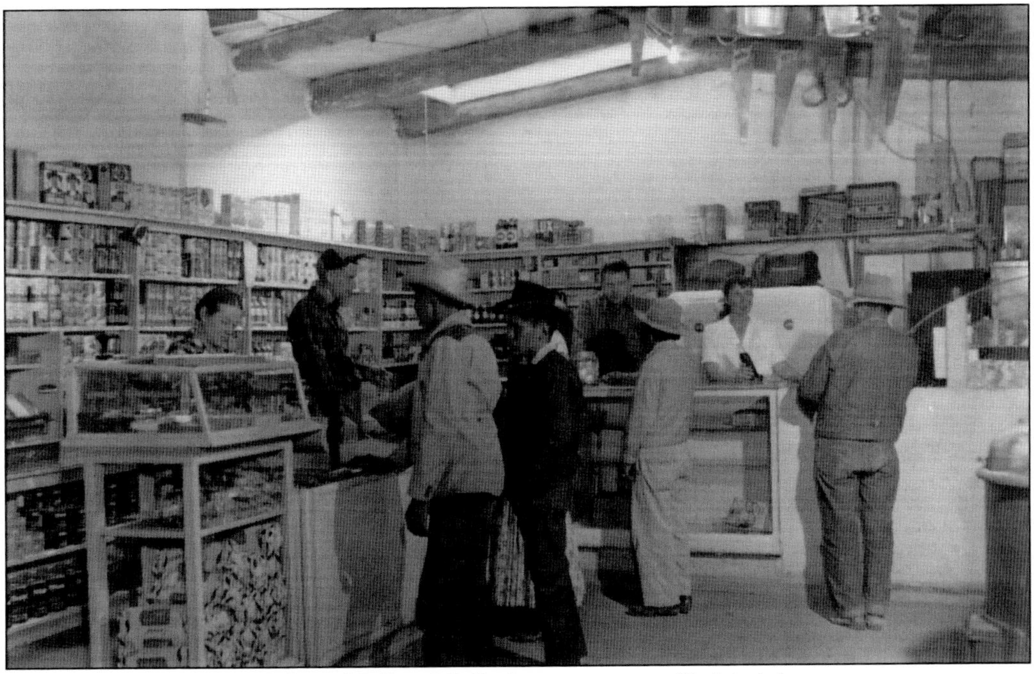

Jean and Bill Cousins, at left, and Bill and Sallie Lippincott stand behind the store counter to serve Navajo customers. Horses and horse-drawn wagons were the common method of transportation in those days. Ledger books from that time show that rugs were bought by the pound, generally at under a dollar per pound. Skins of coyotes, goats, badgers, and cattle were also taken in trade. Wide Ruins was located on a section of deeded land that the Lippincotts sold to the Navajo tribe in 1950. Various owners operated the store until the death of the last manager in 1982. Shortly after, Wide Ruins Trading Post burned down, and today, there are few traces of this store, which was such an important part in the revitalization of Navajo weaving and home to some of the finest weavers of the Southwest. (Both, courtesy of Mary Tate Engels.)

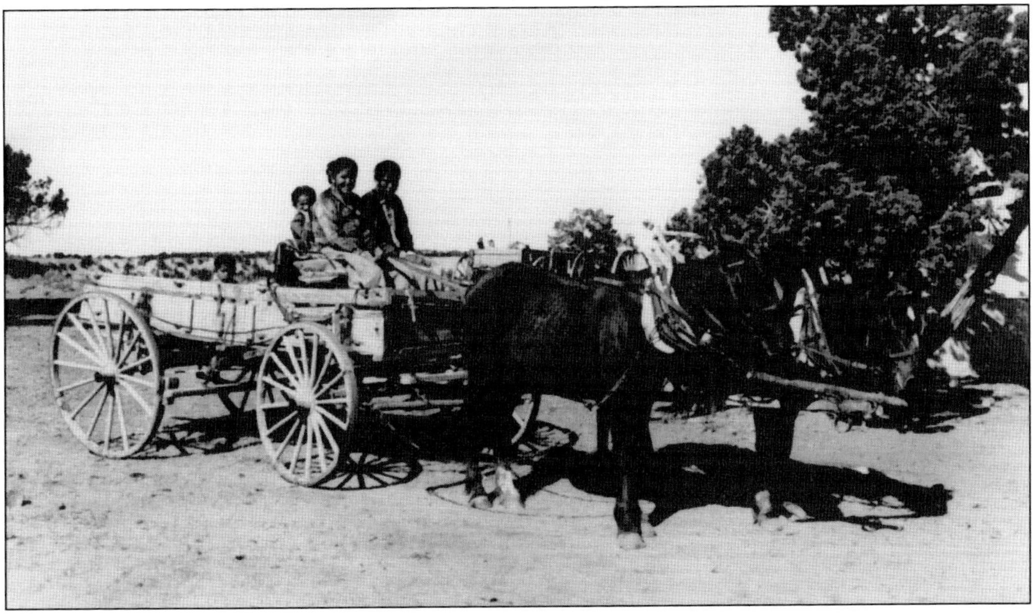

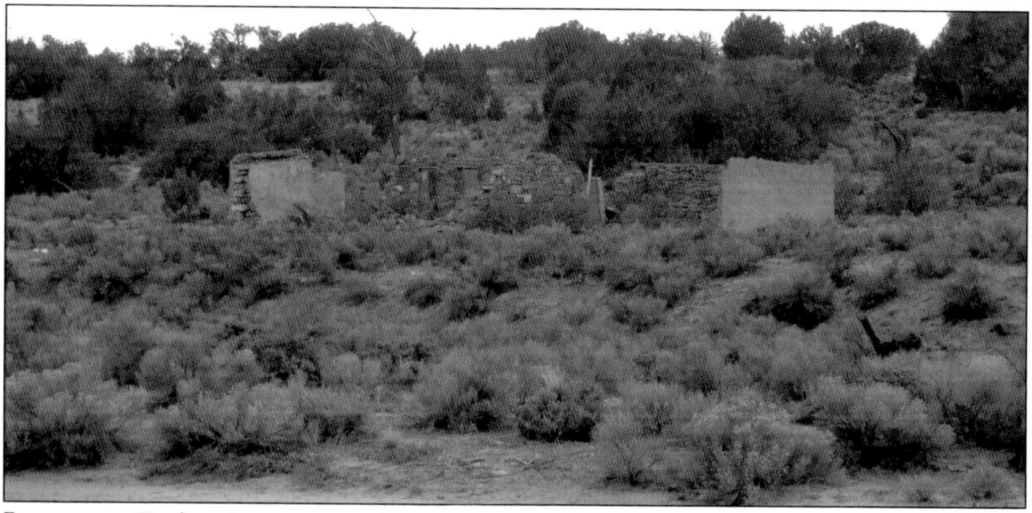

Burntwater Trading Post was north of Sanders. Burris N. Barnes built the store in the early 1900s. The post got its name when a shade ramada caught fire and burning logs fell into the water. Navajos soon renamed the place "Burnt Water." Ruins of the original store are across the wash. In 1930, the business was moved into a Quonset hut, which is still standing, although the store has been closed and abandoned since the early 1980s. Weavers in the Burntwater area developed a remarkable rug style using vegetal-dyed wools in dozens of shades. According to trader Bruce Burnham, weavers may use up to 40 to 60 colors, and some designs are so complex there is virtually no background on the rug. Burntwater rugs have been called the rarest and most desired of all vegetal-dyed rugs.

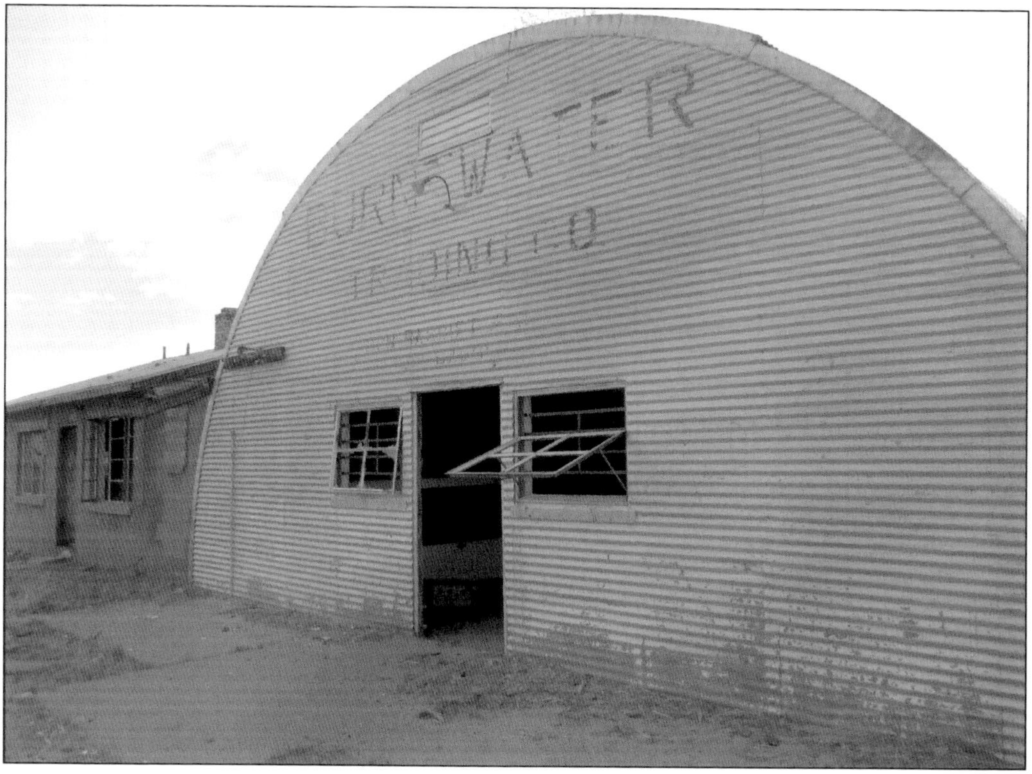

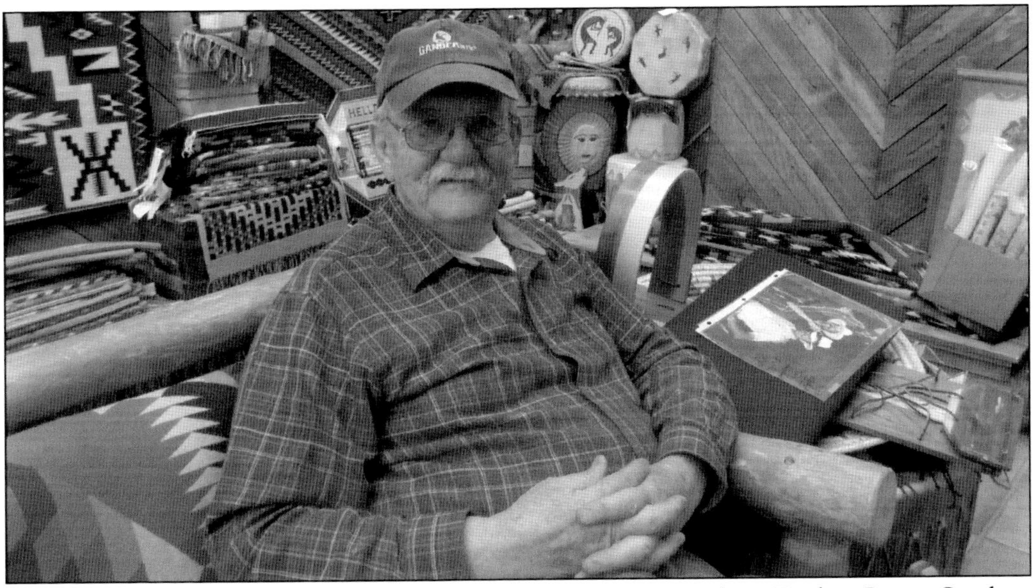

Since 1971, Bruce and Virginia Burnham have operated R.B. Burnham Trading Post at Sanders. Virginia Kaskoli Begay's father was Hopi, and her mother was Navajo. Virginia was raised as a traditional Navajo; her mother and siblings moved seasonally, following her mother's herds of sheep and cattle. Their only permanent home was a winter hogan. Bruce is a fourth-generation trader; his Mormon great-grandfather established a trading route to visit his three wives. Bruce courted Virginia while working at a trading post, and after five years, they were married by a Navajo medicine man in a traditional ceremony. Bruce recalled that his boss negotiated the bride price: a cow, a concho belt, and a car. The photograph of Bruce, above, shows some of the traditional arts in the trading post. Pictured below, Virginia folds piñon bags, and behind her are hanks of vividly colored wools used by Navajo weavers.

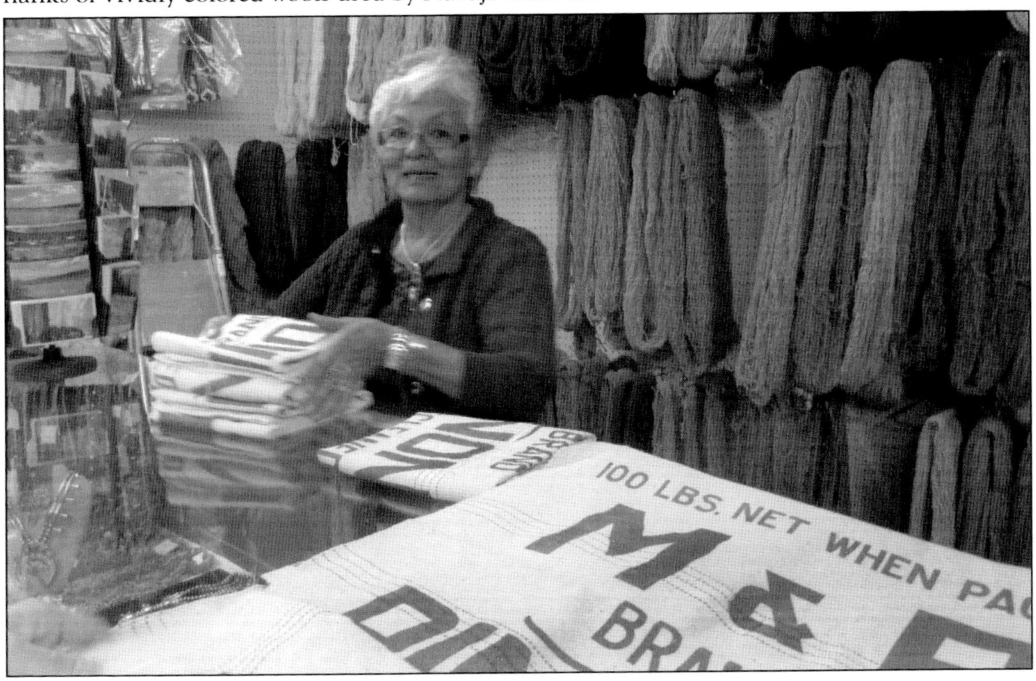

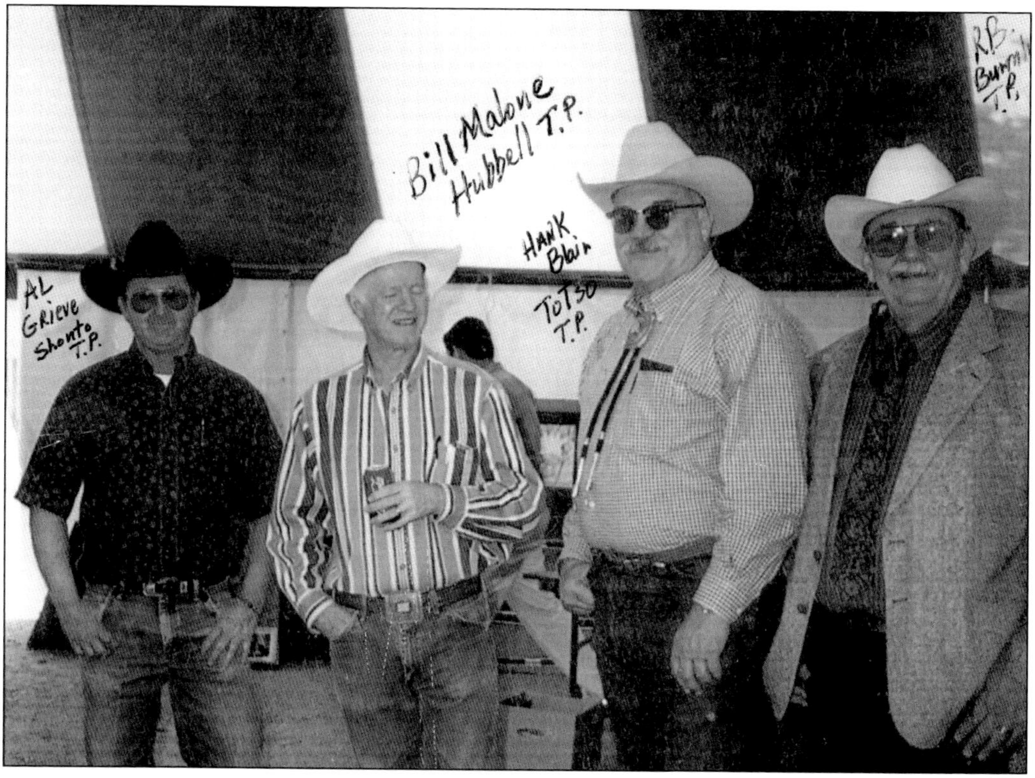

As the trading business changed, Bruce Burnham saw more weavers traveling to town to sell their rugs. He was one of the first to take rugs to auctions and shows around the country. In this 2002 photograph taken at a rug auction, Burnham (right) is joined by longtime traders, from left to right, Al Grieve, of Shonto Trading Post; Billy Malone, of Hubbell Trading Post; and Hank Blair, of Totsoh Trading Post. (Courtesy of Al and Margaret Grieve.)

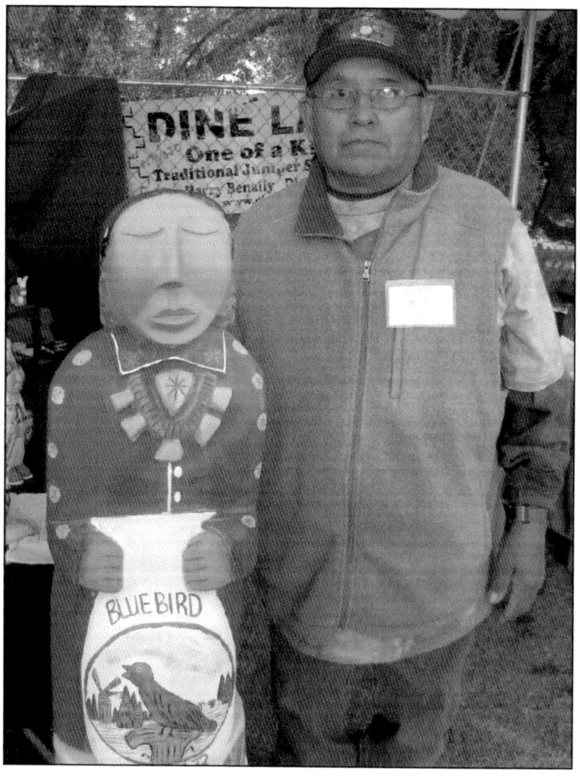

Every reservation store has a stack of Bluebird Flour bags piled on a skid. Bluebird Flour is not only the flour commonly seen across northern Arizona, but the bluebird is also a popular design element in Navajo folk art, Hopi quilts, and souvenirs. Navajo artist Harry Benally (pictured) from Sheep Springs, New Mexico, created the sculpture *Diné Lady*. Harry's wife, Isabelle, painted the carving.

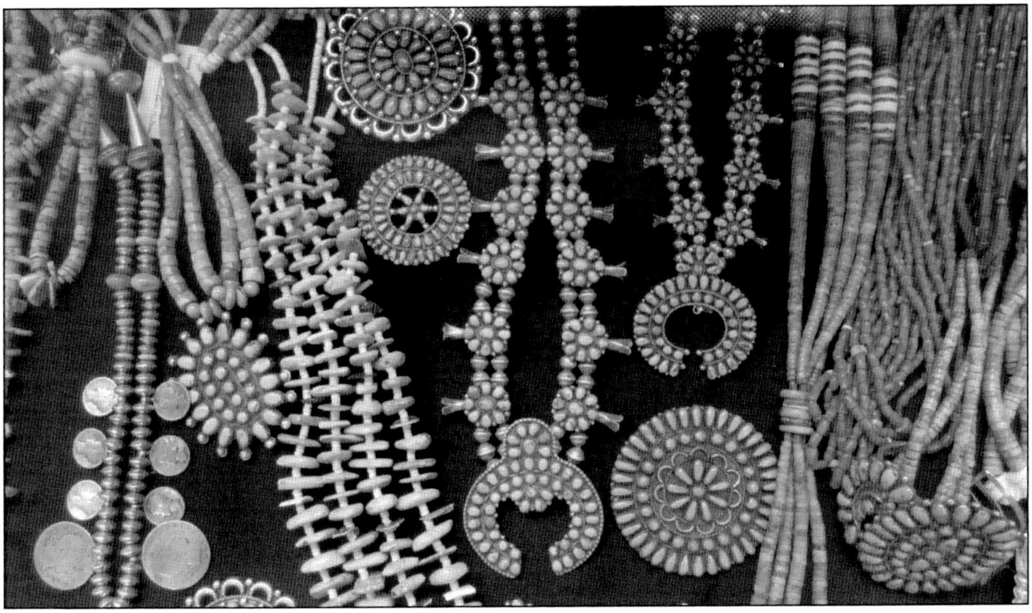

Navajo traders brought in jewelry-making supplies, including turquoise, coral, and silver, for Navajo jewelers. Several traders also developed turquoise mines in the Southwest. In 1899, the Fred Harvey Company began ordering quantities of jewelry for resale to tourists. Over the years, Navajo silver and turquoise jewelry has become popular across the country. Below, trader Billy Malone stands in front of racks of Navajo pawn jewelry in the vault at Shush Yaz Trading Company in Gallup, New Mexico. Pawn is no longer found at the reservation trading posts, with the single exception of Van's in Tuba City. However, off the reservation, especially in the Gallup area, pawn is still a part of the trading business. In addition to jewelry, other pawn items are Pendleton blankets, saddles, rifles, and baskets.

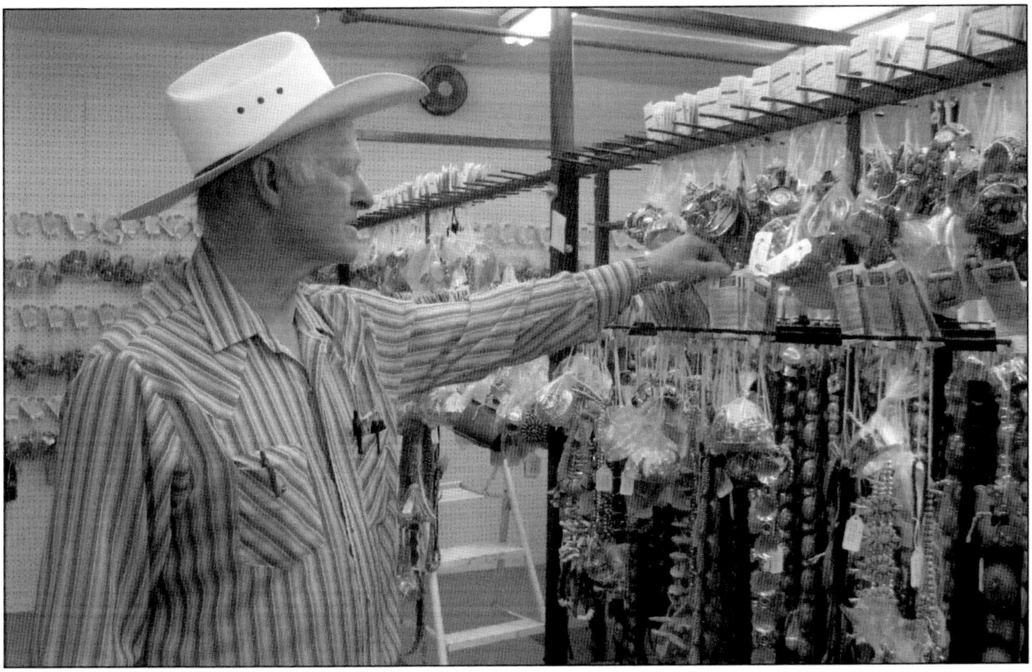

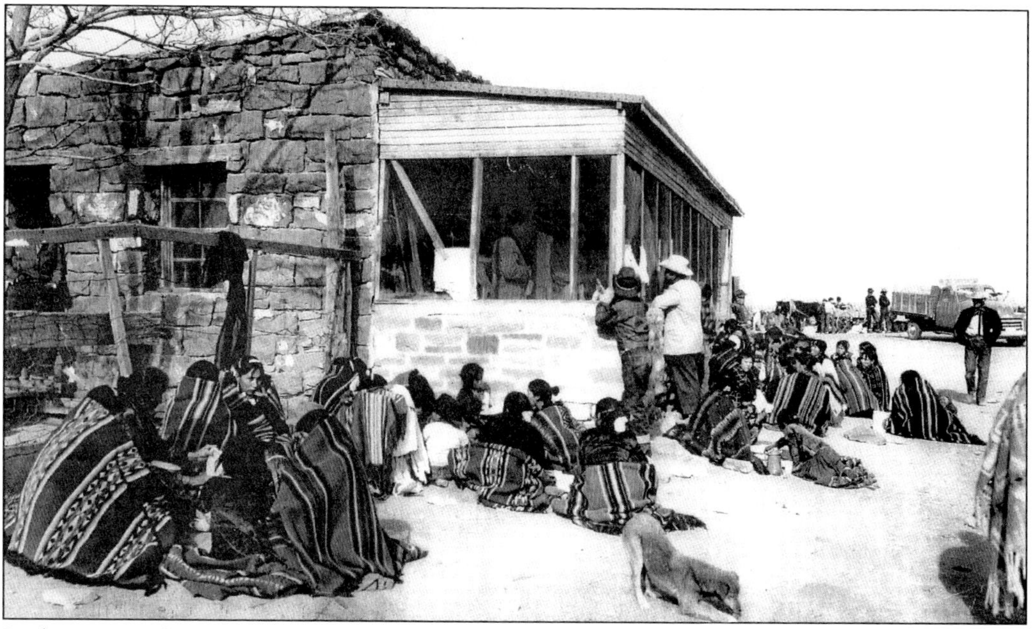

In the 1960s, when Clifton and Bill McGee owned Piñon Trading Post, the store had the highest volume of merchandise on the Navajo Reservation. Lorenzo Hubbell built the large rock post in 1916. There was a full basement for storage and to hold supplies during the winter when roads were often impassable. Betty McGee said that Piñon was a piñon store: one year they bought so many bags of piñons that the floor collapsed and all the bags fell into the basement. At one time, a Laundromat, café, and a car wash existed there. More recently, the store sold hardware, automobile supplies, and cell phones. At Christmas, Clifton McGee dressed as Santa Claus and gave out bags of fruits, nuts, and toys to local children. Piñon Trading Post has since closed. (Both, courtesy of Clifton and Betty McGee.)

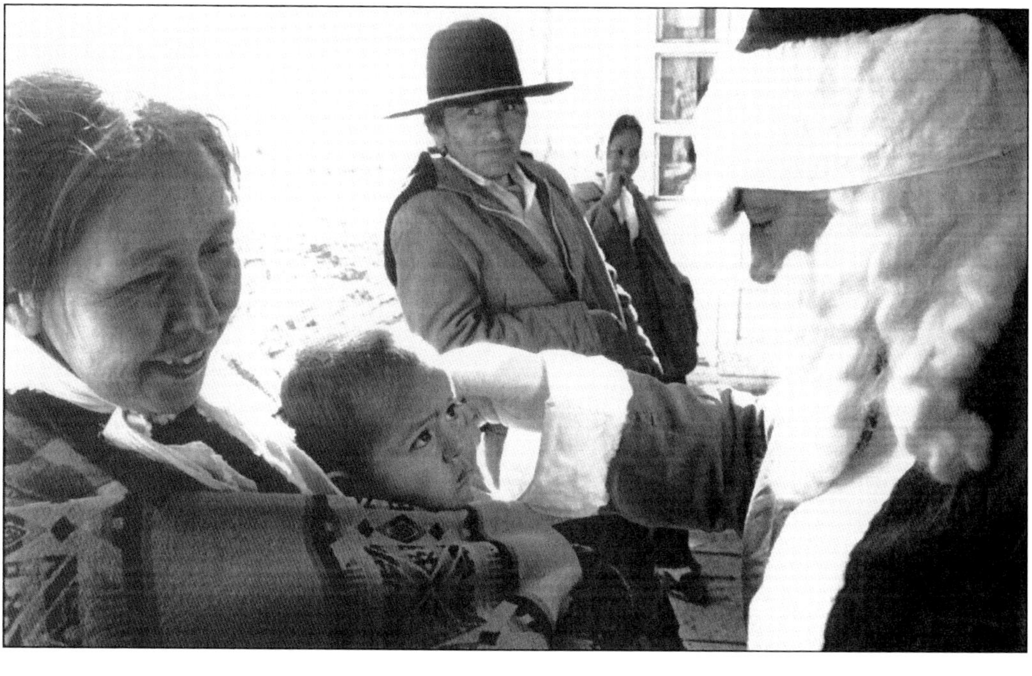

Shine Smith, center, was a Presbyterian preacher who was released from the church after it was apparent that he supported Indian belief and culture, at a time when missionaries were attempting to Christianize Native Americans and eradicate their traditional religions. Shine stayed on the reservation after he was defrocked, working in trading posts. He also organized huge Christmas parties with donated food and gifts. A Christmas gathering at Piñon in 1950 was attended by hundreds of Navajos. Another Christmas, the McGees recalled that there were 500 wagons at the trading post for the annual party.

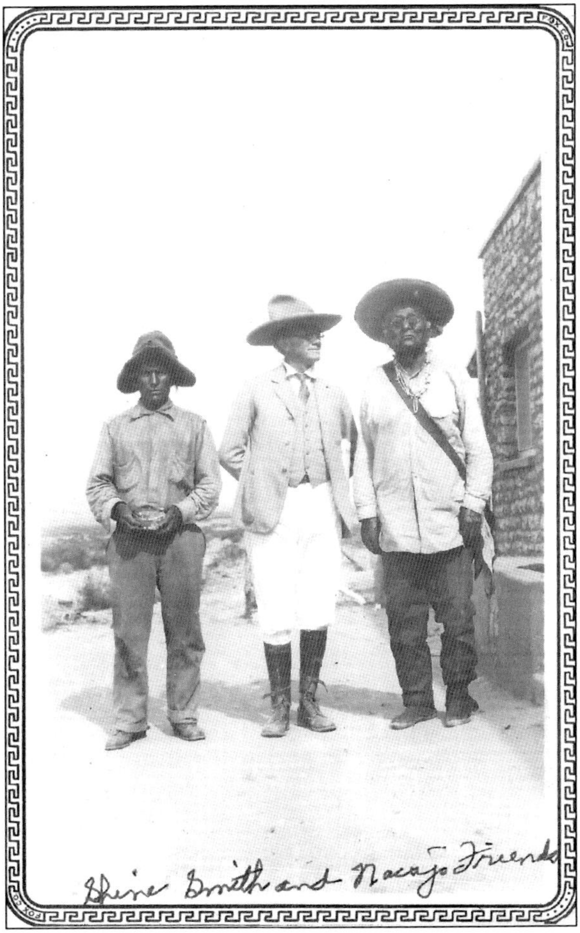

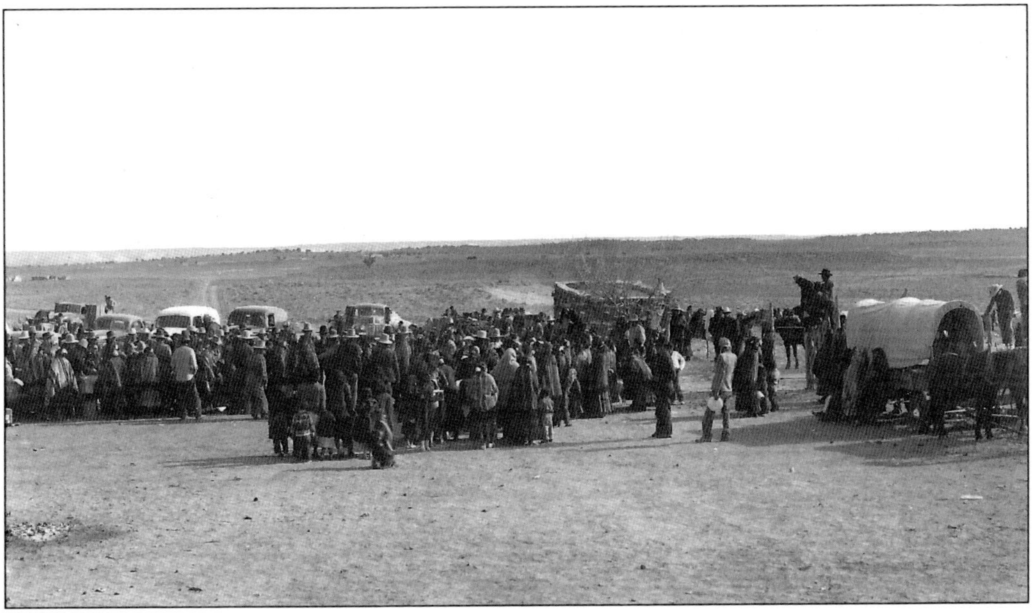

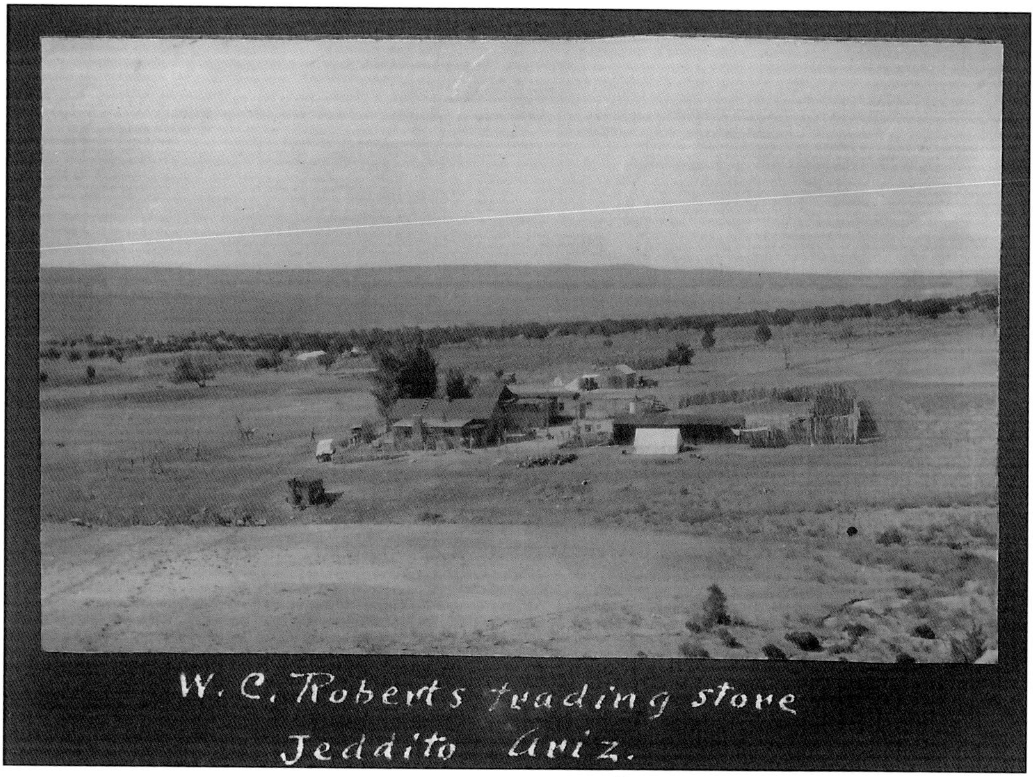

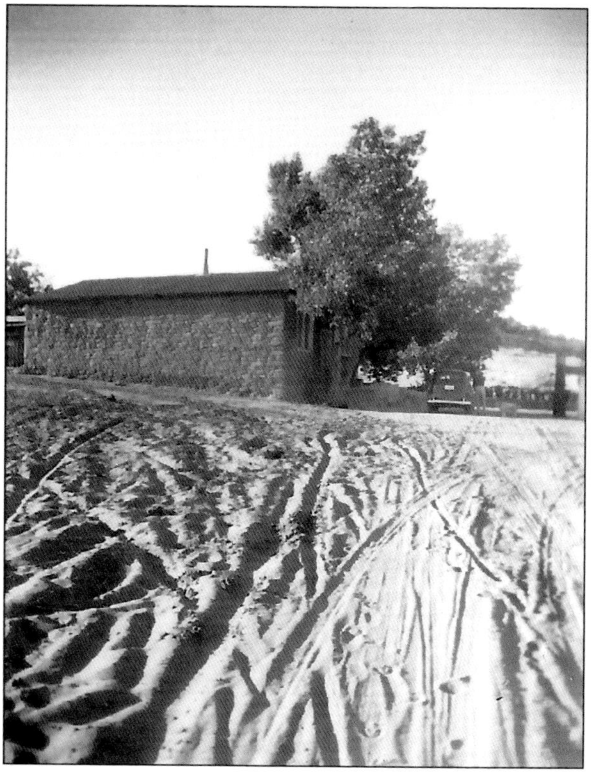

From 1936 to 1939, Harvard University's Peabody Museum sponsored an expedition to Awatovi, an abandoned Hopi village on Antelope Mesa. Jeddito Trading Post was four miles east of Keams Canyon. Managed by Wilmer "Chi" and Alma Roberts, it was the nearest store to the excavations. Supplies were shipped from Winslow to Jeddito. The archaeologists often visited Jeddito for an evening of musical entertainment. Alma played piano, Chi played the drums, and neighboring Navajos brought native instruments. C. Burton Cosgrove took the photograph above in 1936. The Peabody Museum expedition to Awatovi ended in 1939. Ten years later, Window Rock resident Editha Watson took the photograph at left. Jeddito closed in 1972 and was eventually torn down. (Above, courtesy of C. Burton Cosgrove; left, courtesy of Martin Link.)

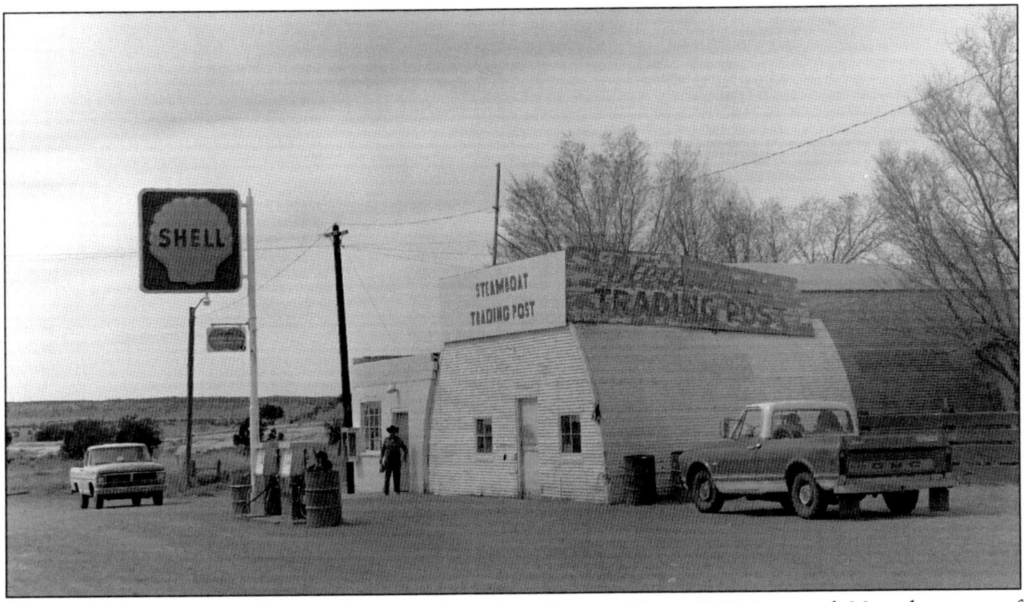

Lorenzo Hubbell owned Steamboat Trading Post from 1912 to 1917. Located 20 miles west of Ganado, the post burned in 1952 but was rebuilt. Today, it is a convenience store. This site was so named because a rock formation north of the highway resembles a steamboat. There are also Spanish inscriptions on the canyon wall, dated 1666, as well as a soldier's 1868 inscription. A nearby spring made Steamboat Canyon an important destination for travelers as well as a watering place for Navajos. The 1974 photograph above was taken by Helga Teiwes. Below, Alvin and Calvin, twin sons of Hubbell traders Al and Margaret Grieve, had stopped in at Steamboat in 1981 when this photograph was taken. Behind the boys, a traditional horse-drawn wagon is visible. (Above, courtesy of Arizona State Museum; below, courtesy of Al and Margaret Grieve.)

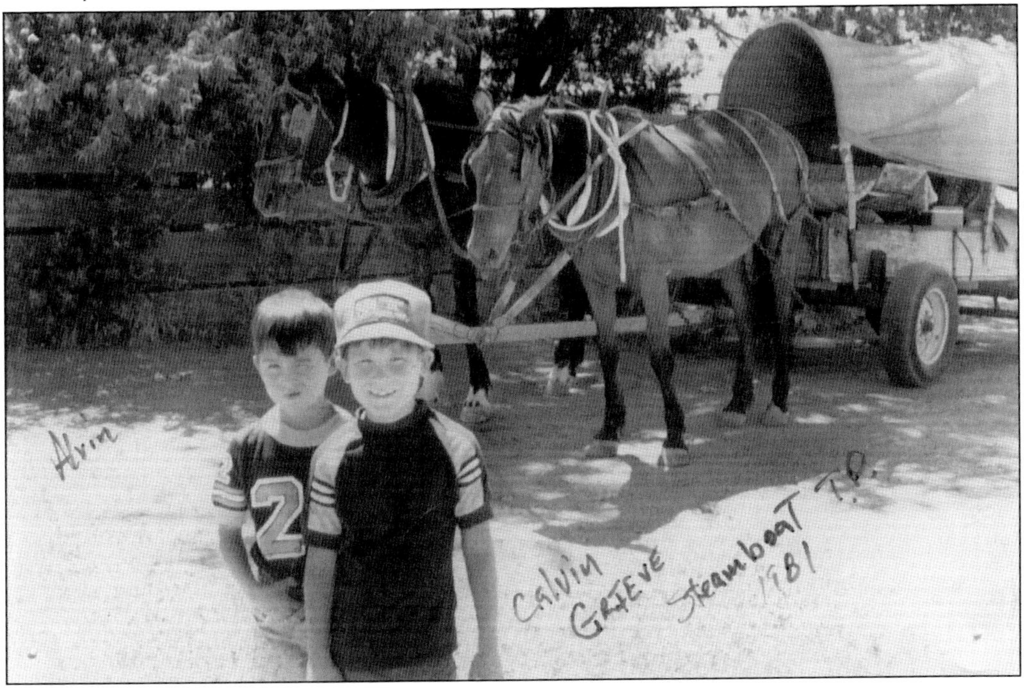

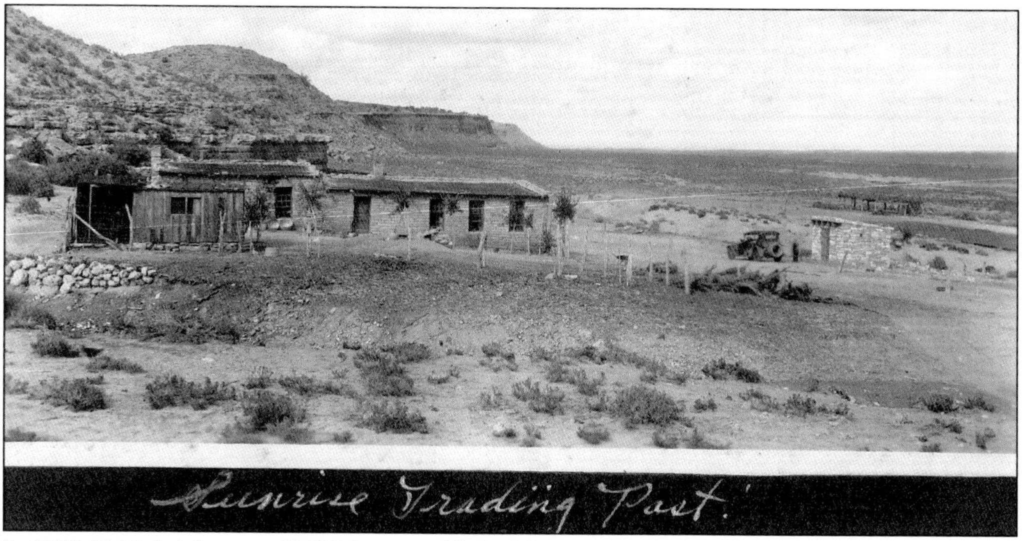

In 1907, J.H. McAdams and E.J. Marty established Sunrise Springs Trading Post, located southwest of Ganado on Highway 15. Lorenzo Hubbell considered this store to be within his trading territory, and he tried to force the traders to leave, giving them until sundown of that day to get out. Marty moved to Gallup, but McAdams stayed on. The following spring, he took two wagonloads of rugs to sell in Gallup to buy out Marty's share. Sunrise Springs had a succession of owners until it closed in 1987. Today, the walls of the post are mostly still standing, but the roof is gone, and the interior of the building is destroyed, as shown in the photograph below, taken in 2006. (Above, courtesy of Harvey Leake.)

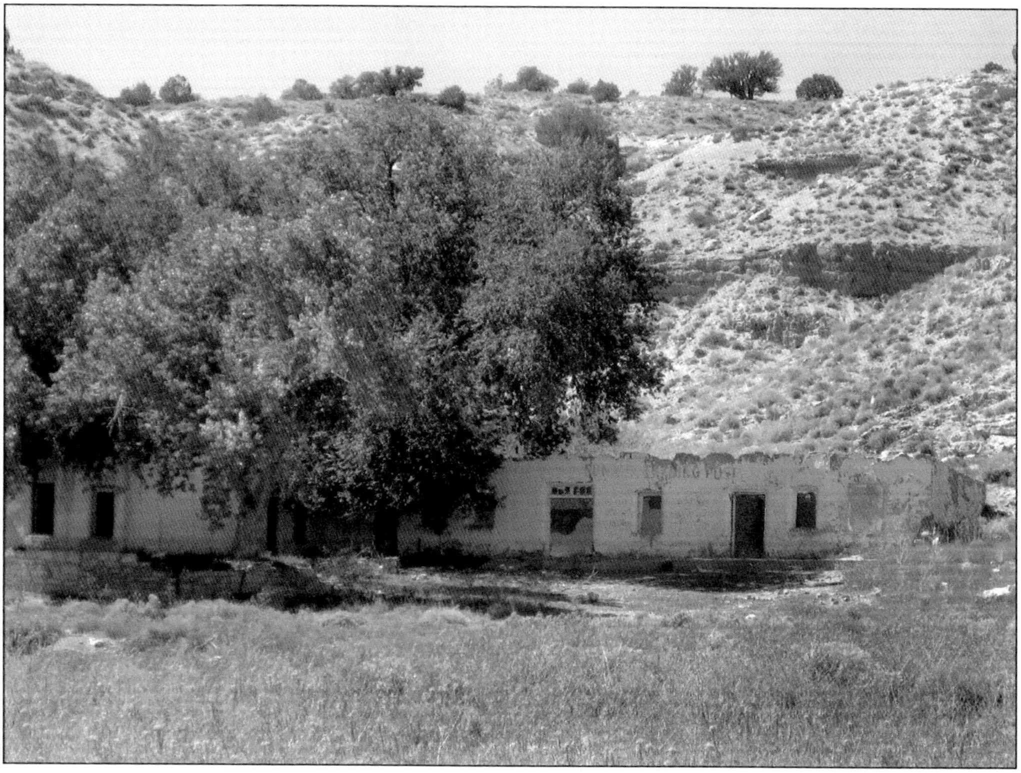

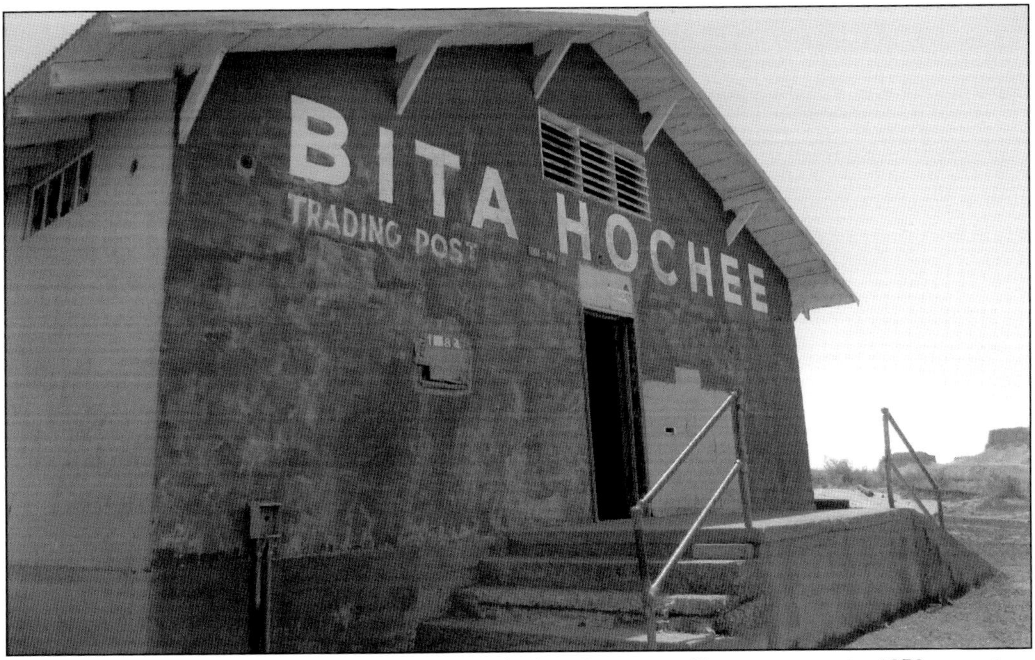

Theodore Thysing was a Prussian from Westphalia, Germany. He came west in 1870 as a cigar maker and soldier, and he was likely one of the first traders, along with Julius Wetzler in 1880, at Bitahochee. It is thought that Bitahochee was a military supply post. Water had to be hauled to the store as it was a dry post, but the traders did a brisk business buying wool. Not much more is known about Thysing, but his white headstone is located behind the post. Thysing was a member of Company C, 4th US Calvary. The Navajo Tribe took over Bitahochee in the early 1990s and closed it in 1994. Today, local Navajo artist Redwing Ted Nez is working to restore the trading post buildings. Below is a vintage wool sign from the trading post.

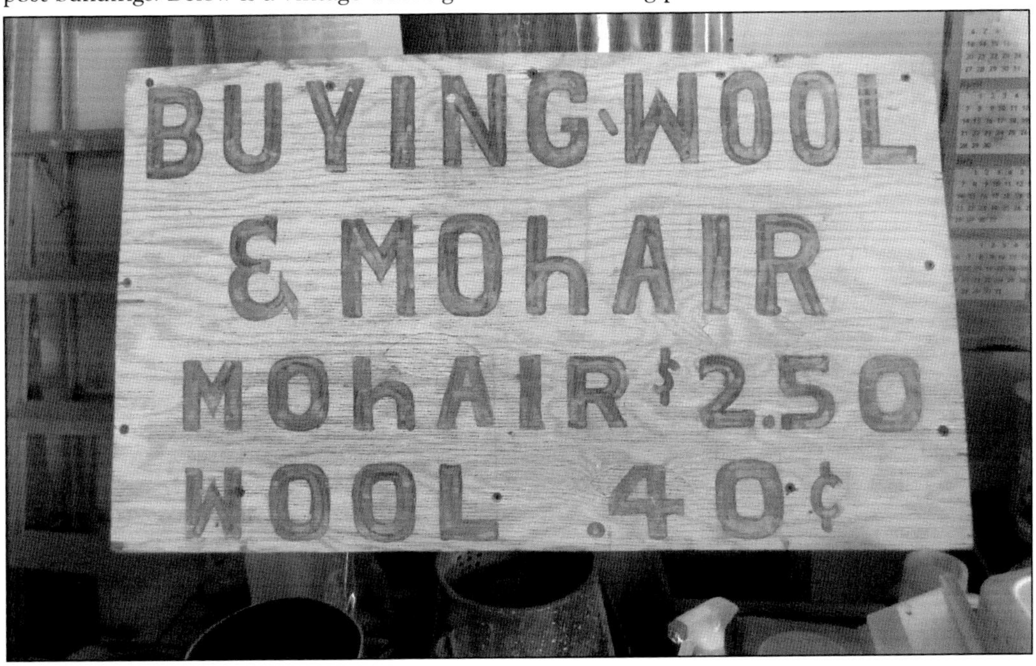

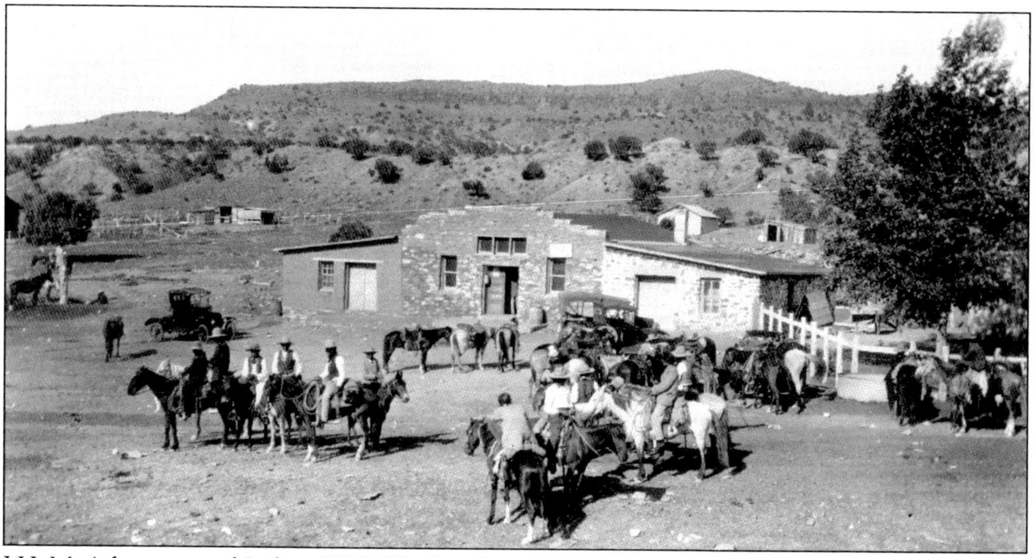

J.H. McAdams owned Indian Wells Trading Post, seen here in 1914. Babbitt Brothers purchased it in the 1930s. Indian Wells is just northwest of the intersection of Highways 77 and 15. The store burned down after it closed in the mid-1970s. Nothing is left today but some traces of the old foundation. (Courtesy of Old Trails Museum.)

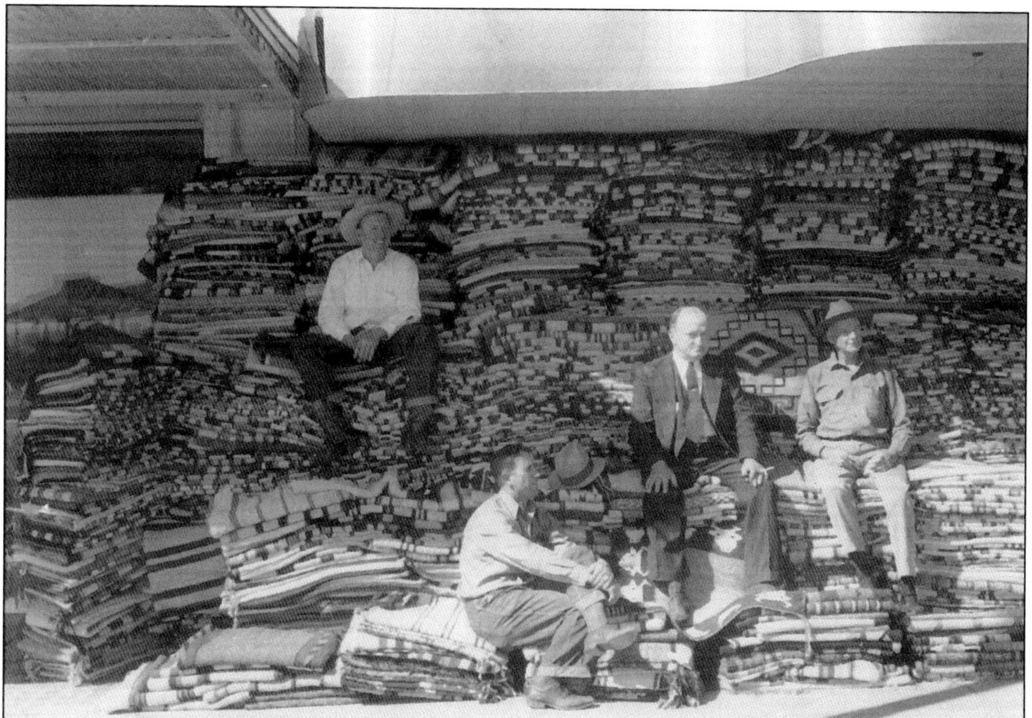

Several traders formed American Indian Crafts in the 1930s. Sitting on stacks of Navajo weavings, Ed Harris is at the left, next to C.A. Wheeler. The two men on the right are unidentified. Based in Phoenix, the association sold rugs to Sears and Montgomery Ward as well as other stores across the country. (Courtesy of Byron Hunter.)

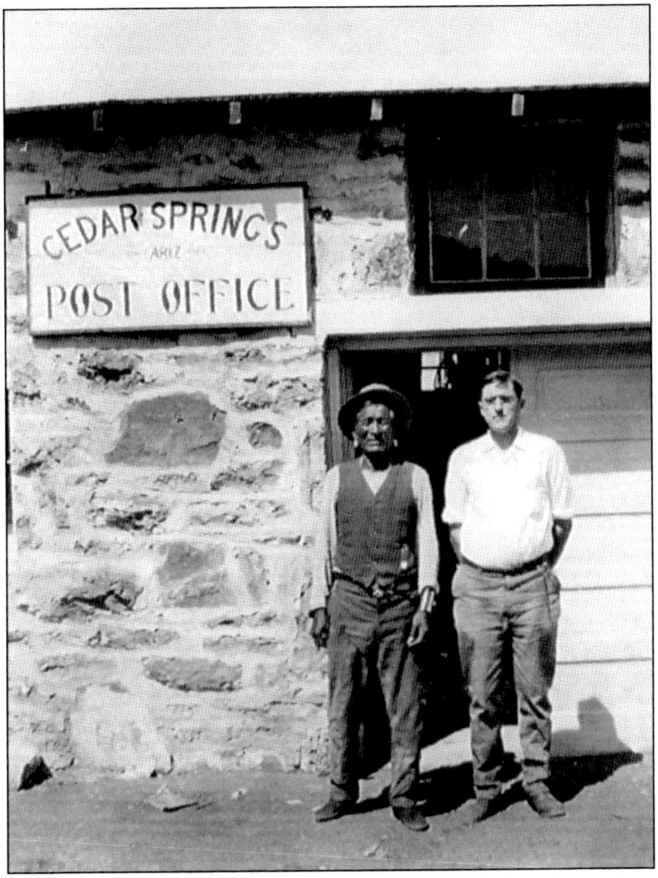

Jake Tobin built Cedar Springs Trading Post in 1885. Lorenzo Hubbell acquired it in 1909, and his younger brother Charles operated the store until he was killed in a 1919 robbery. Lorenzo was strongly against liquor, but according to his biographer Martha Blue, he was aware that Charles had a drinking problem. His solution was to send Charles as far away from alcohol as possible. Charles bitterly complained about the isolation. In 1919, two Navajo brothers came to the post and argued with Charles over the price of some cookies. Charles was shot in the head and then burned, along with the trading post. The store was rebuilt, and Arthur Bailey purchased it the following year; his brother and business partner Wallace is pictured at the right. Below is a merchandise tag from Hubbell's Winslow store. (Right, courtesy of Old Trails Museum.)

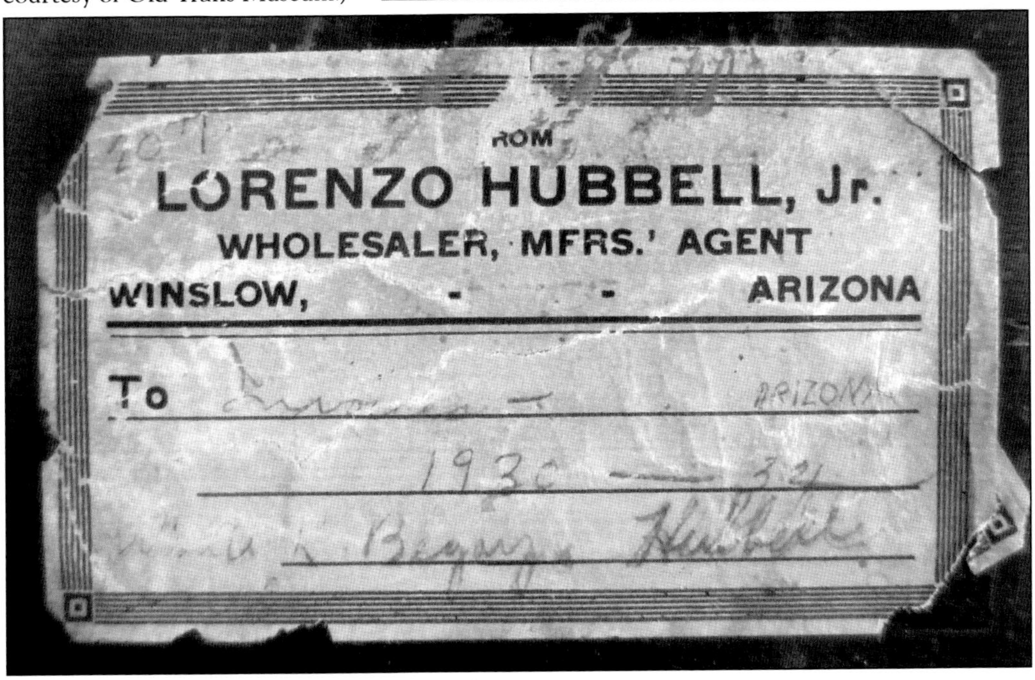

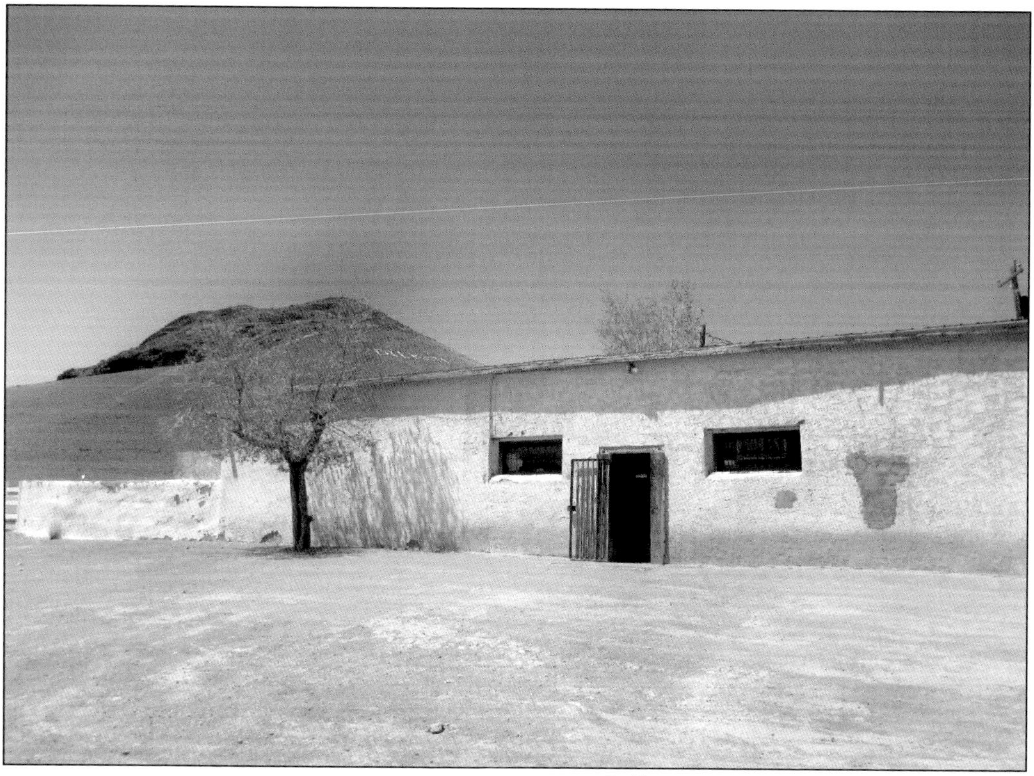

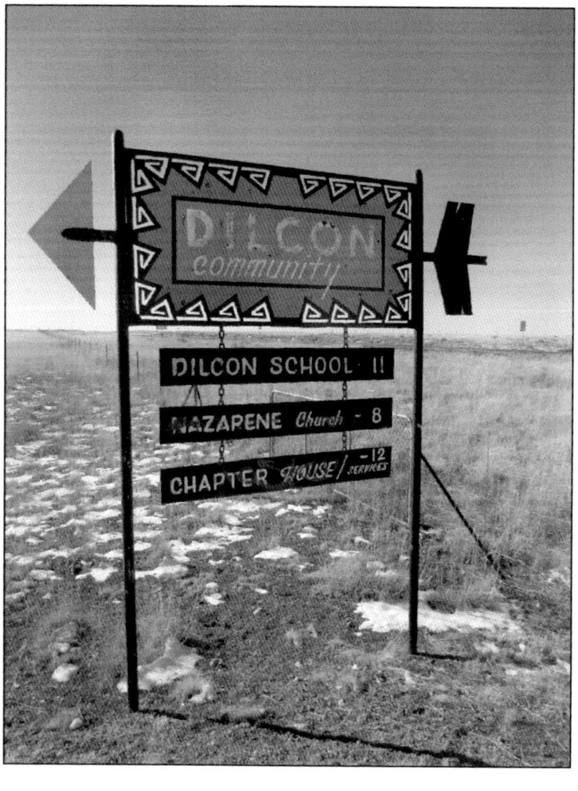

Dilkon Trading Post is closed, although the present owner plans to open it again after the building is remodeled. J.W. Bush established the post in 1919, and Lorenzo Hubbell Jr. owned it for a time in the mid-1930s. The store currently has no signage, but Dilkon is spelled out in white, painted rocks on the hillside, and the elaborate road sign on Highway 15 indicates the direction of the community to the east.

Jot Barnett Stiles, shown here about 1920, worked at Piñon Trading Post for Lorenzo Hubbell and then at Tuba City Trading Post until 1932, when he acquired Castle Butte Trading Post. Jot sold Navajo saddle blankets to J.C. Penney and Montgomery Ward and freighted wagonloads of wool south to the railhead at Winslow. Jot's daughters were never allowed to work in the trading post, as it was not considered proper. His son Roger, who was fluent in the Navajo language, helped with the trading. During World War II, Jot helped many Navajos enlist in the military. Sadly, his own son was killed in Germany. The Stileses left Castle Butte in 1960, and the store was abandoned in the 1980s. All that remains of Castle Butte Trading Post today are traces of the stone foundation. (Right, courtesy of Mary May Bailey.)

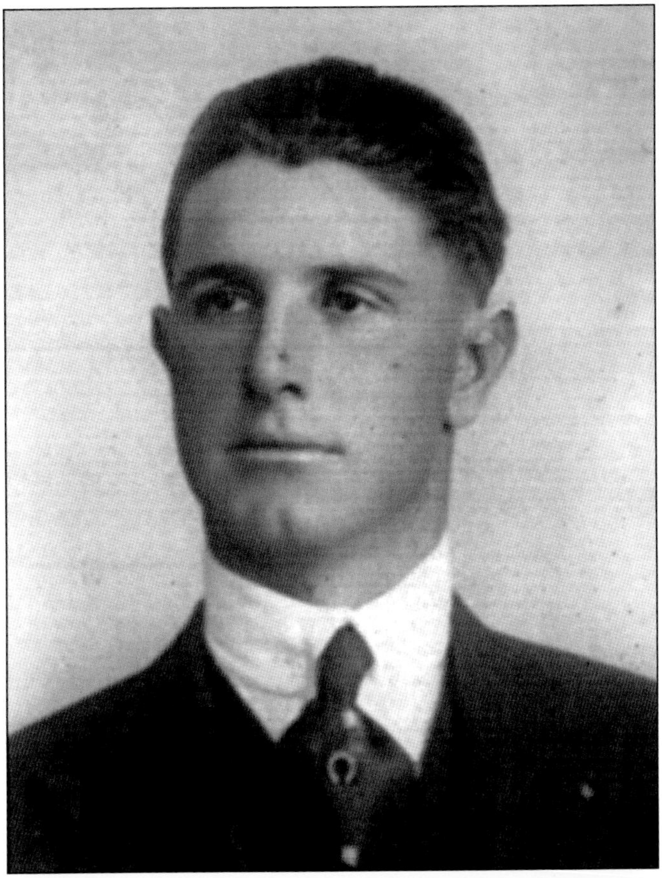

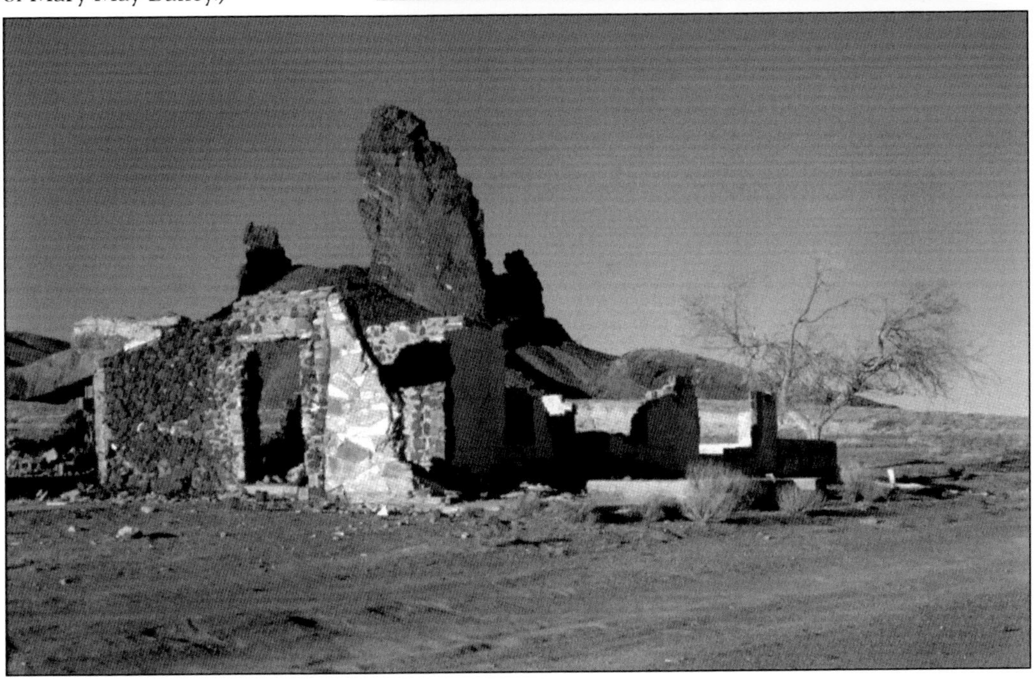

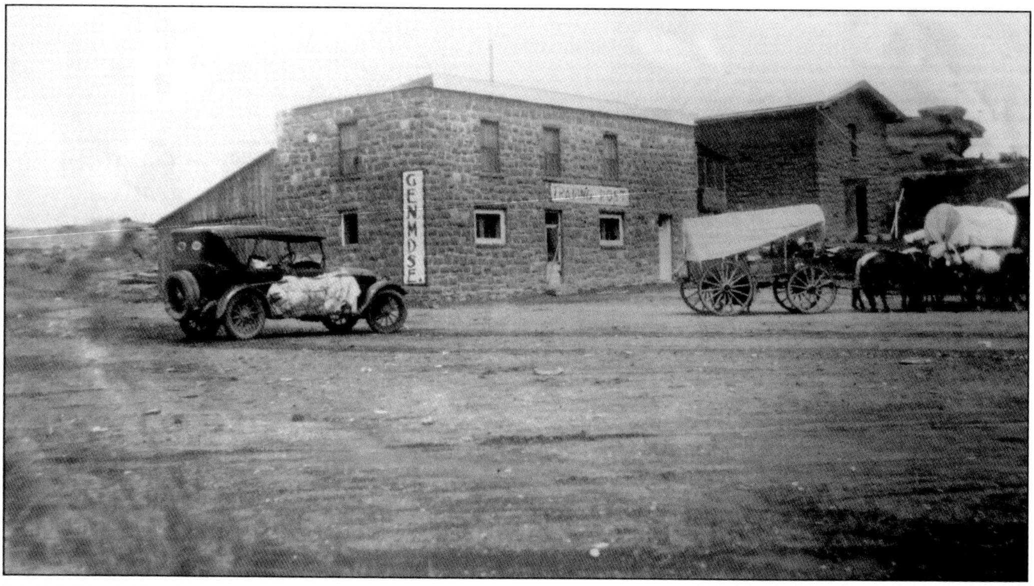

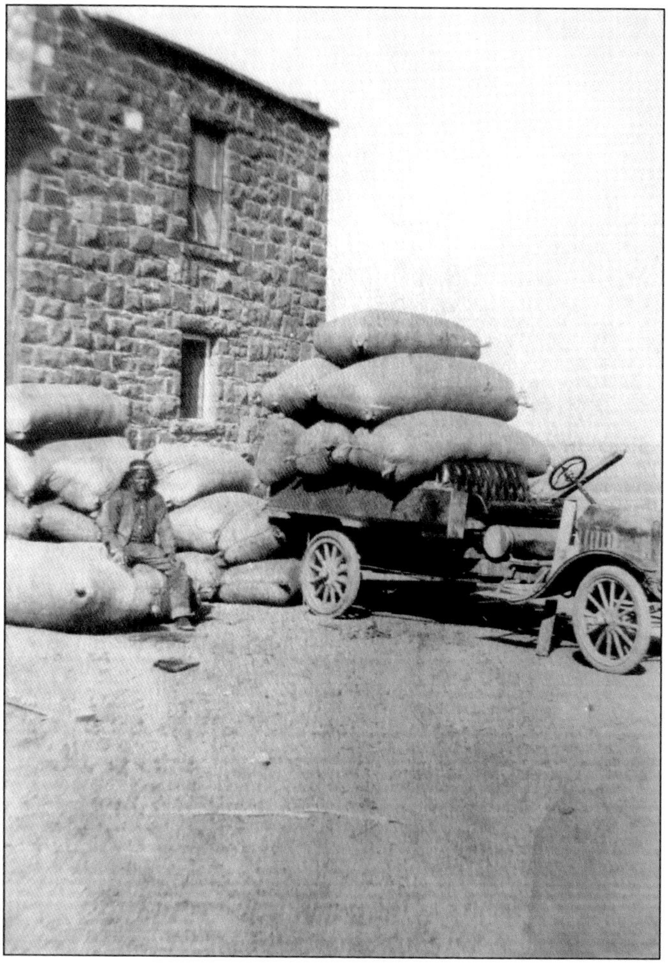

John Walker started Tolchaco Trading Post in 1905 and later sold to Babbitt Brothers. Carl Steckel managed the post after World War I. Located northwest of Leupp, Tolchaco was a busy, large, stone, two-story store with two Anglo employees and one part-time Navajo. While Carl Steckel managed Tolchaco Trading Post, the store shipped three railcars of wool annually to Boston, Massachusetts. Steckel's Ford truck could carry eight bags of wool, each weighing about 250 pounds. This trading post was later dismantled, and the stones were transported by wagon to build another store near Leupp. (Both, courtesy of Veran Steckel.)

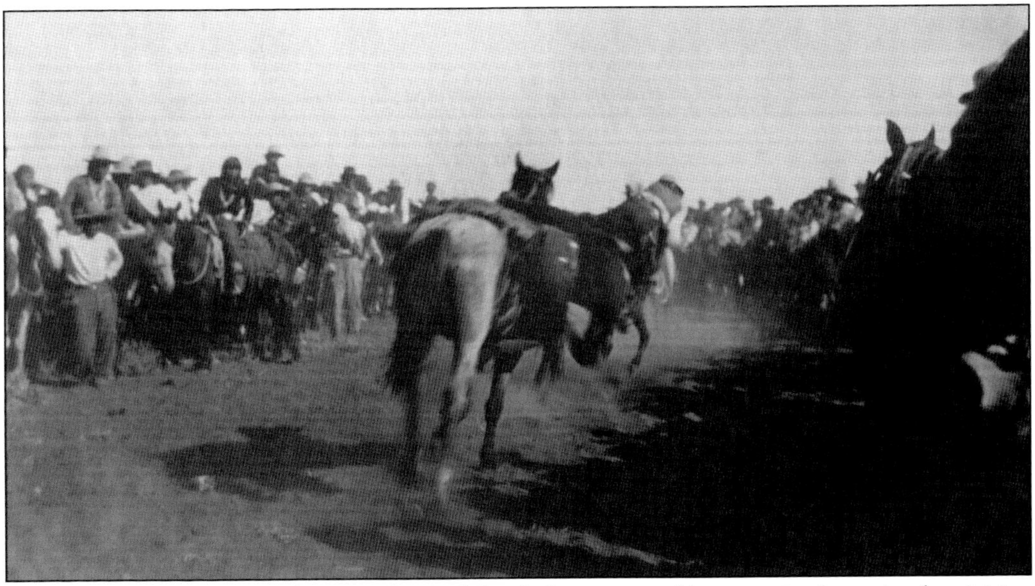

Known as "Blue Eyes," Tolchaco trader Carl Steckel encouraged business in the spring by visiting neighboring hogans and informing people that he would buy their rugs and wool and that there would be a chicken pull with prizes and gifts and a meal. In earlier times, a live chicken was buried up to its neck in the sand, but later on, the prize was a bag of coins partially buried. Riders took a number for their turn and galloped by, attempting to lean from their horses and pull out the sack—without falling off their horse. The trader gave a first prize of a leather saddle, a silver bracelet was second prize, and a Pendleton blanket was third, followed by a big feast. The rider below would have been a typical trading post customer. (Above, courtesy of Veran Steckel.)

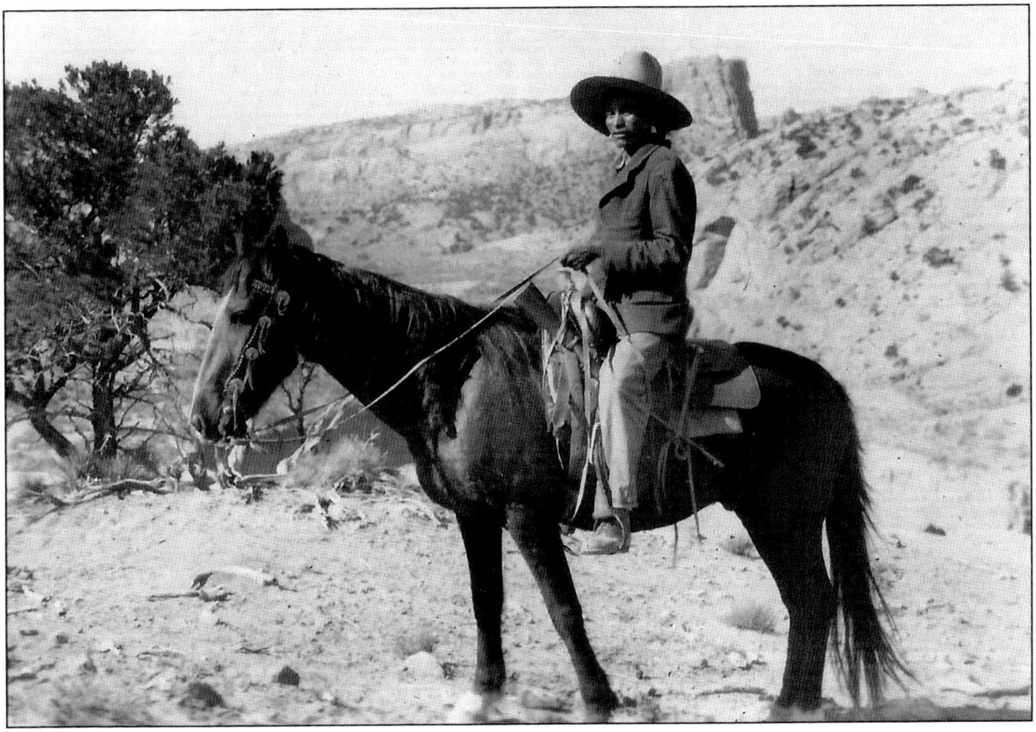

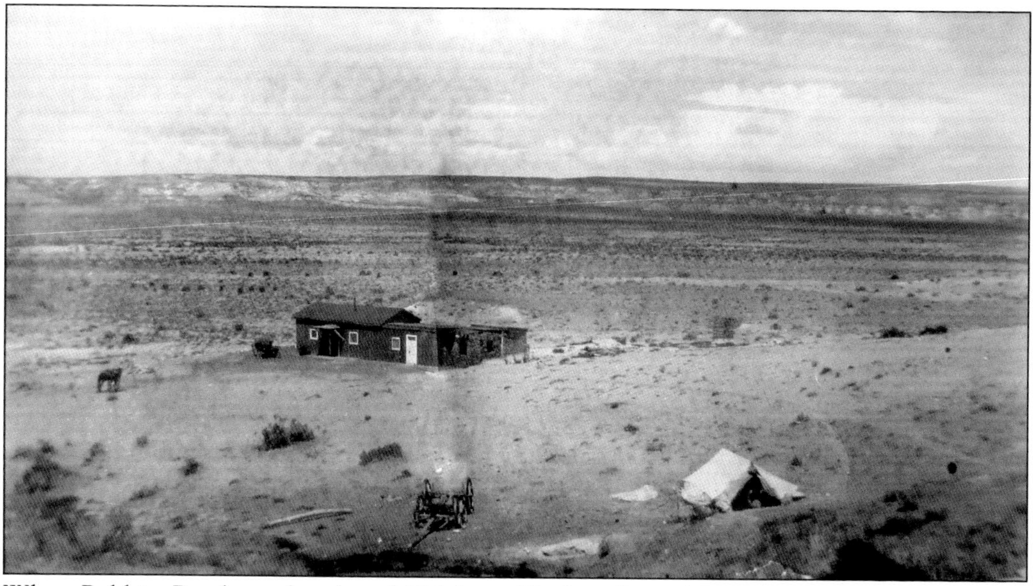

When Babbitt Brothers abandoned Tolchaco Trading Post about 1920, store manager Carl Steckel built Sandwater Trading Post in the same general area at a spring called Say-be-tow, "Sandy Water." Carl used materials from the Tolchaco Presbyterian Mission School to erect his trading post. Steckel recalled that he slept on the ground for three months while building the post, eating only sardines and crackers. The store closed a few years later, and nothing remains today. (Courtesy of Veran Steckel.)

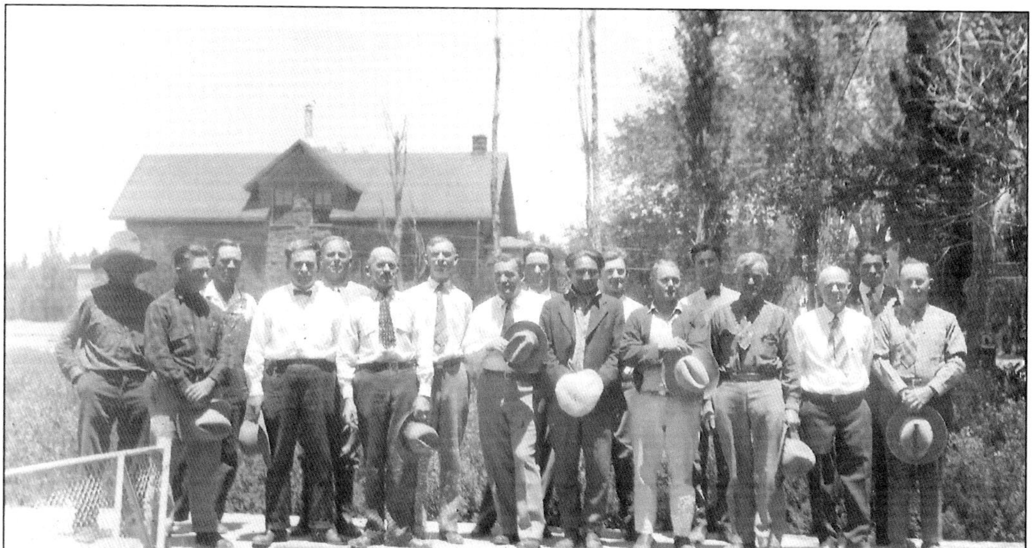

This group of traders gathered at Tuba City about 1930 to discuss business practices and mutual issues. All are unidentified except for John Wetherill from Kayenta, fourth from the right, and Jot Stiles, standing just behind and to Wetherill's right.

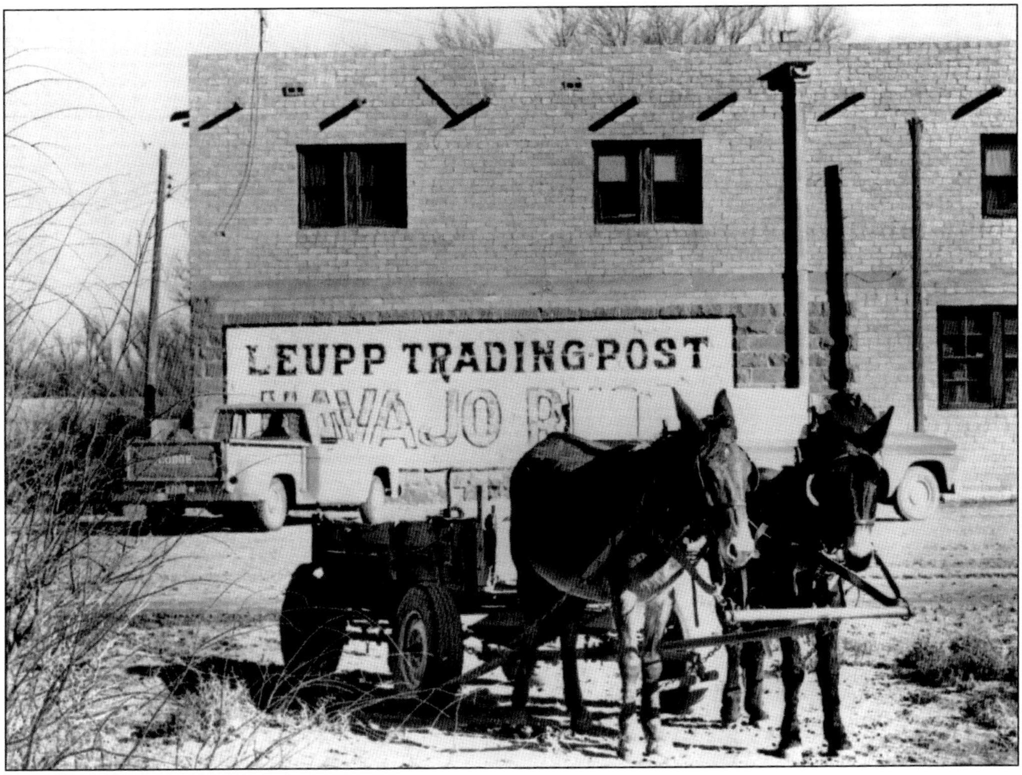

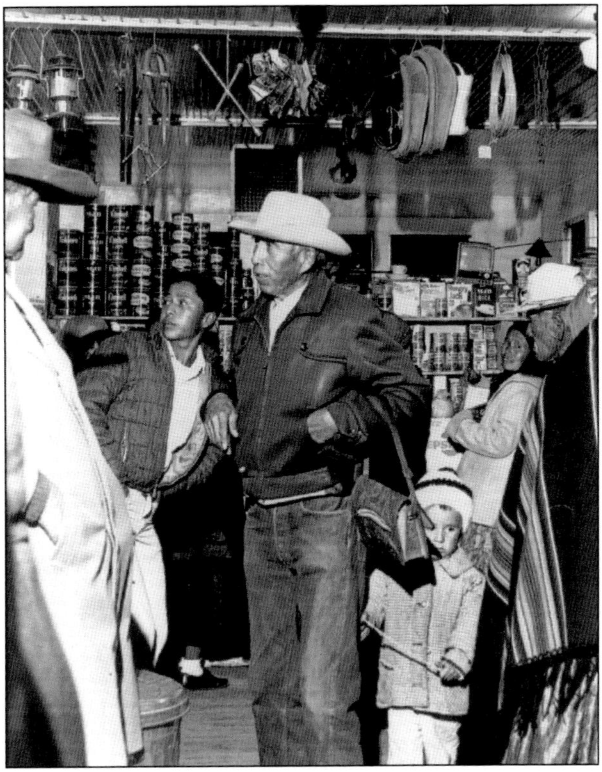

The old Leupp Trading Post was located two miles southeast of Leupp. The store was built in 1910 by John Walker and was later owned by Hubert Richardson, Stanton and Ida Mae Borum, William and Lucille McGee, and then Ralph and Ellen McGee, who operated the post from 1967 to 1982. Living quarters were above the store on the second story. The 1960s photograph at right shows the interior of the store, and, from left to right, Hasten Bitsuie, Lamar Slowtalker's son, John Billy, John Billy's small grandson, Beth Chee, Hosteen Mark Keyonnie, and Ason Kayonnie. During World War II, an isolation center for interned Japanese Americans was located nearby in the buildings of an abandoned Indian boarding school. The store remained open, selling to Navajos and soldiers. Leupp Trading Post closed in 1980, and nothing remains today. (Both, courtesy of Old Trails Museum.)

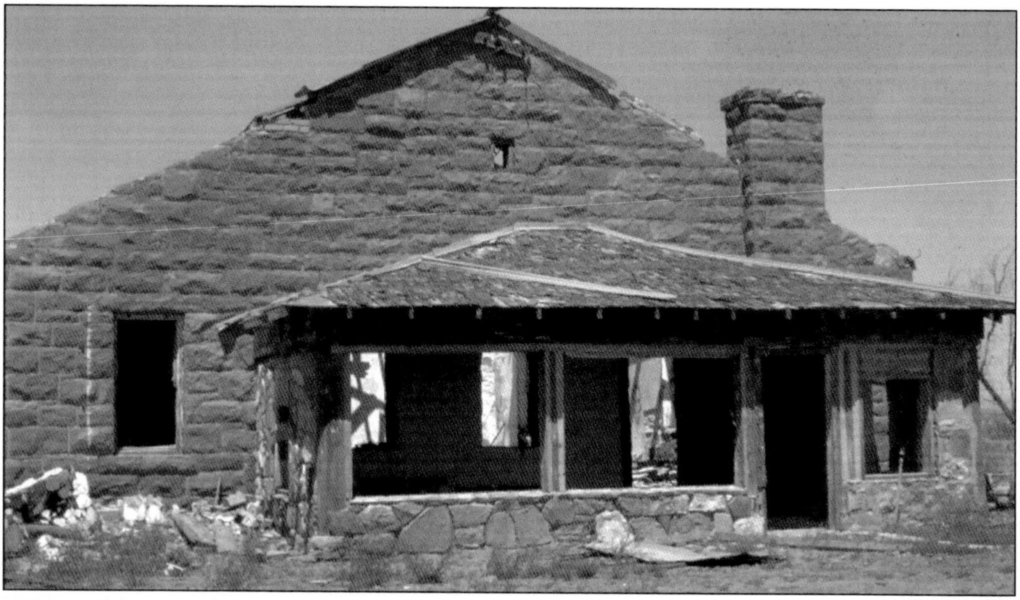

H.W. "Nebby" Smith, an employee of Babbitt Brothers, built Sunrise Trading Post in 1920. The Babbitts owned another trading post at Tolchaco, but it did not get much business after the bridge was built near Leupp. Unknown to the Babbitts, Smith dismantled the Tolchaco store stone by stone, and then carried them south near the Little Colorado River to construct Sunrise Trading Post. In the 1930s, the trader bought about 10 rugs a day.

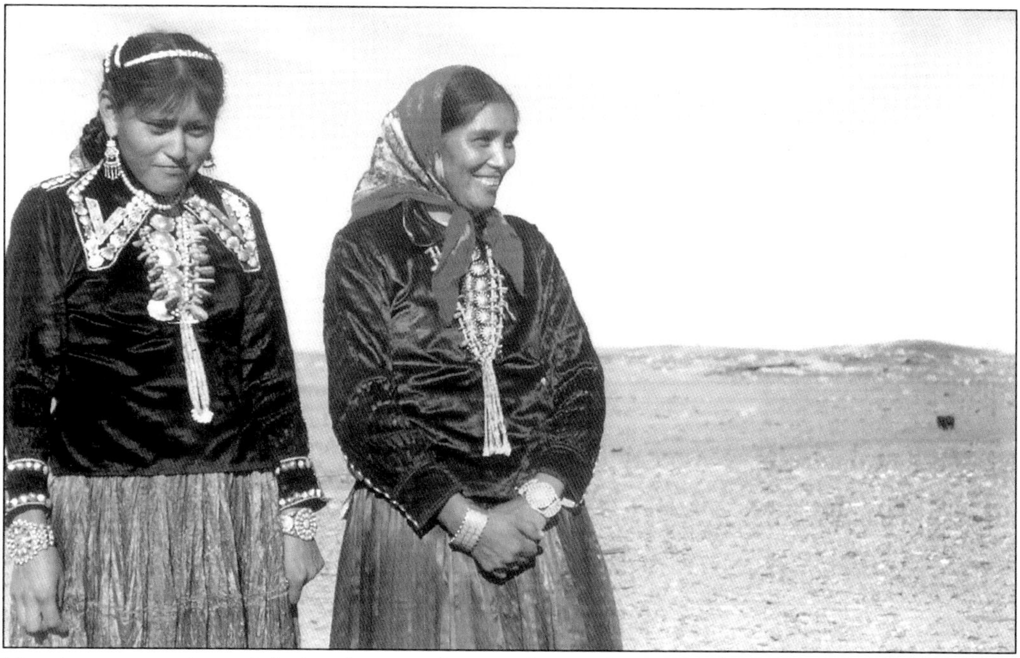

Navajo women adorned their velveteen shirts with coin buttons. The buttons were silver coins that were reshaped and curved with a loop attached on the back. If a trading post purchase required a bit more cash, the button could be snipped off to make up the difference. Banks did not like the coin buttons because even without the loop, the coin was not flat and would not fit in a coin roll. (Courtesy of Lois McMindes.)

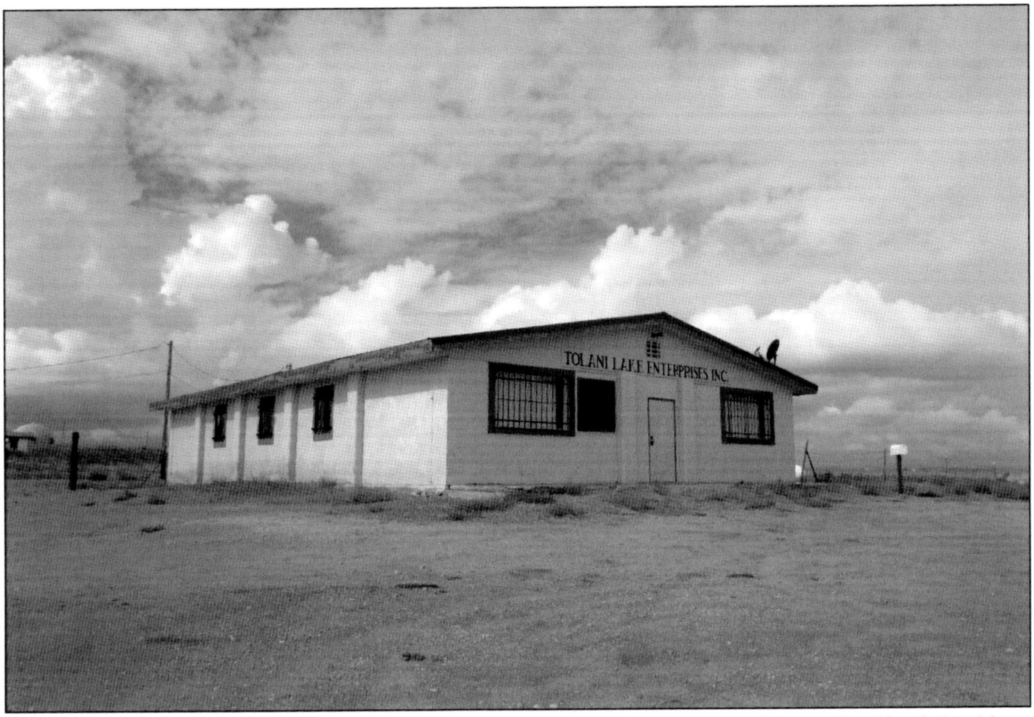

Tolani Lake Trading Post has operated in several locations. Today, the cinder block building houses Navajo-run Tolani Lake Enterprises.

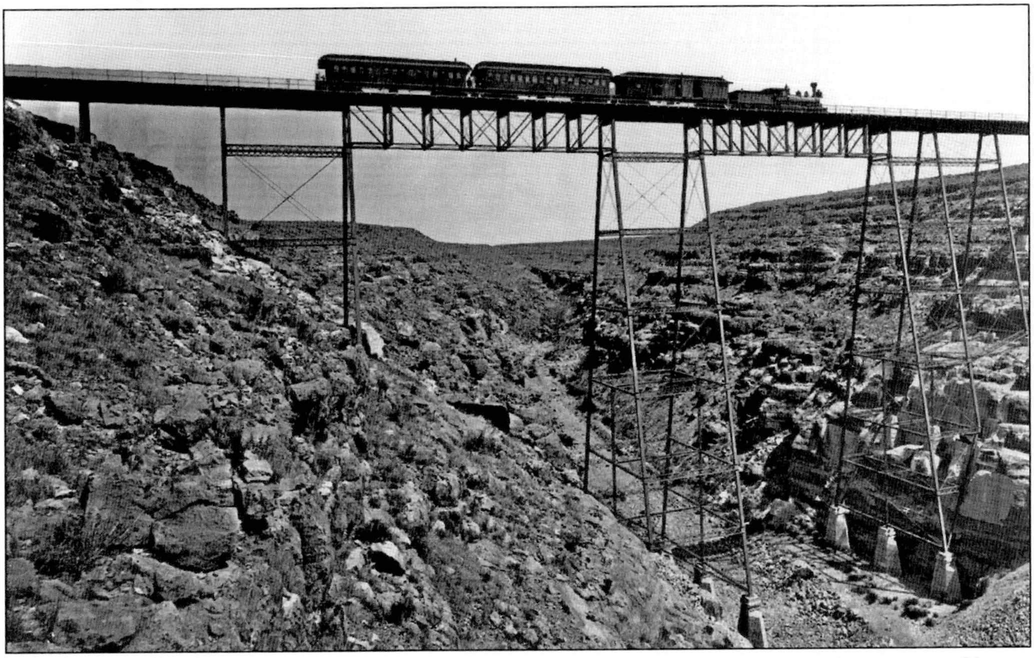

The Atlantic & Pacific Railroad built the iron bridge across Canyon Diablo in 1882. Trains often stopped on the bridge to allow passengers to see the view and the sheer drop into the steep canyon. Businesses painted advertisements on the rock walls in the canyon, an early version of advertising billboards.

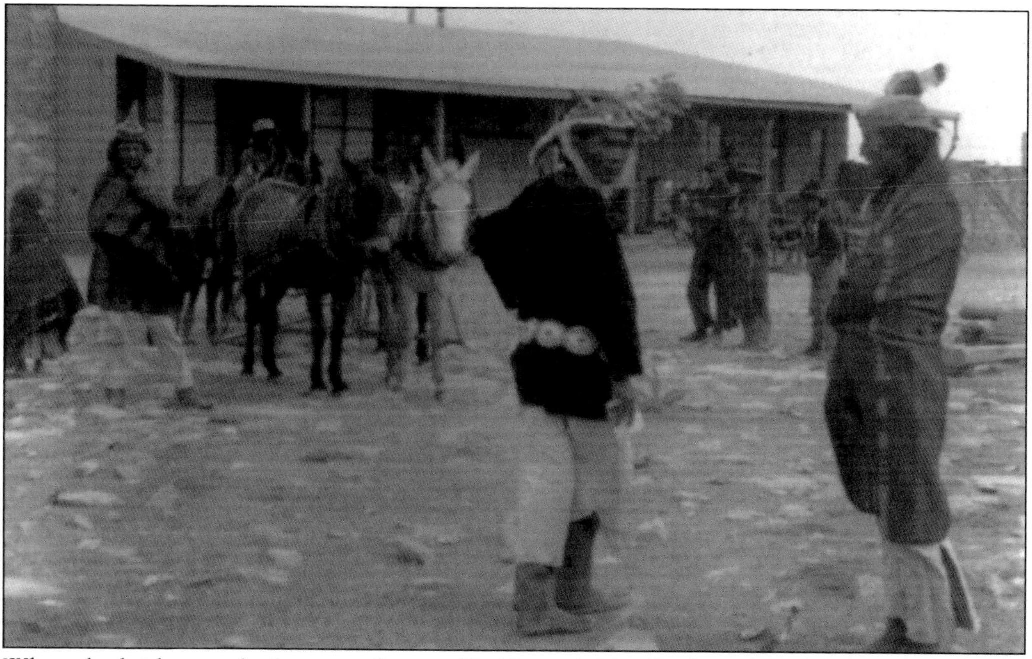

When the bridge was built across Canyon Diablo in 1882, Charles Algert opened a store in an abandoned boxcar. With 14 saloons, 10 gambling houses, and 4 houses of prostitution, Canyon Diablo was known as the toughest town in the Southwest, with daily robberies and killings. The first marshal, sworn in at 10:00 a.m. in the morning, was shot dead by 3:00 p.m. in the afternoon. Train robberies were common, and stories of hidden loot still persist. After the railroad workers moved on, a large stone trading post was built, operating until the 1940s. Stone ruins are all that remain today. (Above, courtesy of the Library of Congress.)

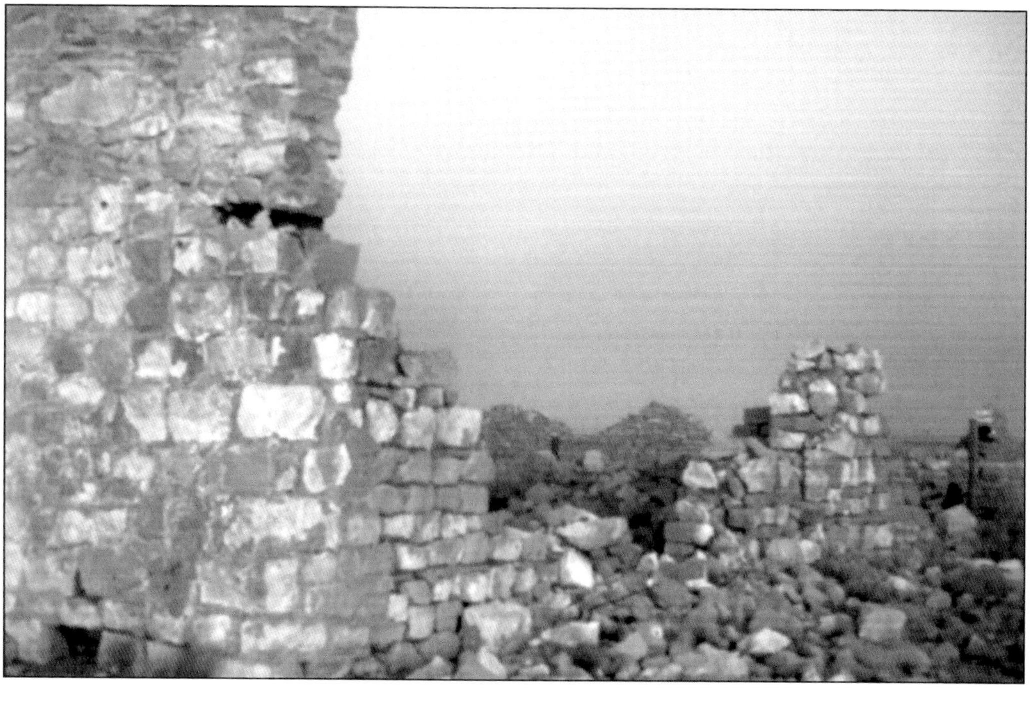

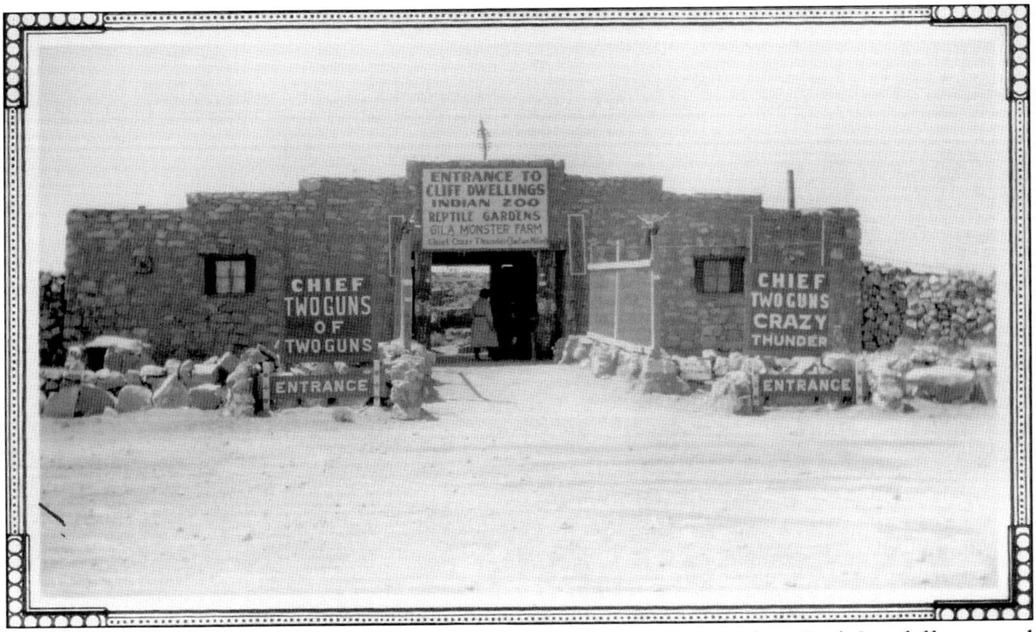

Two Guns Trading Post was a Route 66 tourist attraction, but before that, Earl Cundiff operated it as a trading post. Harry "Chief Crazy Thunder" Miller, an Apache, leased the store in 1925, called it Fort Two Guns, and started a wild animal zoo. Miller also promoted an old cave in the area as a tourist attraction known as the Apache Death Cave. The cave was reportedly where a group of Apaches died when they took refuge from attacking Navajos who built fires at the cave entrance and suffocated the Apaches. In 1926, after numerous disputes, Miller shot and killed Cundiff, his landlord and the owner of Two Guns. Although Cundiff was unarmed, Miller claimed self-defense. Miller was acquitted but soon left the area due to unpopularity with local people who did not support his innocence in the shooting.

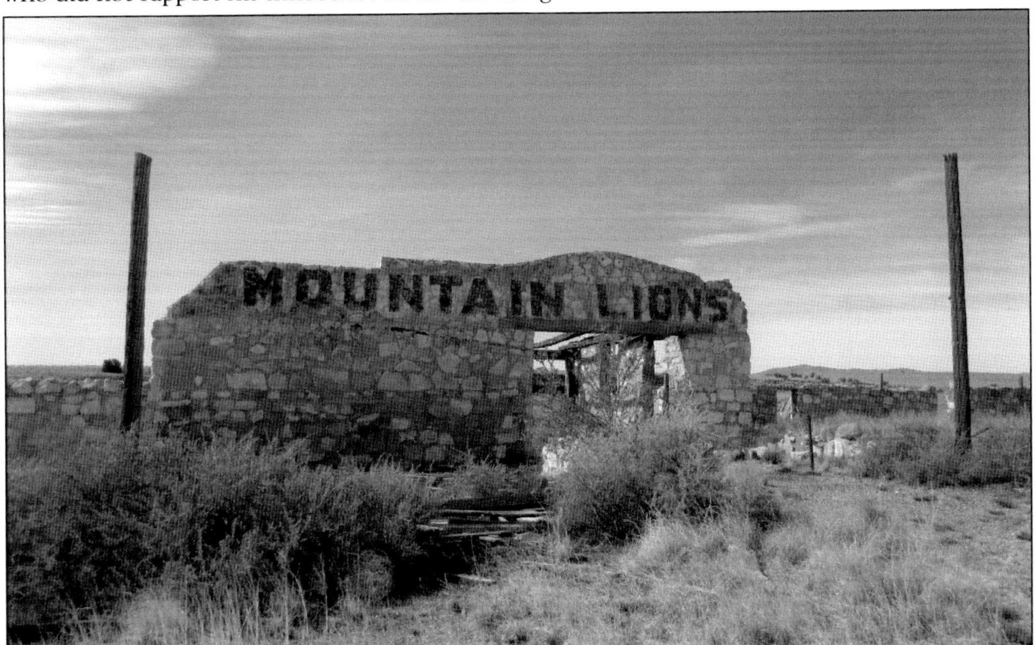

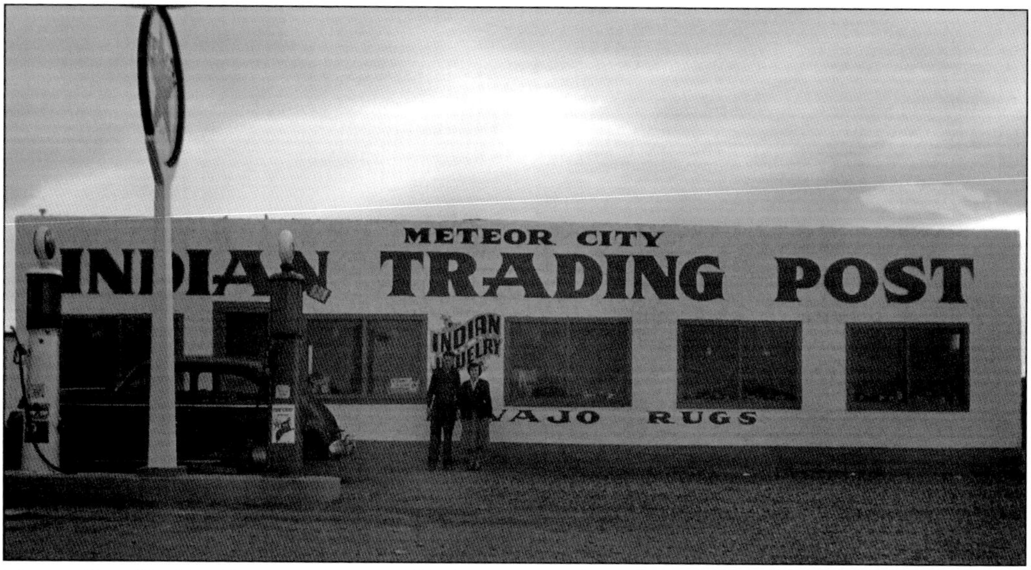

Meteor City Trading Post may have sold Indian arts and curios, but it was not a traditional trading post. On Route 66, thirty-seven miles east of Flagstaff, Jack Newsum took over an existing service station and then opened a trading post and souvenir shop in 1941. After the store burned in the 1960s, the business was moved to a geodesic dome. The store was named for the huge crater nearby that was created by a meteor that fell 50,000 years ago. For many years, the crater was thought to have been caused by a volcanic eruption. Mining engineer Daniel Barringer was ridiculed for his theory that a meteor created the feature. Beginning in the early 1900s, Barringer spent much of his life digging at the bottom of the crater, searching in vain for the meteorite. His theory was proven correct many years after his death. (Above, courtesy of Old Trails Museum.)

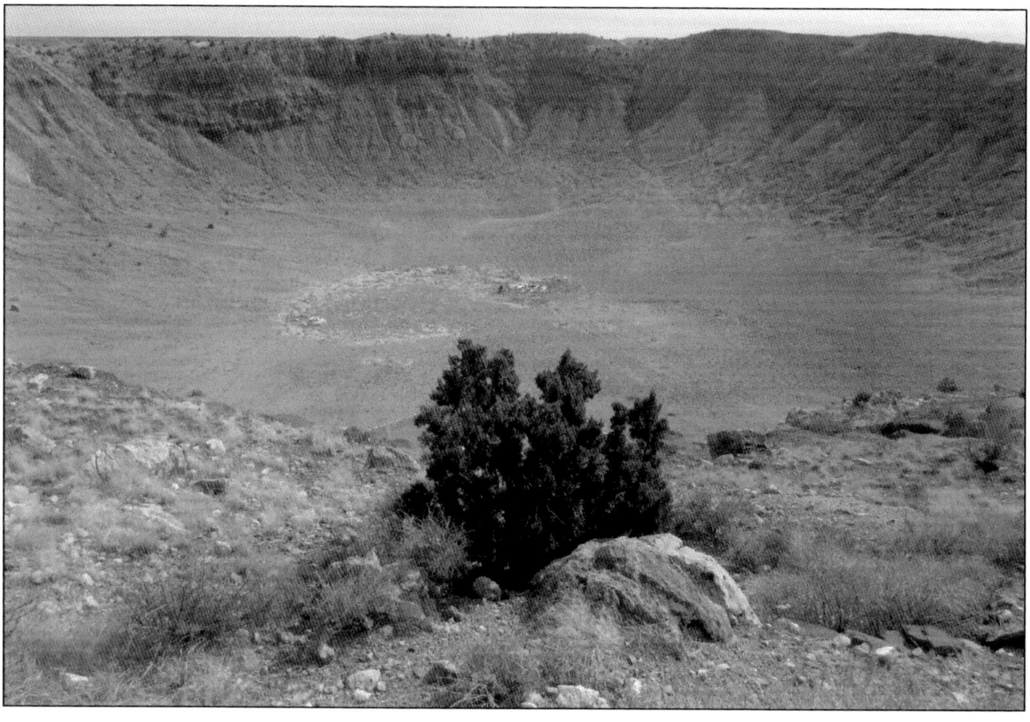

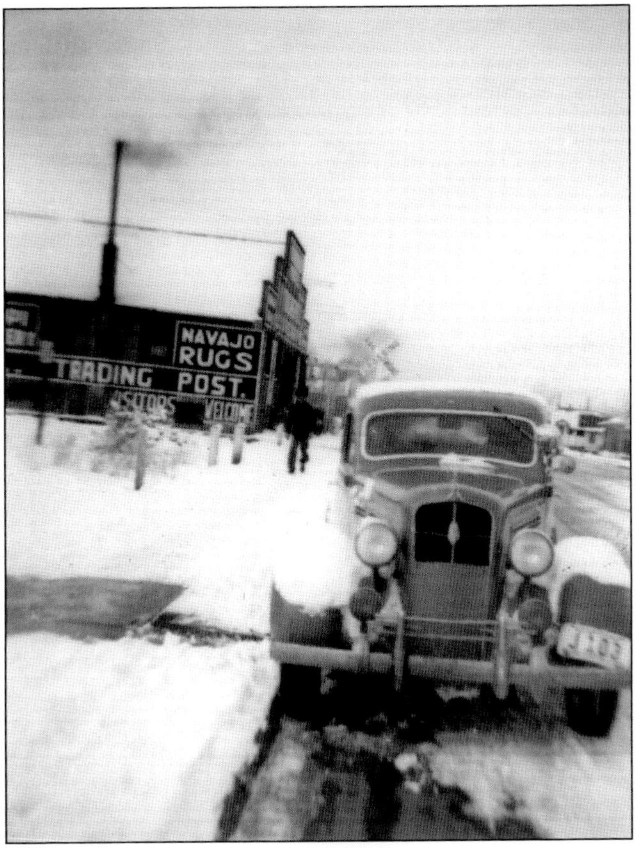

Lorenzo Hubbell Jr. purchased Richardson's Trading Post on West Second Street in Winslow in 1924. This large building served as a warehouse for the many Hubbell-owned trading posts. It was located on the Atchison, Topeka & Santa Fe Railway line, making it convenient to store goods and then load or unload them directly into a railcar. Roman and Dorothy Hubbell managed the store from 1942 until 1953. Today, the building, now listed in the National Register of Historic Places, is owned by the City of Winslow and serves as the Winslow Chamber of Commerce and Visitor's Center. (Both, courtesy of Old Trails Museum.)

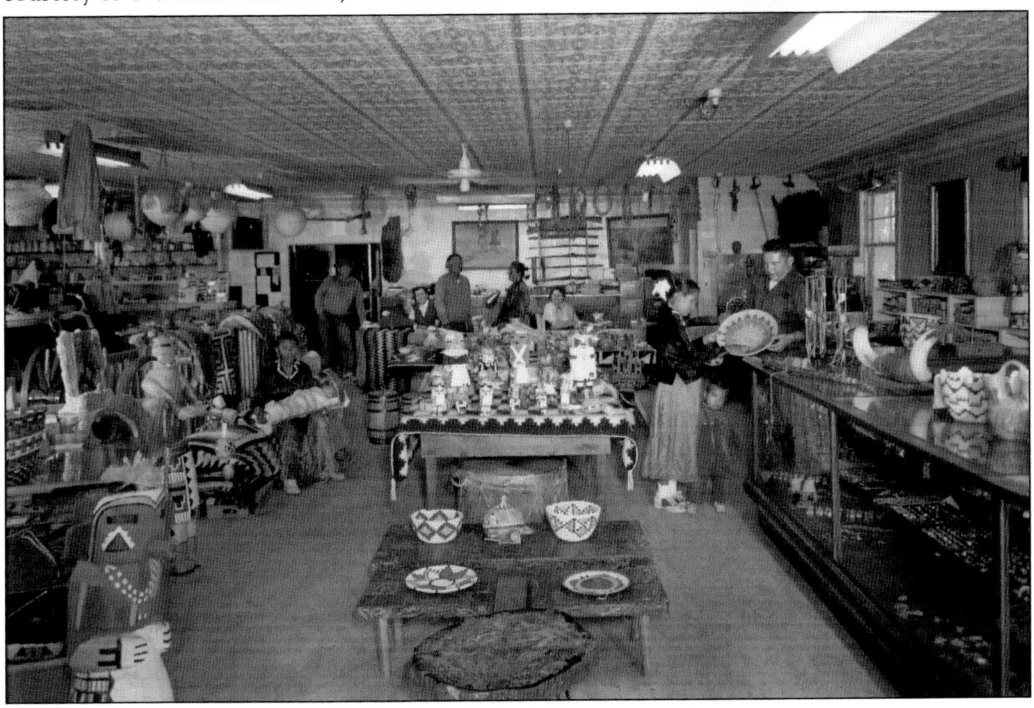

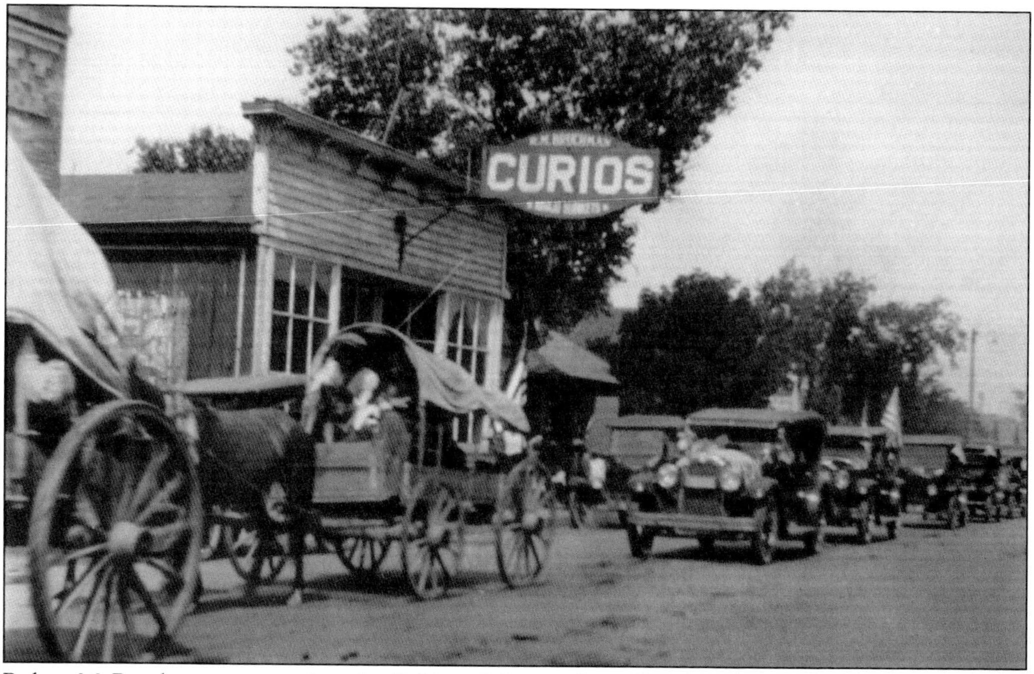

Robert M. Bruchman was employed at Babbitts Mercantile in Winslow about 1902 and then operated Bird Springs Trading Post. He returned to Winslow 20 years later and established R.M. Bruchman Indian Curios on East Second Street. Bruchman was a German immigrant who spoke fluent English, Navajo, Spanish, and, of course, German. (Both, courtesy of Old Trails Museum.)

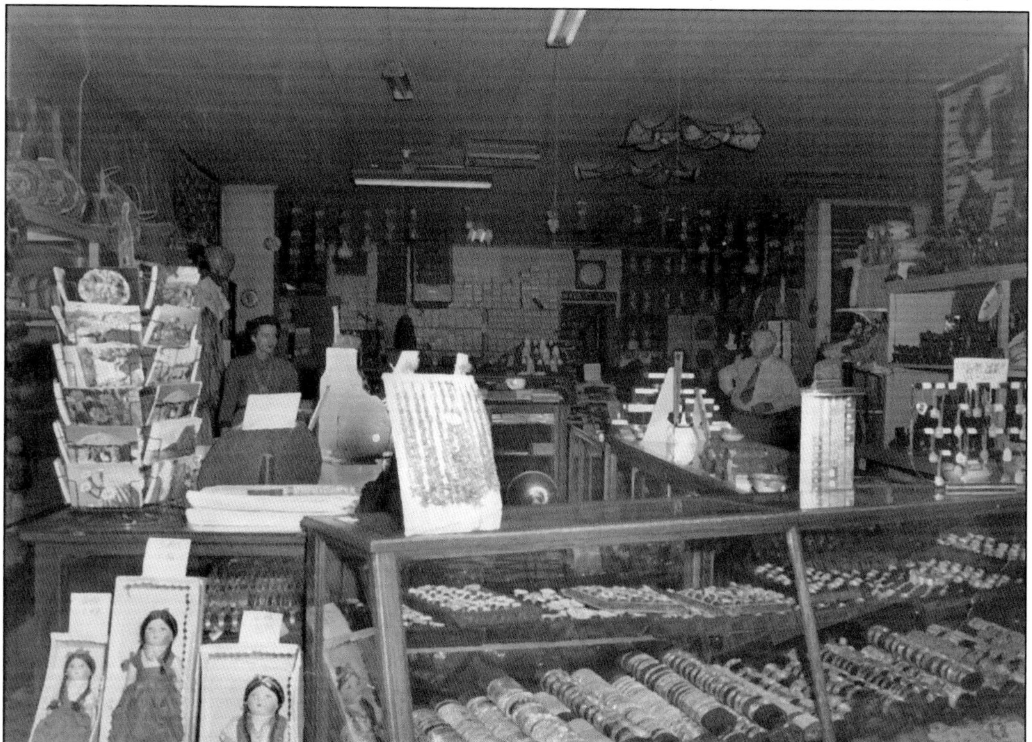

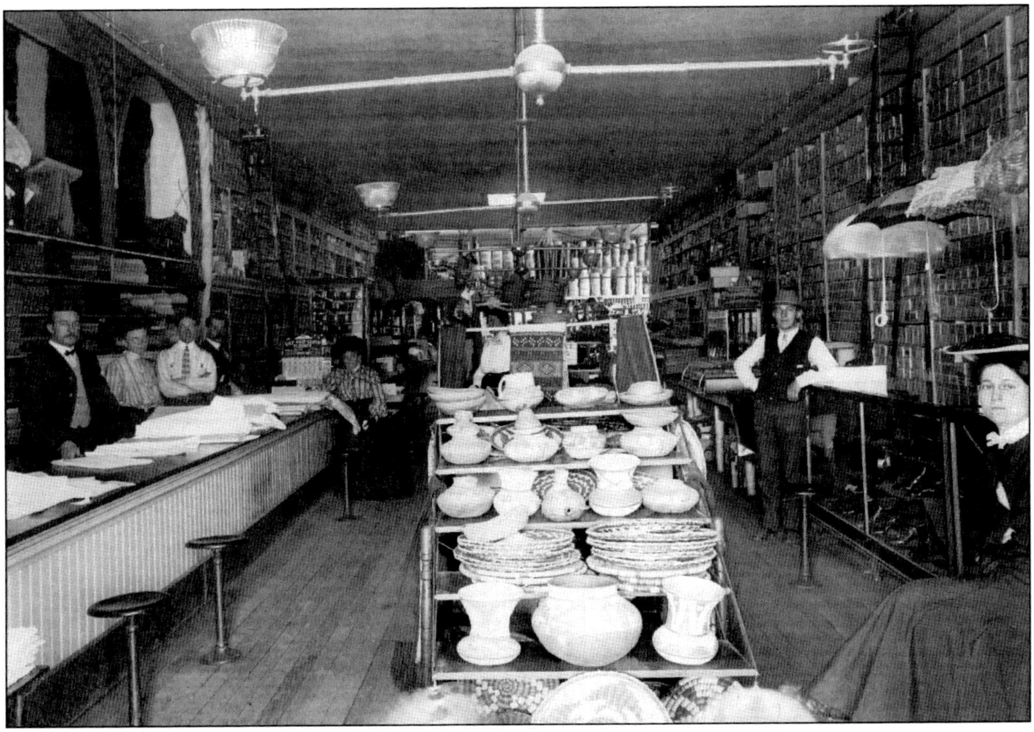

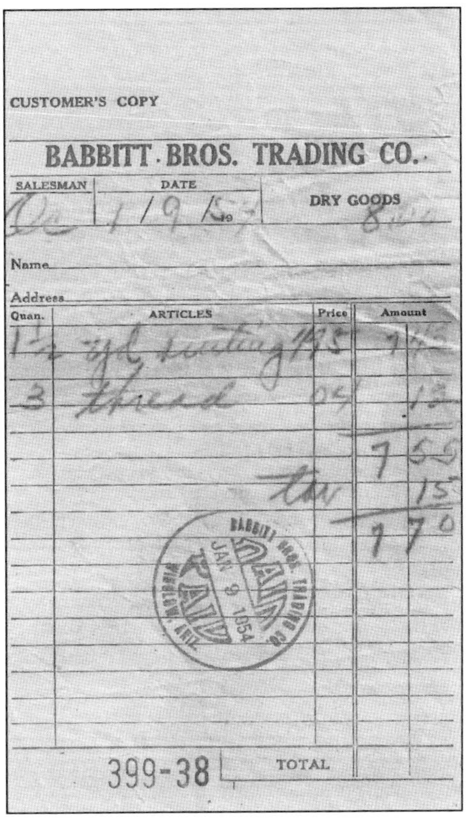

CUSTOMER'S COPY

BABBITT·BROS. TRADING CO.

SALESMAN	DATE	DRY GOODS
	1/9/54	

Name

Address

Quan.	ARTICLES	Price	Amount
1½	yd suiting	1.95	
3	thread	.04	.12
			7.59
	tax		.15
			7.70

399-38 TOTAL

Babbitt Brothers Mercantile Company, owned by the five Babbitt brothers in Flagstaff, managed various businesses, ranches, and many trading posts in northern Arizona. It opened the Winslow store on Railroad Avenue in 1898. In this 1902 interior view of the store, clerk Richard M. Bruchman stands third from the left. In addition to the typical dry goods found in town stores, Indian arts were offered for sale. According to information on the back of the 1954 sales receipt at right, the store carried groceries, drugs, meats, "gents' furnishings," millinery, boots, and shoes, as well as Navajo blankets and curios. (Above, courtesy of Dona Bruchman Harris and Old Trails Museum.)

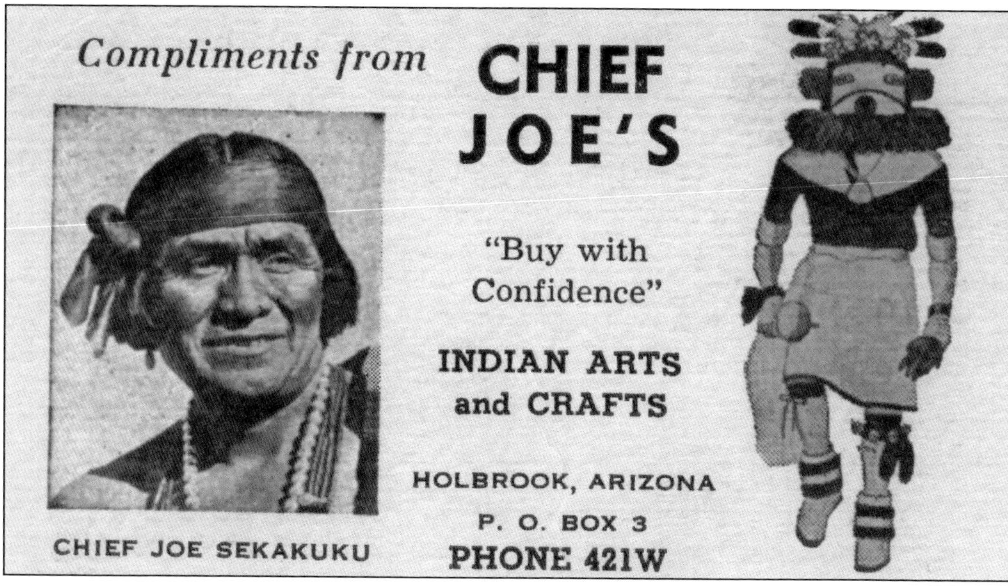

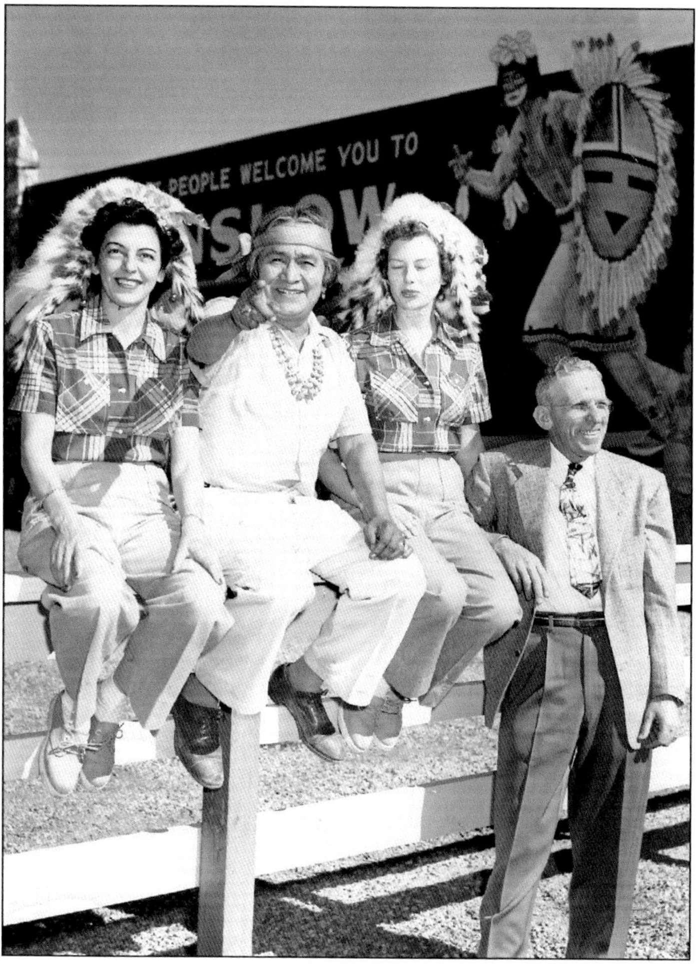

"Chief" Joe Secakuku was born about 1896 in a Hopi village on Second Mesa. In the early 1920s, he worked for Fred Harvey at the Grand Canyon. When Harry Miller opened the zoo at Two Guns in 1925, Secakuku was hired to operate the Indian arts store. Joe later moved to Holbrook and then Winslow, where he had Indian arts stores. In Winslow, he added "Chief" to his business cards. In 1950, Secakuku poses for a Winslow publicity photograph with Mayor Whipple and two young women who were ushers at the Chief Theater. Barbara Aragon is at the left, and 16-year-old Phyllis Gould Sirrine is to Secakuku's left. This was the first job for shy, young Phyllis. She did not want to be in a photograph, she did not want to put on a feathered headdress, and she would not smile. (Both, courtesy of Old Trails Museum.)

Two

HOPI
THE ANCIENT PEOPLE

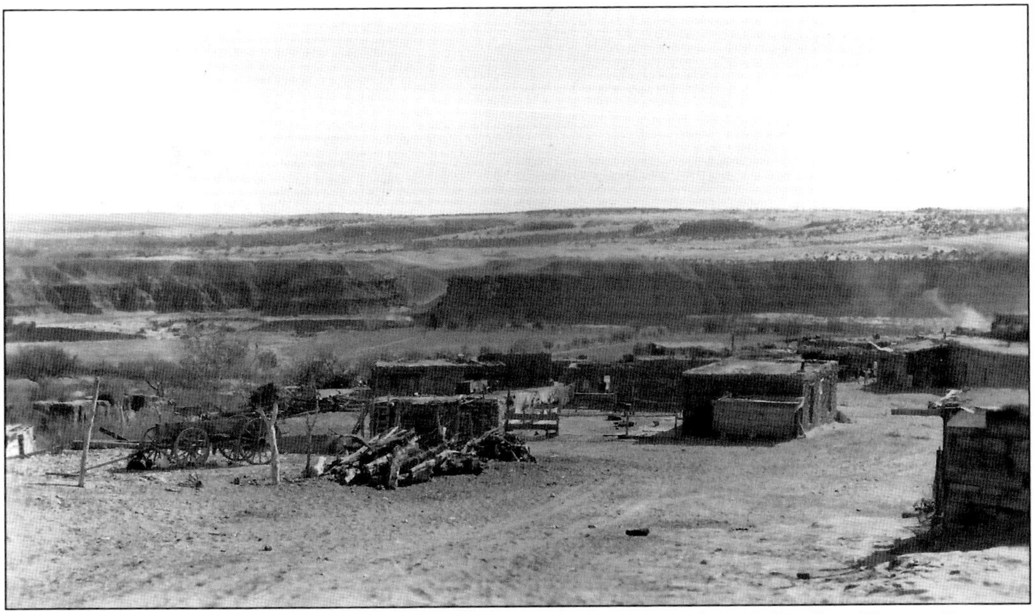

According to the 1910 superintendent's report of the Moqui Indian School in Keams Canyon, there were seven traders operating on the Hopi Reservation. Three traders were Anglos, and four were Hopi. Two Hopis, the James brothers, operated the trading post at Moencopi, and Joe and Hale Secakuku had a store at Second Mesa, between Shipaulovi and Mishongnovi. The traders mostly sold necessities, like canned foods and hardware, to locals, while tourists bought rugs, baskets, silver jewelry, and kachina carvings. Navajo customers also purchased corn, peaches, and piki bread.

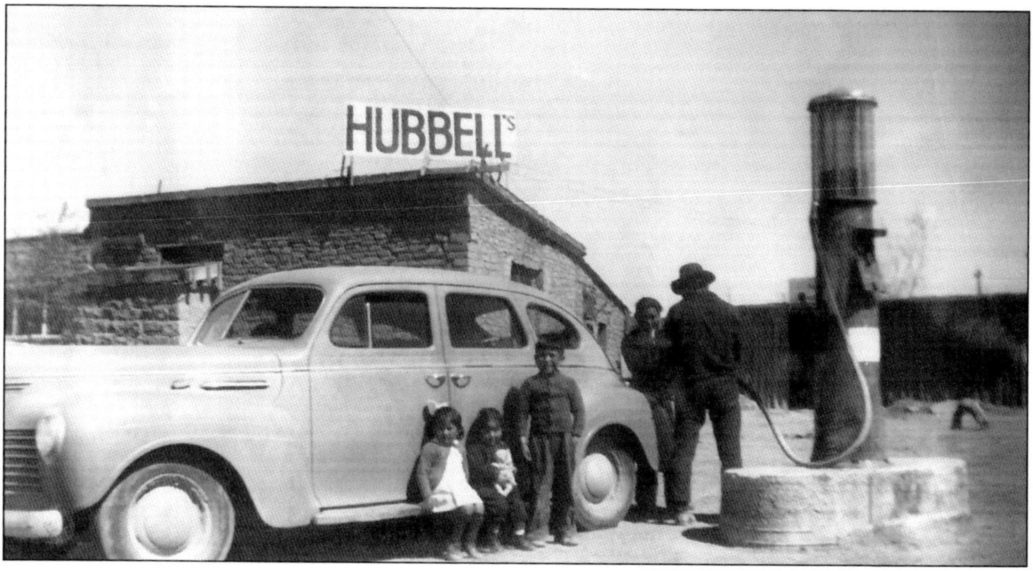

F.W. Volz started Oraibi Trading Post in the village of Kykotsmovi about 1897. Lorenzo Hubbell bought it in 1905, and his son Lorenzo Jr. took it over in 1920. Lorenzo Jr. was one of the first traders to deal extensively in Hopi pottery. He was also one of the first to try to pay with coin, but locals did not trust coins, so he offered copper bracelets in trade. The Hubbells lost the store in 1951 when Roman Hubbell speculated on the price of wool. Because of the Korean War, he thought that the price of wool would soar and that the military would buy wool for uniforms. That never happened, and with the huge debt, Babbitt Brothers bought out the store. Below, Lorenzo Hubbell Jr. shows a rug in his showroom in 1932. (Below, courtesy of Frashers Fotos Collection.)

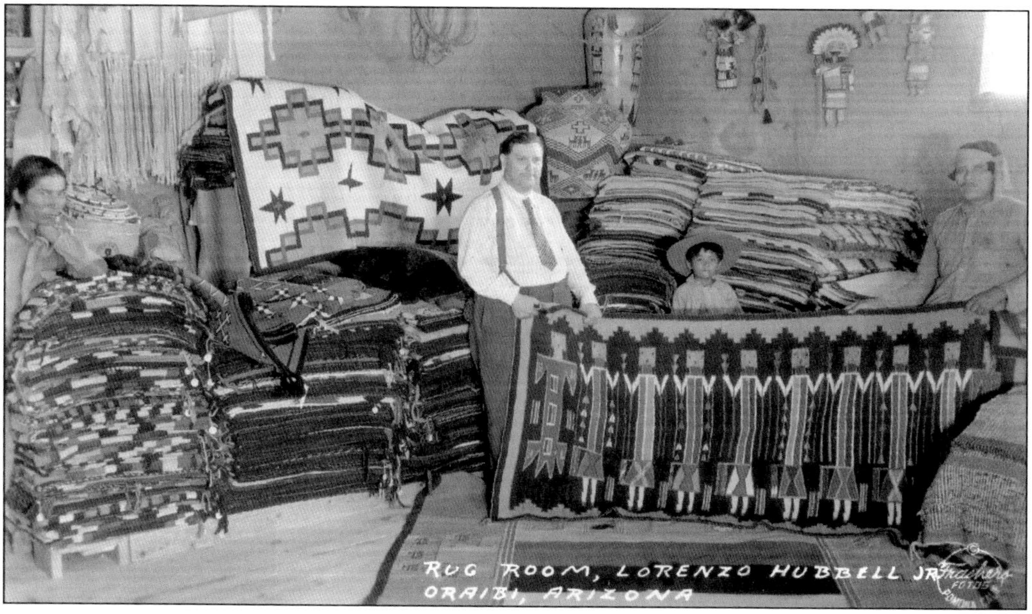

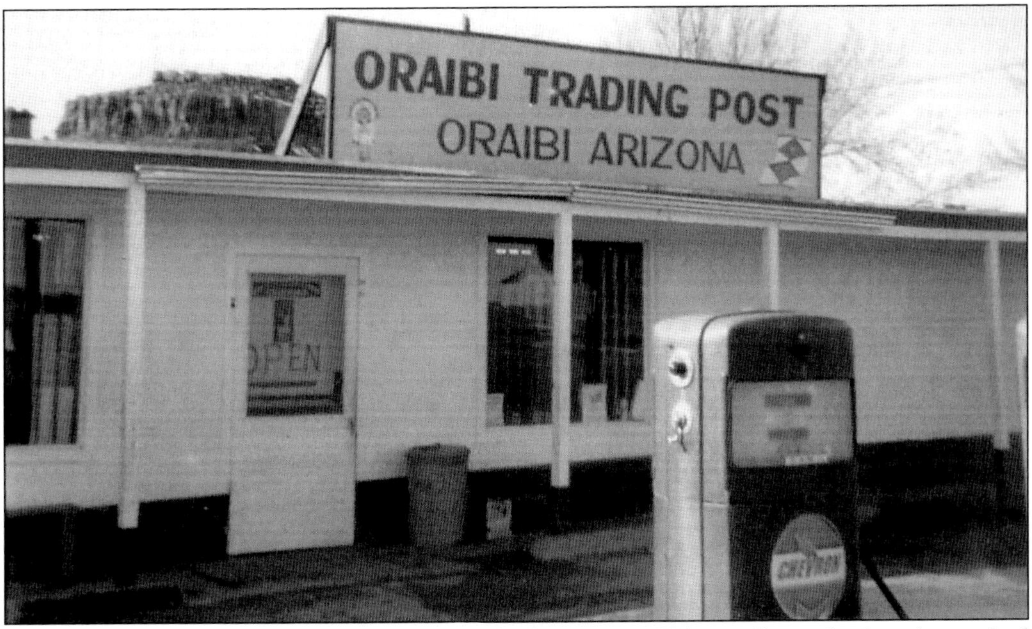

Lorenzo Hubbell Jr. was well liked. Once he asked a Navajo, "What will you do if you have a bad winter? You may get hungry." The man looked at Hubbell and said, "Why? Where are you going?" Hubbell was a trader who would buy a poor quality rug from an elderly and infirm weaver because he was there to serve the needs of the people. After Babbitt Brothers acquired Oraibi Trading Post, the name was changed to Kykotsmovi. Bruce and Delna Powell operated the store from 1966 to 1976, living in a house behind the trading post. Delna recalled that all the roads were dirt at that time and "some were mostly just sand." The village of Kykotsmovi acquired the store in 1996, and today, it is still in operation, under the management of Tommy and Julie Canyon. (Above, courtesy of Bruce and Delna Powell.)

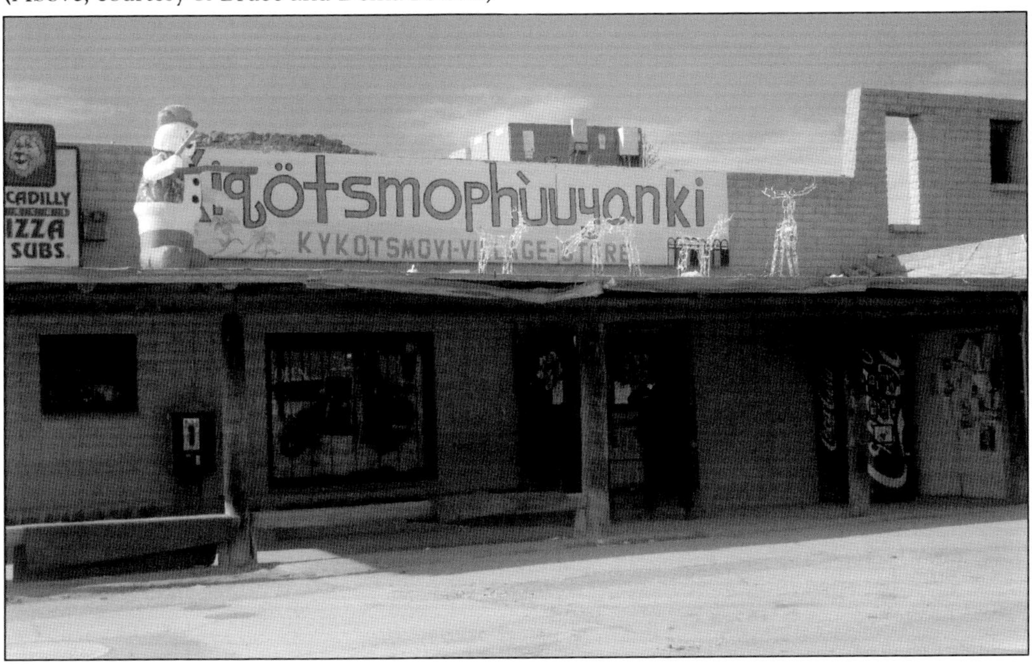

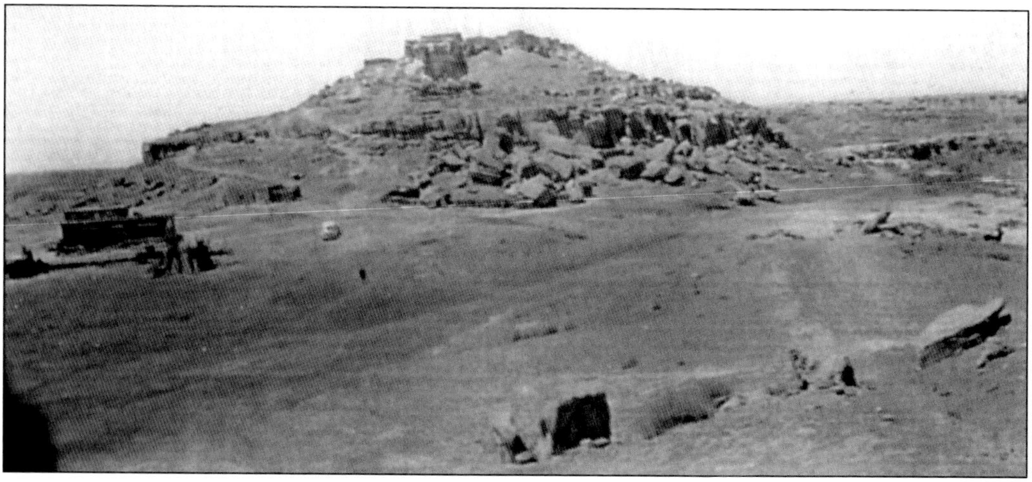

Hopi entrepreneur Hale Secakuku opened a trading post near his home at Second Mesa on the Hopi Indian Reservation. The store was near the top of the mesa between the villages of Shipaulovi and Mishongnovi, as shown in this 1927 photograph taken by writer Florence Crannell Means. Twenty years later, Editha Watson visited the Secakuku store at Second Mesa. The building still stands and is currently a residence. In 1960, Hale Secakuku and his son Ferrell built a large store down by the intersection of Highways 264 and 87. It mostly sold groceries and is now closed. (Above, courtesy of Eleanor Means Hull; below, courtesy of Martin Link.)

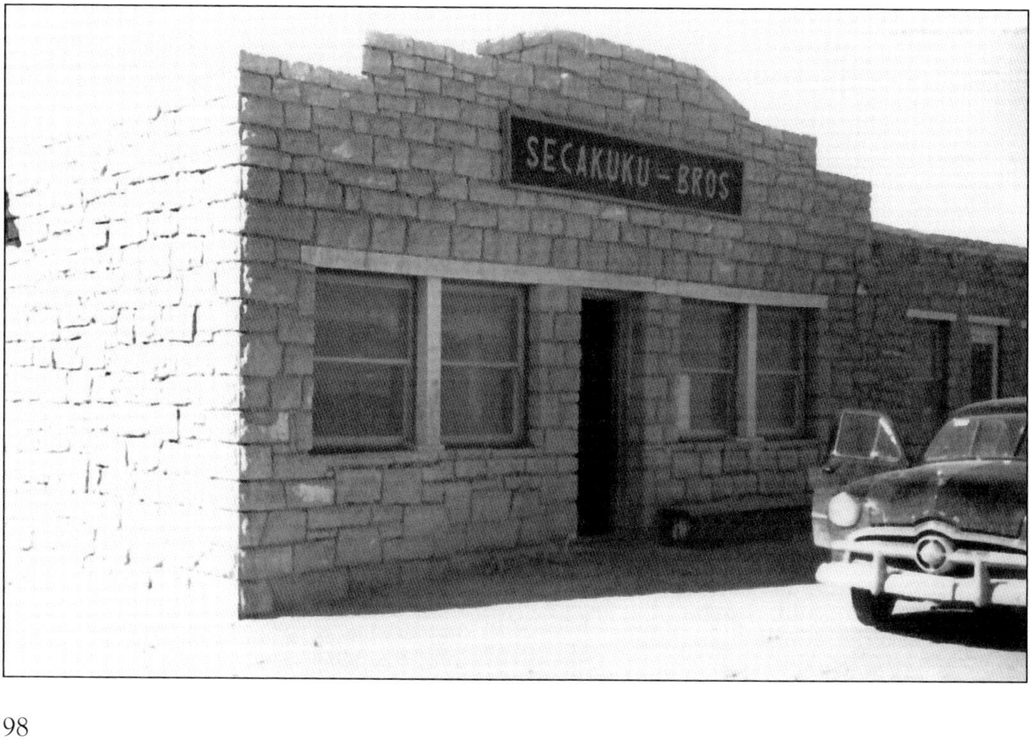

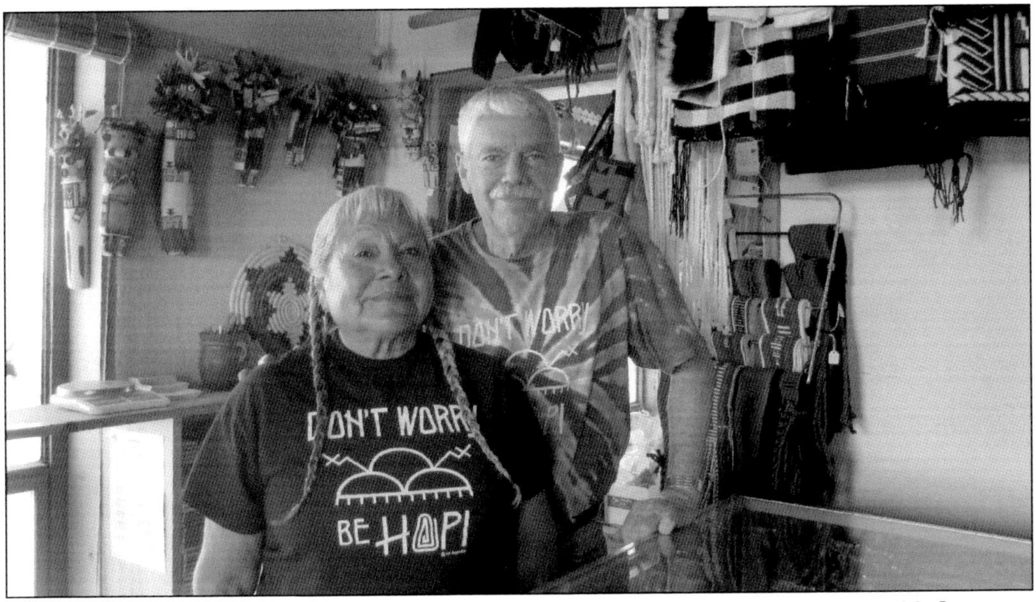

Joseph and Janice Day opened Tsakurshovi Trading Post on Second Mesa in 1988. Janice, a member of the Bear Strap Clan, is from the Hopi village of Shungopavi; Joseph is from Kansas. Tsakurshovi carries Hopi arts such as kachina carvings, woven baskets and plaques, silver overlay jewelry, and weavings. Additionally, it stocks items used by local craftsmen, like cottonwood root (for carving kachinas), deer hooves, fox tails, turtle shells, rattles, sashes, mineral pigments, and pelts. These traditional items are sold to Hopis preparing for ceremonies. The Days' first store was an old trailer on Highway 264. Proceeds from their famous "Don't Worry—Be Hopi" T-shirts financed construction of the current store. Hundreds of photographs just inside the door show famous or far-traveled Tsakurshovi customers wearing the distinctive shirts.

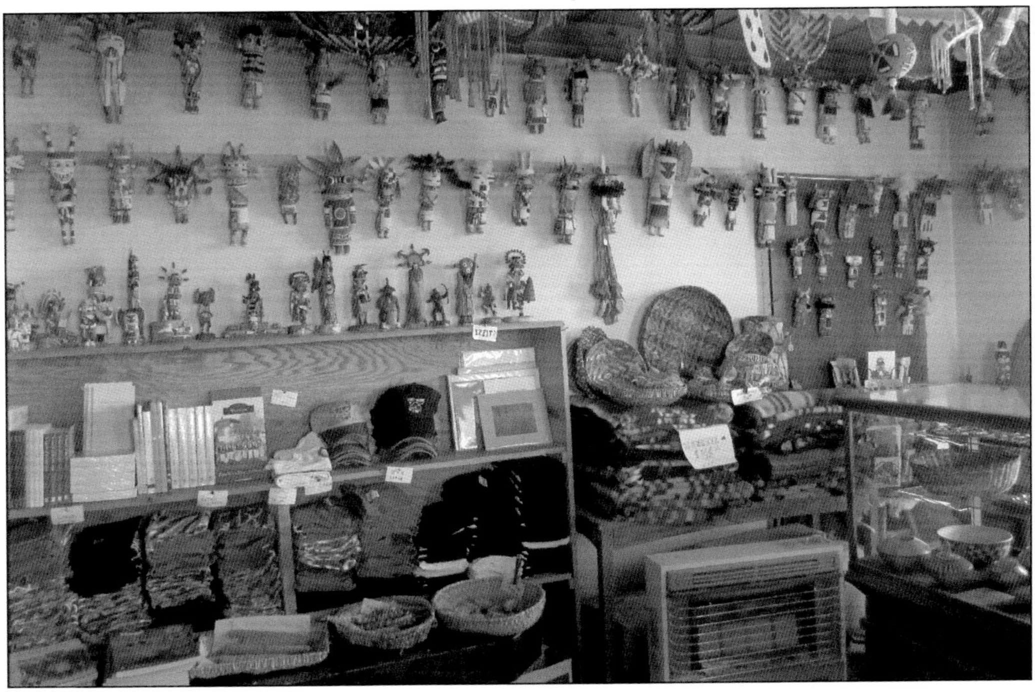

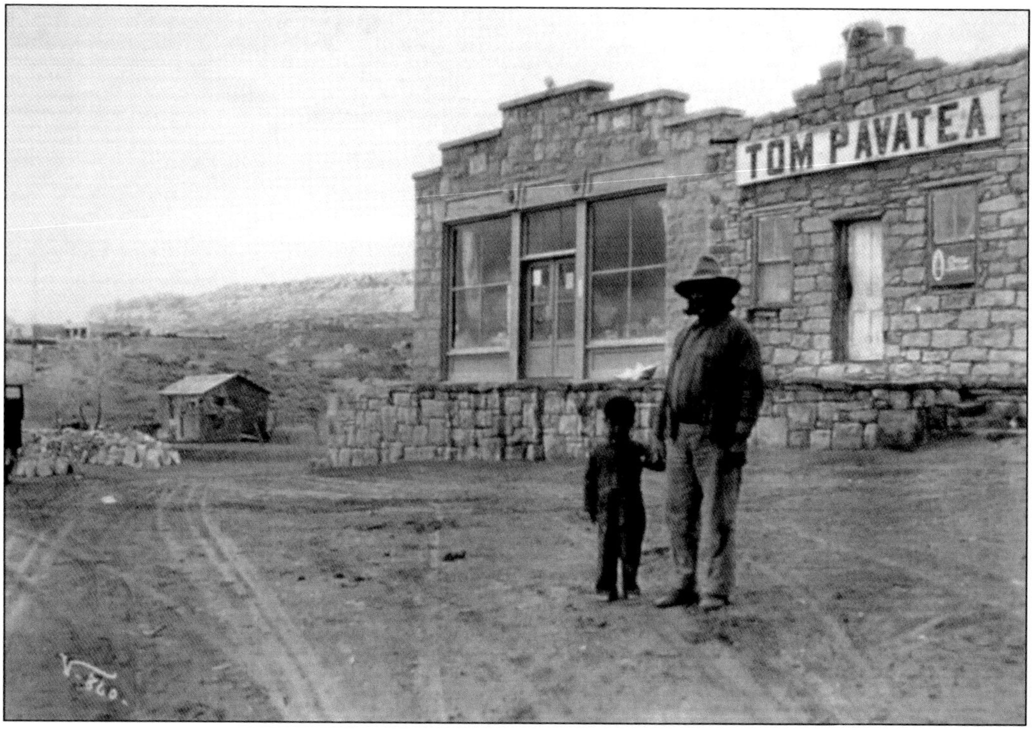

Hopi Tom Pavatea started his store in 1896 in a stone building at the bottom of First Mesa on the Hopi Indian Reservation. As a boy, Pavatea was taken to the Keams Canyon boarding school. He ran away and never learned to read and write. Pavatea worked for Thomas Keam herding sheep for 15 years, earning 25¢ a day plus food. Pavatea saved his money and went to Holbrook, where a wholesaler staked him for goods to open a store at First Mesa. Pavatea became a successful trader and was known for his help and generosity to his Hopi neighbors. Tags like the one shown below were attached to rugs and textiles in Tom Pavatea's store. (Above, courtesy of Florence Crannell Means; below, courtesy of Byron Hunter.)

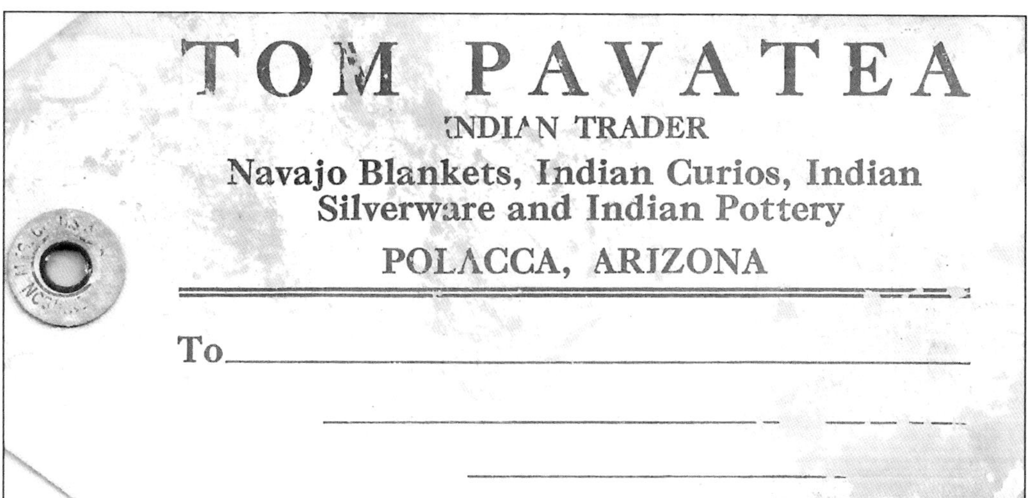

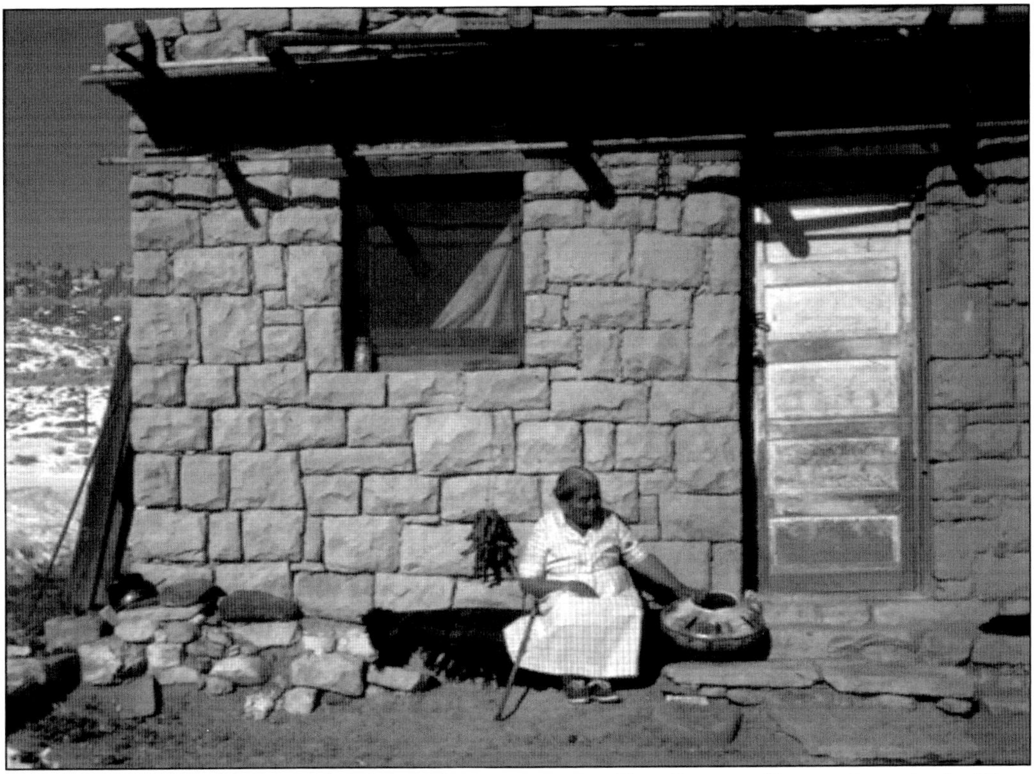

Grace Chapella, "White Squash Blossom," was married to Tom Pavatea. She was born in the Tewa village of Hano on First Mesa. She was a master potter, and her pots were sold in her husband's store as well as at nearby Keams Canyon Trading Post. Grace Chapella's beautiful pottery is valuable and highly collectible today. (Above, courtesy of Byron Hunter; below, courtesy of Harvey Leake.)

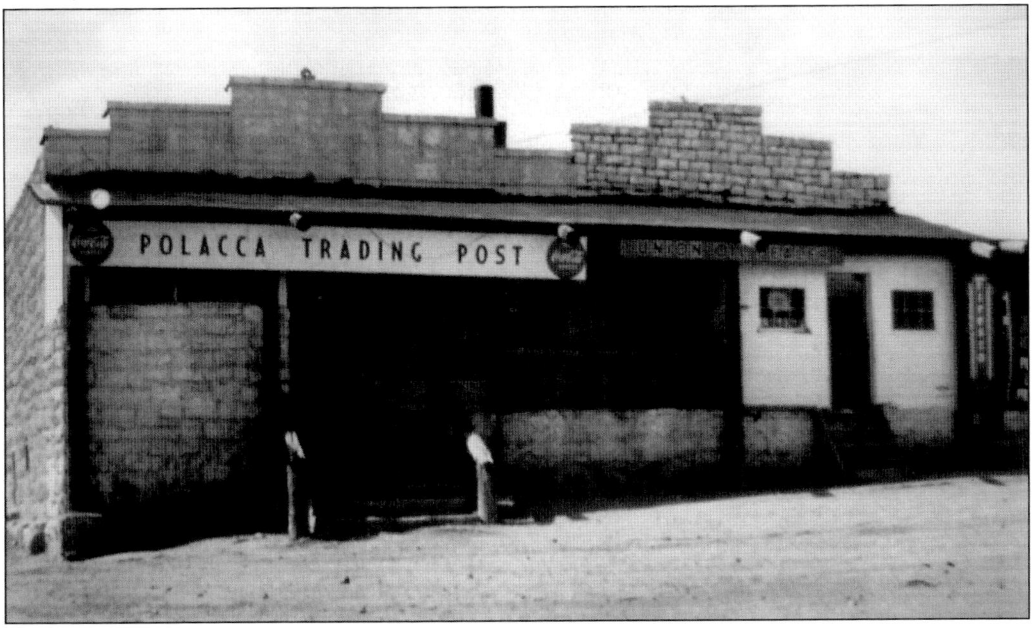

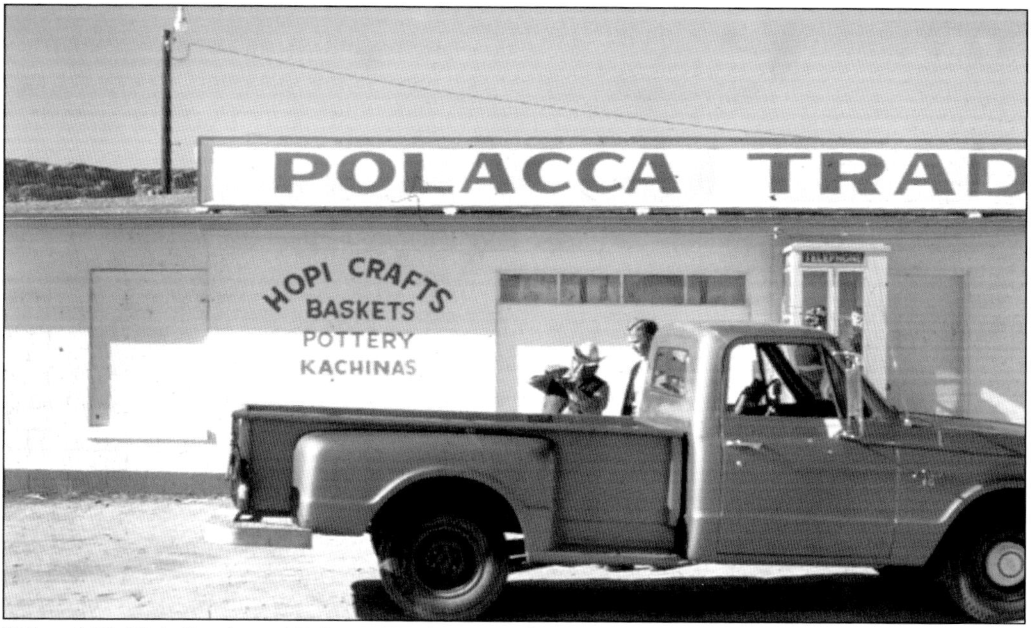

Bill and Cliff McGee leased Polacca Trading Post from Tom Pavatea and then purchased the store in 1950. After burning down in 1969, the store was rebuilt to the east on Highway 264. Trader Byron Hunter managed the store from 1963 to 1970. In earlier times, traders purchased rugs by the pound, and kachinas, as seen here on the wall of Polacca Trading Post, were bought by the inch. (Both, courtesy of Byron Hunter.)

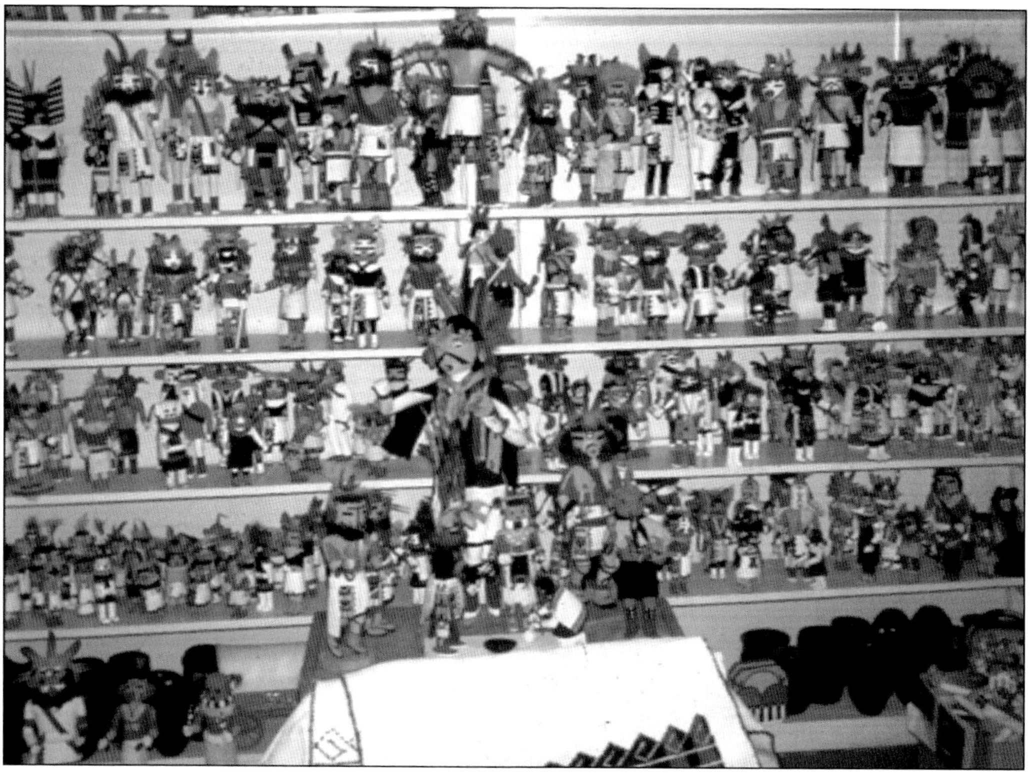

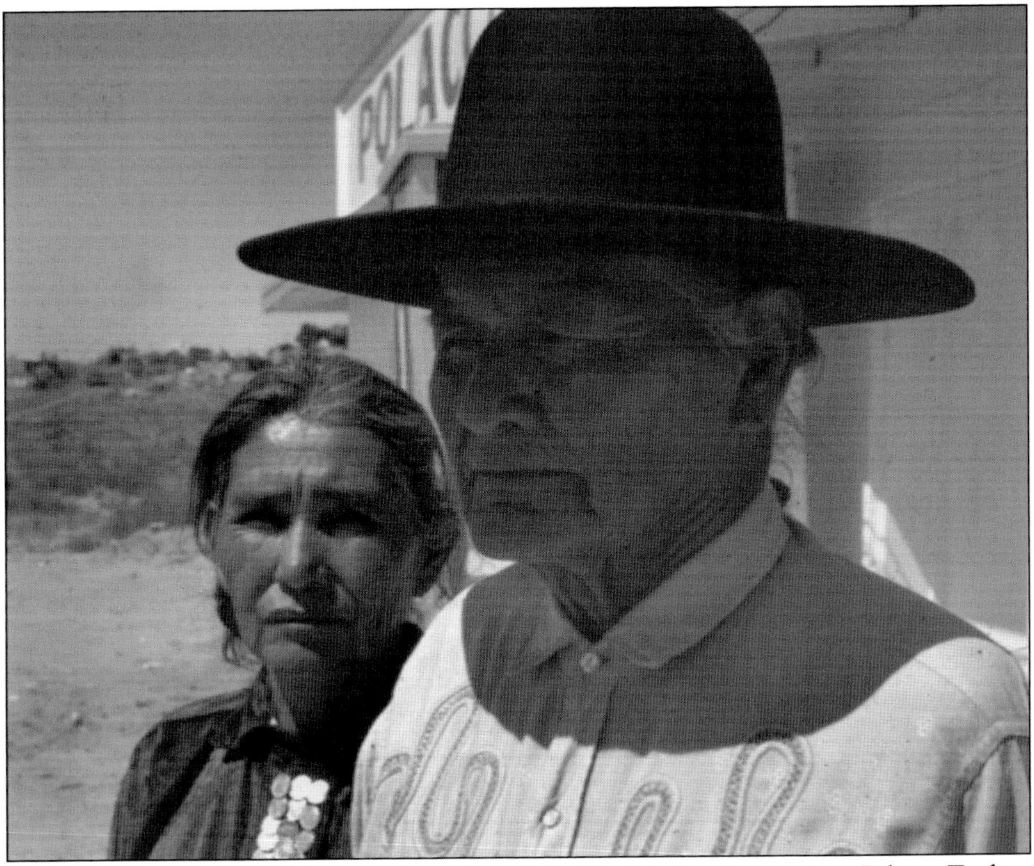

Because it was located at the eastern boundary of the Hopi Indian Reservation, Polacca Trading Post served Navajo as well as Hopi customers. Navajo customers Ann and Frank Nez, pictured above in 1970, are at Polacca Trading Post. Ann's velveteen shirt is embellished with a triple row of silver coin buttons. Seen below, Flora Ray Koyquaptewa (left) and Alice Kabotie were from First and Second Mesa, respectively. Alice may have walked some of the eight miles from her home at Second Mesa, carrying goods to trade or her purchases in the bundle tied across her back. (Both, courtesy of Byron Hunter.)

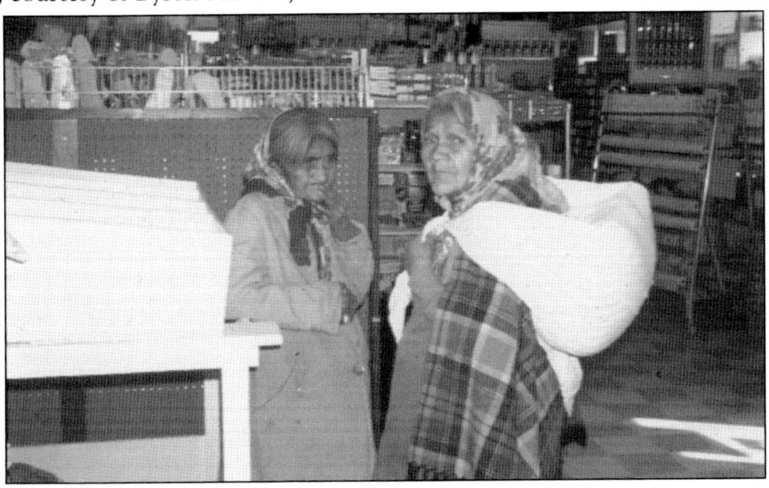

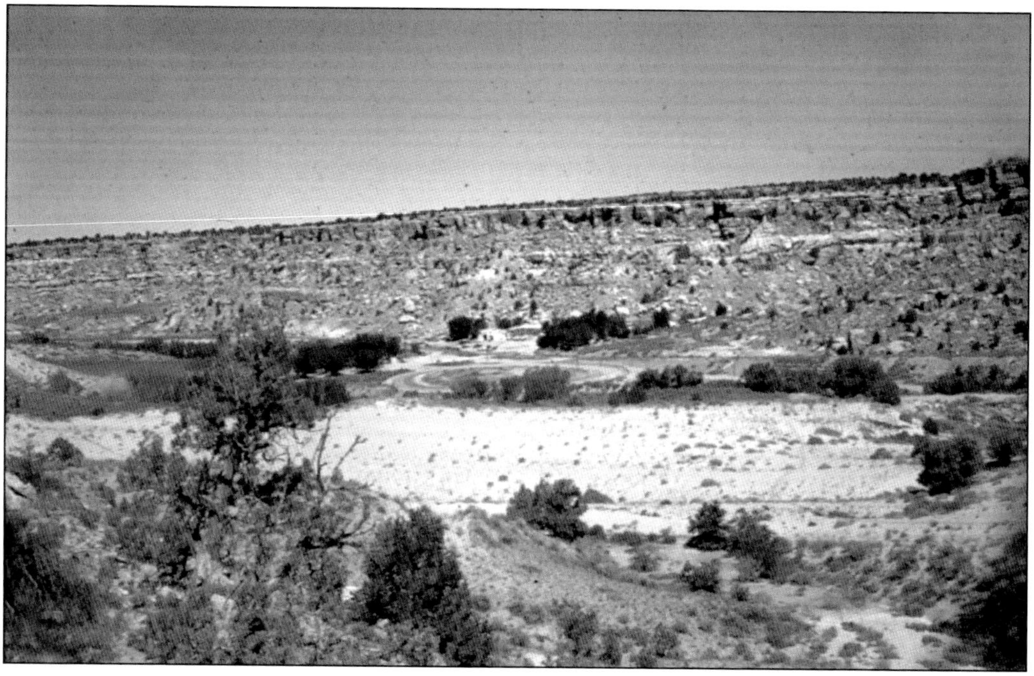

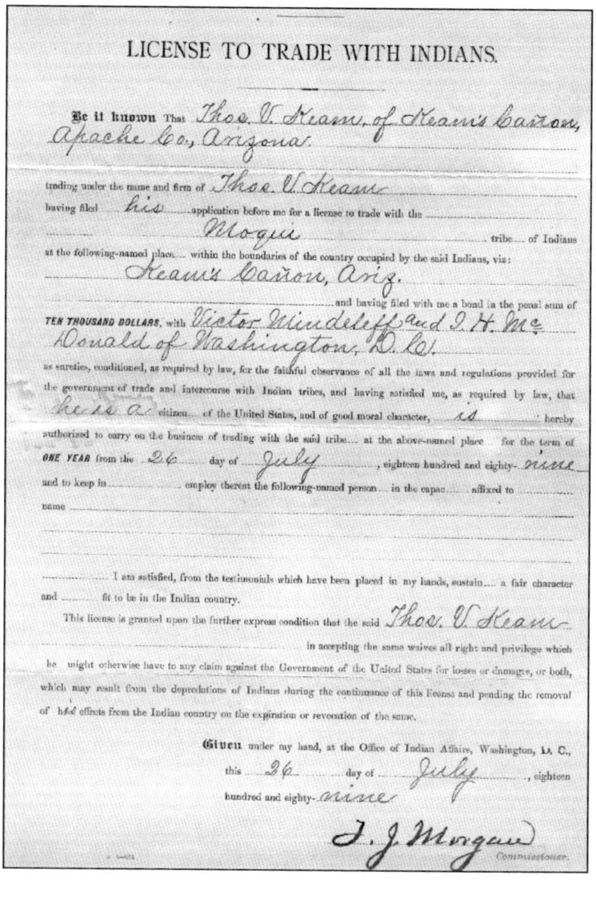

LICENSE TO TRADE WITH INDIANS.

Be it known That Thos. V. Keam, of Keam's Cañon, Apache Co., Arizona.

trading under the name and firm of Thos. V. Keam having filed his application before me for a license to trade with the Moqui tribe... of Indians at the following-named place... within the boundaries of the country occupied by the said Indians, viz: Keam's Cañon, Ariz. and having filed with me a bond in the penal sum of TEN THOUSAND DOLLARS, with Victor Mindeleff and I. H. Mc Donald of Washington, D.C. as sureties, conditioned, as required by law, for the faithful observance of all the laws and regulations provided for the government of trade and intercourse with Indian tribes, and having satisfied me, as required by law, that he is a citizen... of the United States, and of good moral character, is hereby authorized to carry on the business of trading with the said tribe... at the above-named place... for the term of ONE YEAR from the 26 day of July, eighteen hundred and eighty-nine and to keep in ... employ thereat the following-named person... in the capac... affixed to name ...

... I am satisfied, from the testimonials which have been placed in my hands, sustain... a fair character and ... fit to be in the Indian country.

This license is granted upon the further express condition that the said Thos. V. Keam in accepting the same waives all right and privilege which he might otherwise have to any claim against the Government of the United States for losses or damages, or both, which may result from the depredations of Indians during the continuance of this license and pending the removal of his effects from the Indian country on the expiration or revocation of the same.

Given under my hand, at the Office of Indian Affairs, Washington, D. C., this 26 day of July, eighteen hundred and eighty-nine

T. J. Morgan
Commissioner.

In 1865, Englishman Thomas Keam enlisted in the 1st New Mexico Volunteer Calvary. He learned to speak Navajo and Hopi and worked as an interpreter at Fort Defiance. In 1875, Keam bought out the original trader who had been trading at the canyon that now carries his name. The original site of Keams Trading Post was up in the canyon beyond Beaver Dam, and Keam later moved the store further down the canyon. Keam married a Navajo, Grey Woman, but was looked down on by Anglo government agents for the relationship. Keam sold his trading post in 1902 to Lorenzo Hubbell and returned to England, where he died shortly after. At left is an image of Thomas Keam's original 1889 License to Trade with Indians. (Above, courtesy of Byron Hunter; left, courtesy of Edgar Busch.)

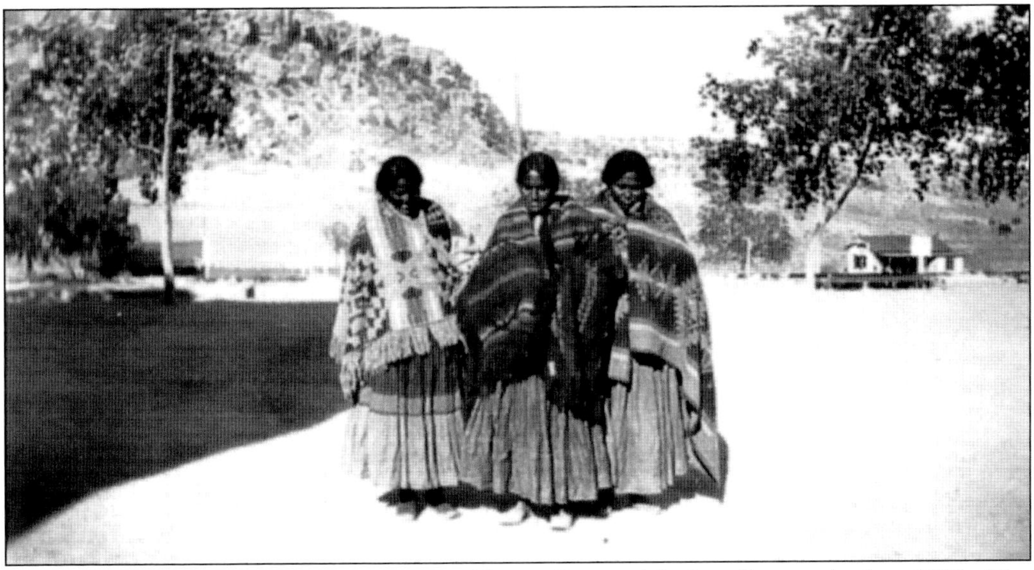

A group of Navajo women is seen visiting Keams Canyon Trading Post in the late 1920s. The ladies are wearing moccasins and at least two gathered skirts apiece, and they are wrapped in colorful Pendleton blankets. (Courtesy of Florence Crannell Means.)

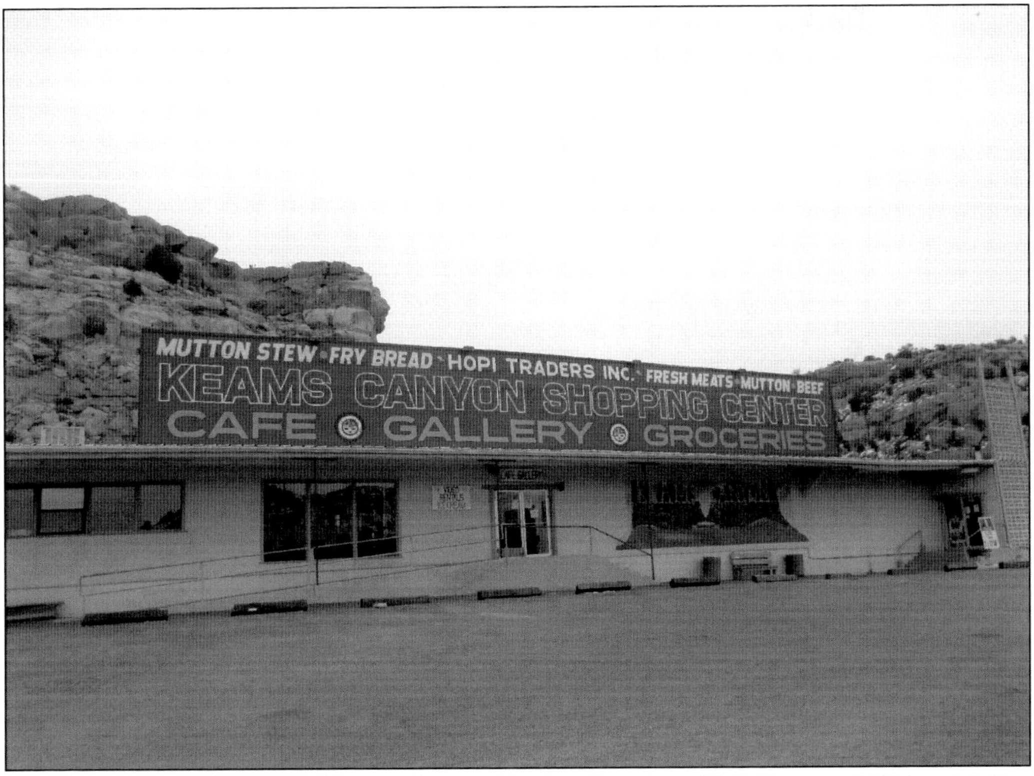

The McGee family has owned Keams Canyon Trading Post since 1941. Betty and Clifton McGee went there to manage the store in 1945. Highway 264 was a dirt road, and they lived in a two-room house next to the gas pumps. Additions were made to the old store, and today, there is a grocery store, Indian art gallery, and a restaurant offering mutton stew and fry bread.

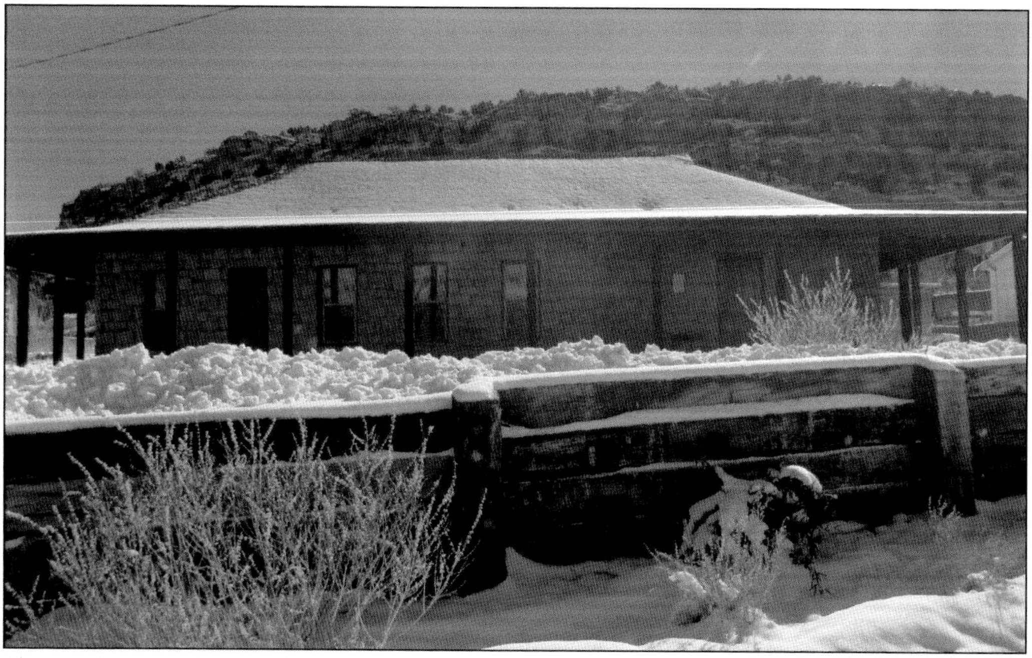

Skeet Stiles started L&A Trading Post in 1930. Located just off Highway 264 near Keams Canyon, L&A was named for Lester and Ann Lee, who had the store until 1949. It was then taken over by Lester's brother Jack Lee, who operated the store until 1975. The post had Hopi and Navajo customers, and because Jack spoke Navajo, he waited on Navajos while his wife, Evelyn, waited on Hopis. Evelyn bought a lot of Hopi pottery and said that, at one time, she sold Nampeyo pottery for 40¢ a bowl. Today, Nampeyo pottery is extremely valuable. Helen Naha, "Feather Woman," shown here in 1969, was a master potter who also sold her pottery at the store. Today, the red sandstone building is a church. (Below, courtesy of Byron Hunter.)

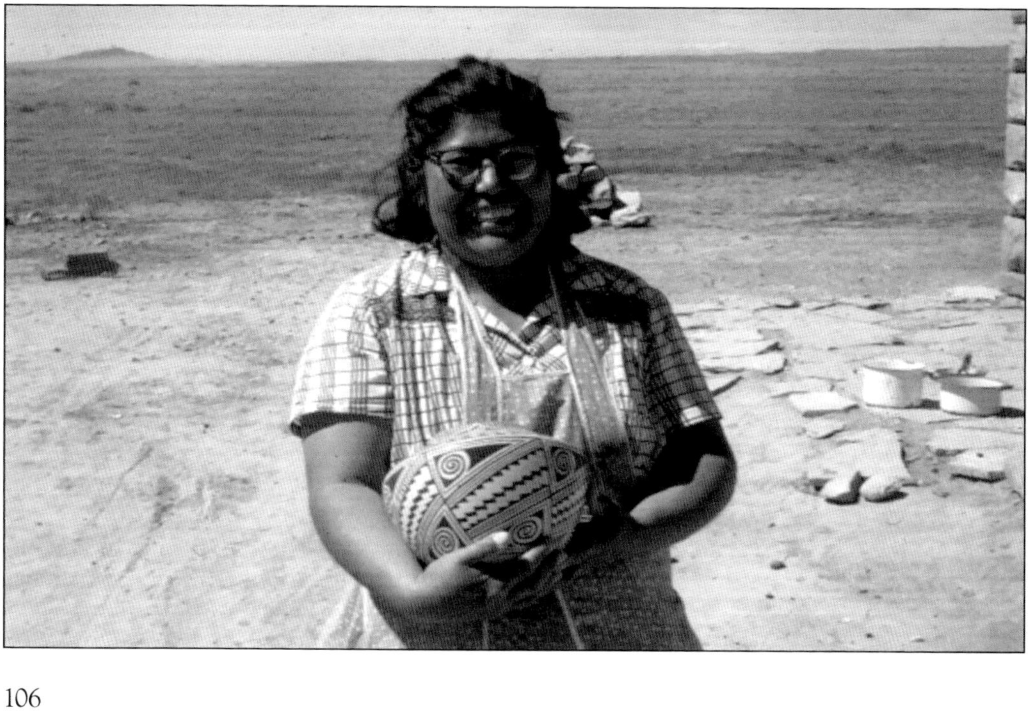

Three

NDEE
THE PEOPLE

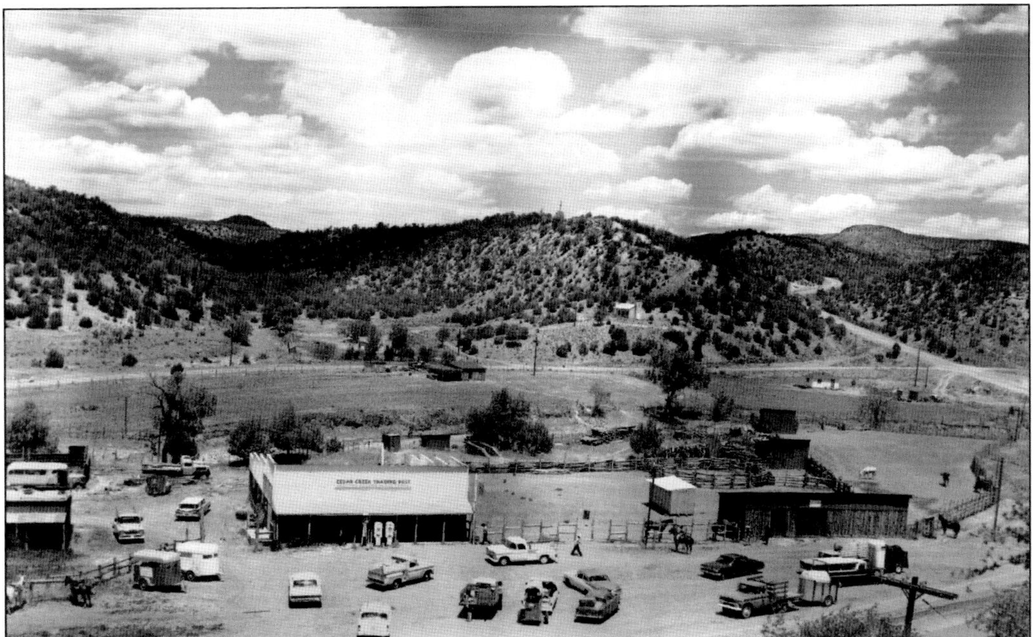

Cedar Creek Trading Post, seen in this 1960s photograph, was located on Cedar Creek on the White Mountain Apache Reservation. Other early Apache trading posts were at Cibecue, Grasshopper, Carrizo, and East Fork. (Courtesy of Mead Publishing.)

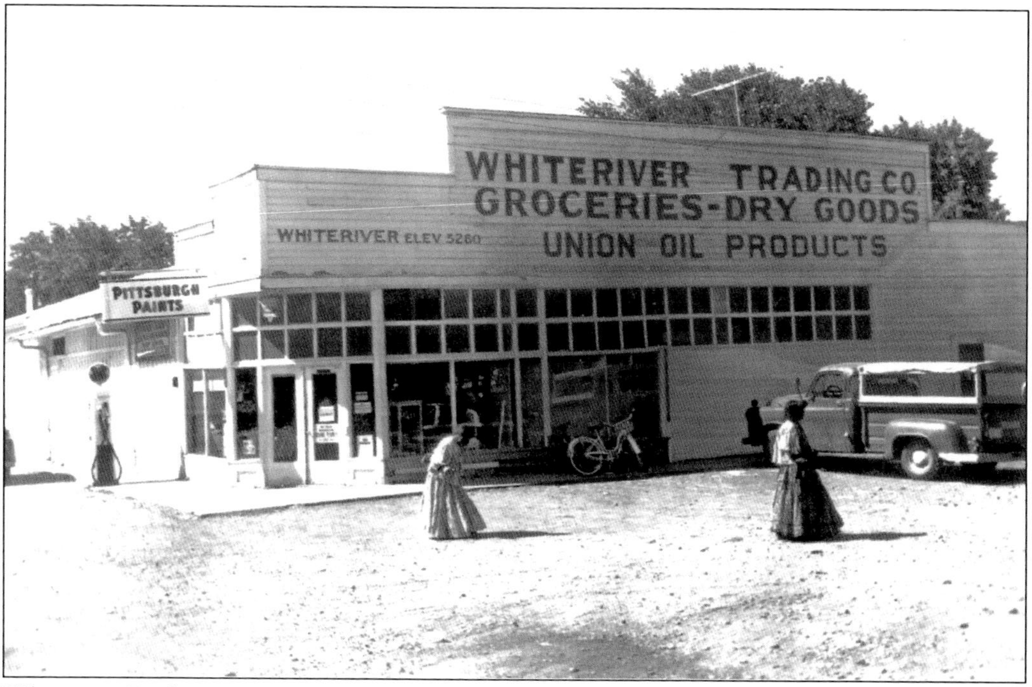

Whiteriver Trading Post was on the Fort Apache Indian Reservation on Highway 73. John Lee, a longtime trader at Whiteriver, recalled that back in the 1920s, when he first began working in his uncle's store, the Lee Mercantile Company, they sold a lot of canvas that was stretched over the traditional brush wickiup. The store also sold cotton calico because the women wore skirts made with 16 yards of material. Ranching was the predominant enterprise, and trading posts extended credit to their customers through the year until October, when cattle was sold and bills were paid. Below is a traditional Apache home, a wickiup, which is a circular, timber-brush structure with a smoke hole in the center top. The floor was dirt with a fire pit in the center. (Above, courtesy of Mead Publishing; below, courtesy of WACC.)

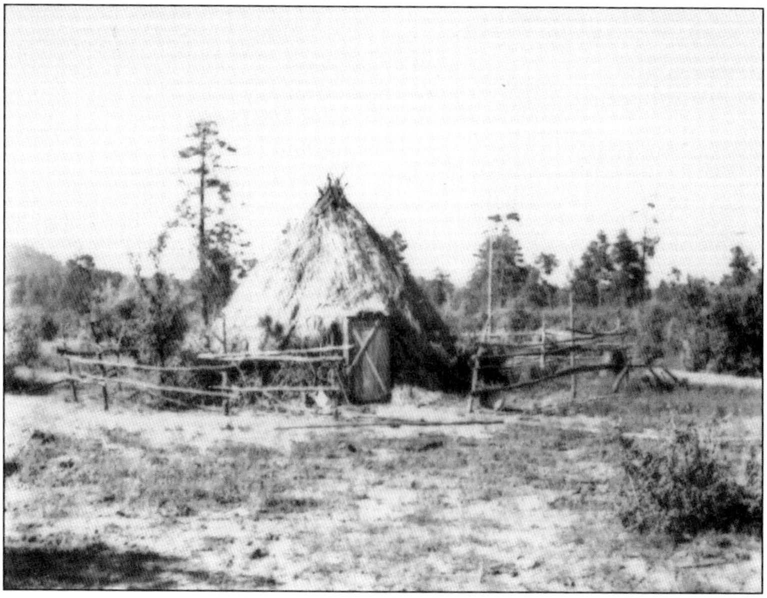

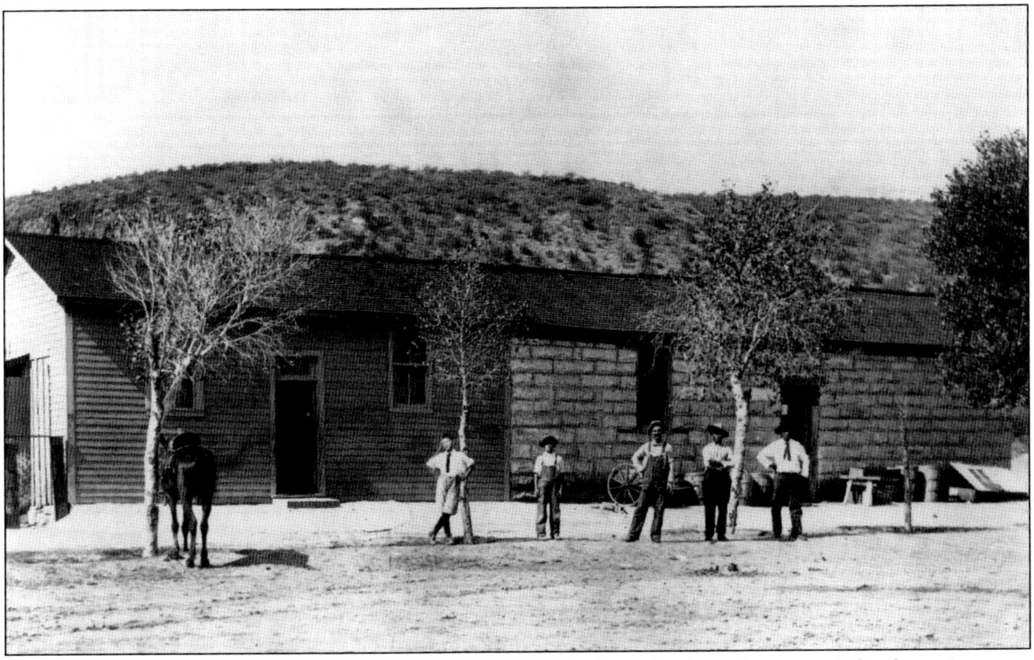

Wid Childress operated the Rice Trading Post near San Carlos, Arizona. The location was originally named Twelve Mile Post and then Talkai in 1880, and the name officially became Rice in 1907. The town of San Carlos eventually absorbed the community. Childress, seen above in about 1914, is the man in the center; his son Charlie is on the left wearing overalls. Others are unidentified. Below, Childress is standing behind the store counter, and young Charlie is at the right. Wid and Rosa Childress had five children; the youngest, George, was born in the family home next to the trading post in 1914. The store burned down in 1916, and the family moved to Globe, Arizona. (Both, courtesy of the Arizona Historical Society.)

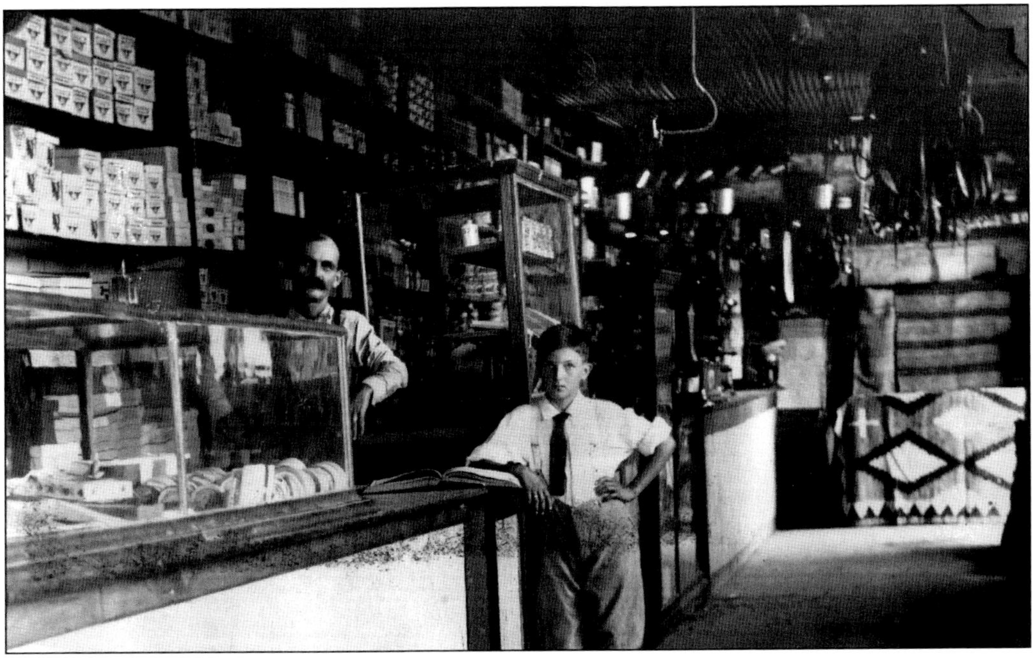

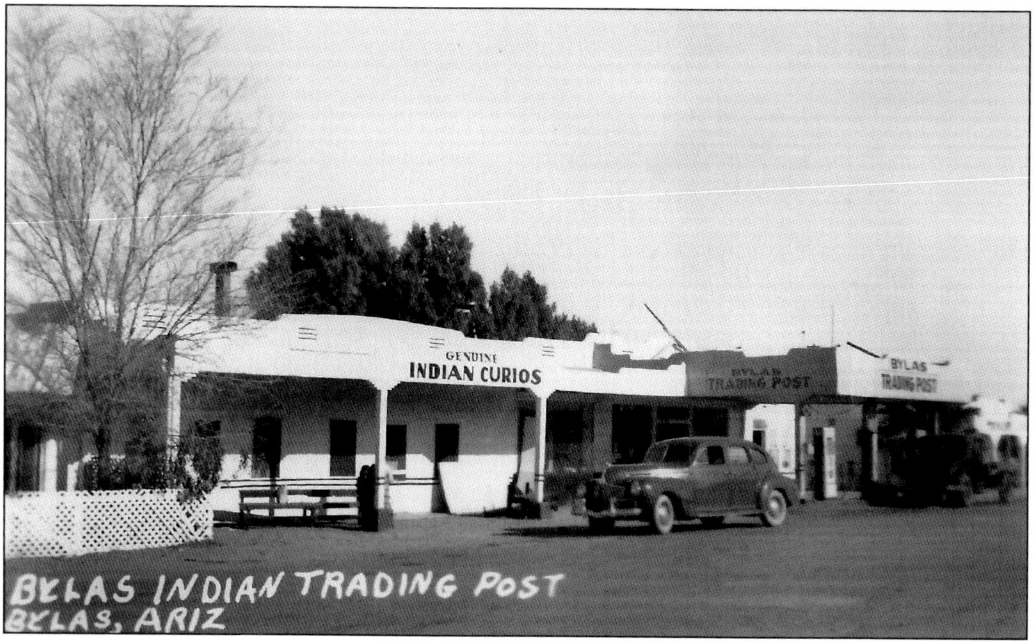

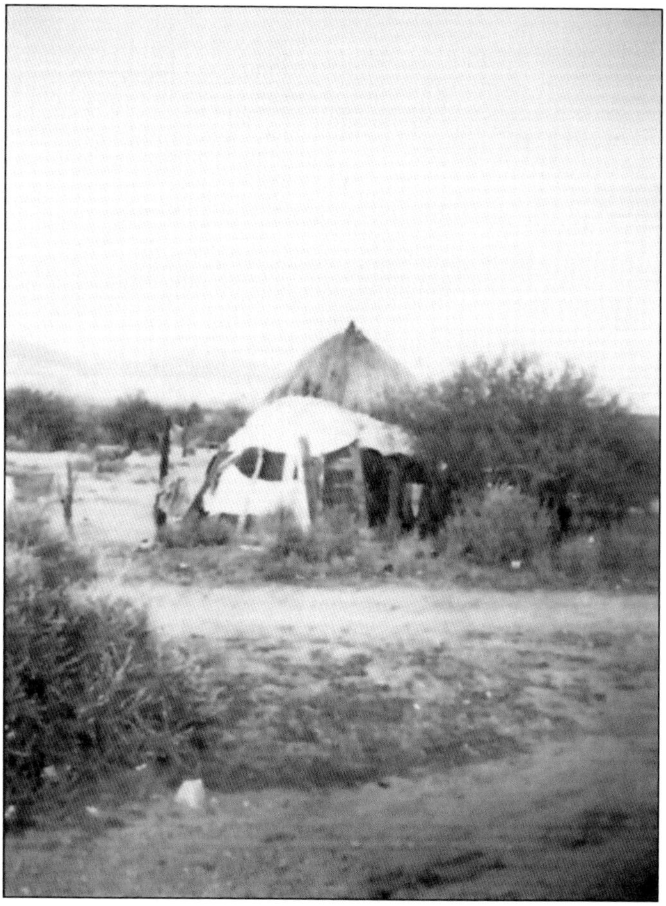

Bylas Trading Post, with an adjacent café, was located on Highway 70, midway between San Carlos and Safford on the San Carlos Apache Indian Reservation. The community is named for Bailish, a chief of the White Mountain Apache. Before construction of the interstate system, Highway 70 was a major east-west route, running from North Carolina in the east to Los Angeles and the Pacific Ocean; it was known as the "Broadway of America." Bylas Trading Post burned to the ground in 1955 as a result of an electrical fire. Store manager Norman Mydlin was able to save the accounts book, but little else could be salvaged as the telephone was out and help had to be summoned from Safford, about 30 miles away. At left is an Apache wickiup near Bylas. (Above, courtesy of Frashers Fotos Collection; left, courtesy of Martin Link.)

Four

Akimel O'odham and Pee Posh People

Gila River Indian Community

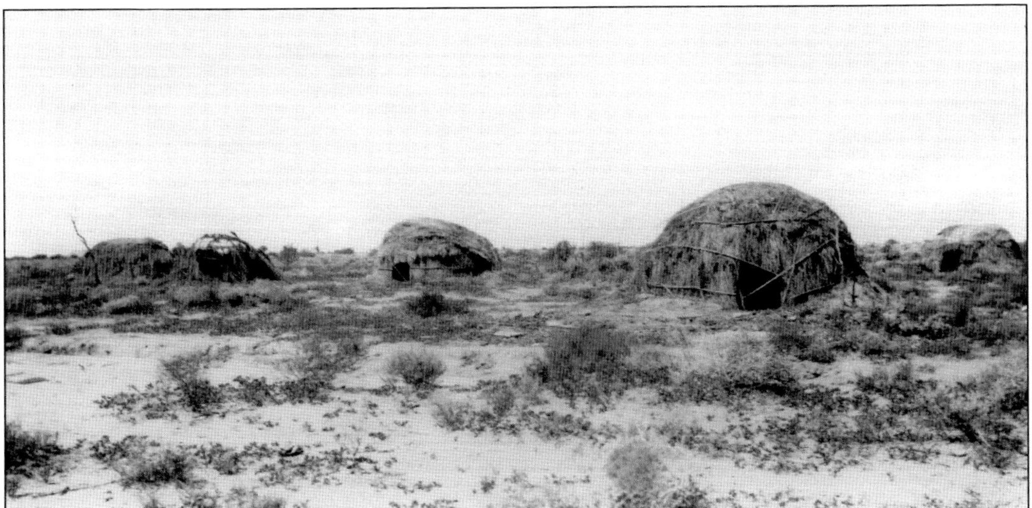

The Gila River Indian Reservation spreads along the Gila River south of Phoenix. The Pima people living in this area were farmers, irrigating through ditches running from the river. The old-time houses, kis, were dome-shaped and were constructed with a framework of bent rods covered with brush, a layer of earth, and a second layer of mud and brush to keep out wind and rain. Openings were small and low, as shown in this 1912 photograph taken at Sacaton. (Courtesy of WACC.)

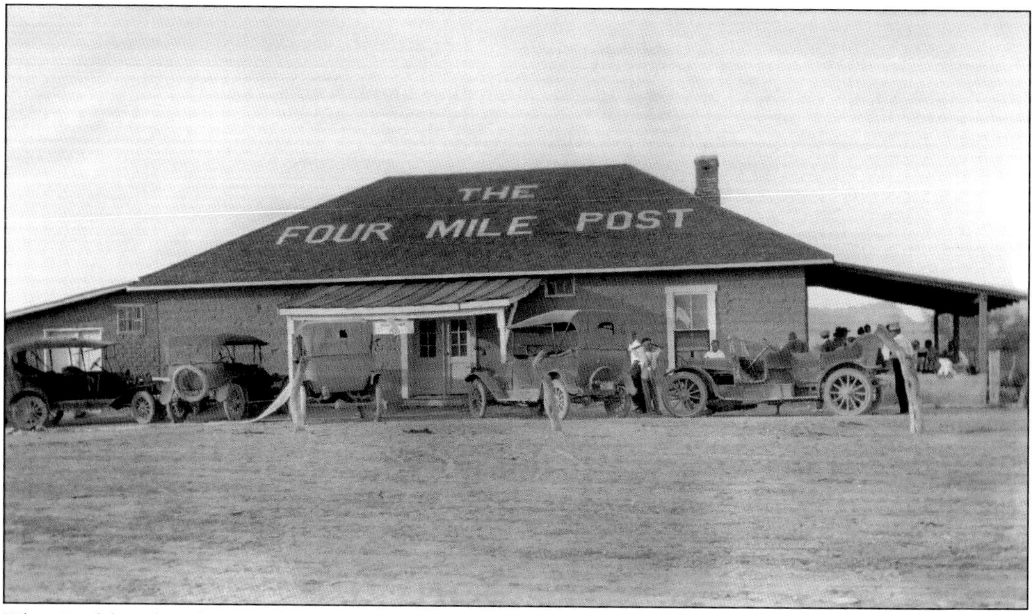

The Pinkley family ran the Four Mile Trading Post at Blackwater on the Gila River Indian Reservation. Young Frank Pinkley came west from Chillicothe, Missouri, in 1900 with the hope of curing his tuberculosis. The year following his arrival in Arizona, 20-year-old Pinkley was named the first resident custodian of the Casa Grande Ruins. While Pinkley worked to protect and stabilize the ruins, his parents ran the trading post. (Courtesy of WACC.)

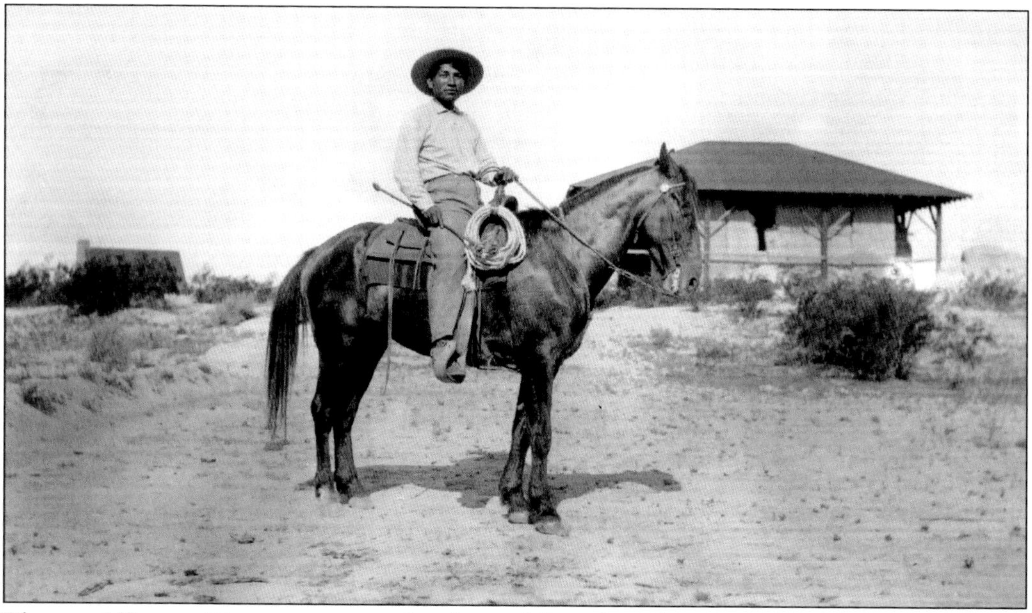

Thomas Allison, a Pima man, is posed in front of Casa Grande Ruins. Through Frank Pinkley's efforts, a roof was erected to protect the badly deteriorating ruins in 1903. The roof was effective, even though some people commented that it looked like a hay shed. In 1918, Pres. Woodrow Wilson named the site a national monument. Pinkley's next efforts were to fence the ruins to prevent grazing animals from trampling the structures. (Courtesy of WACC.)

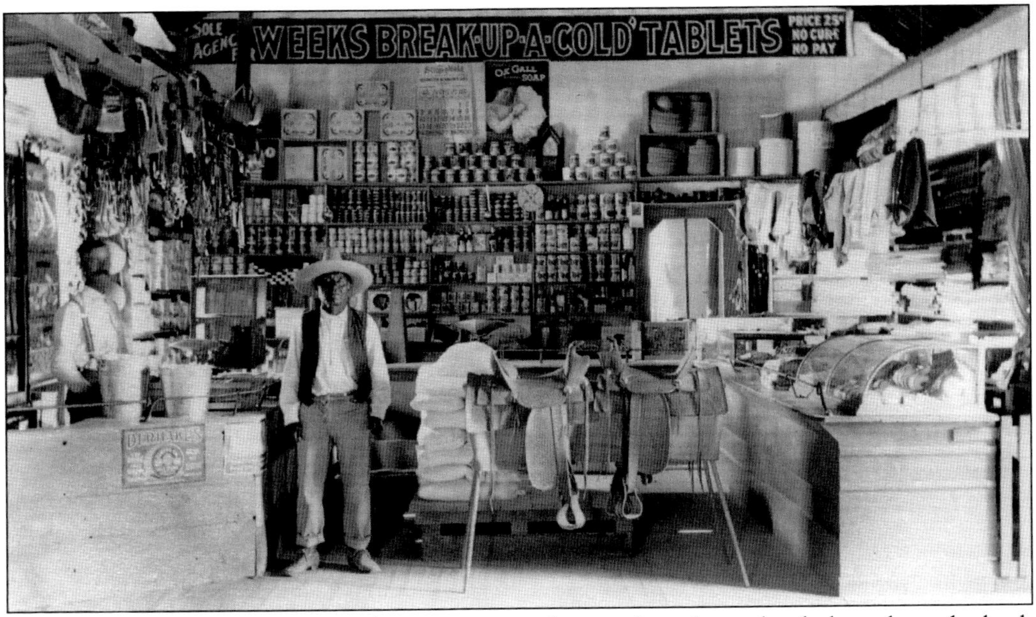

The interior of the Pinkley store shows a variety of canned goods on the shelves along the back wall, bags of flour on a wooden skid in front of the counter, and also saddles. Horse tack and bridles are hanging at the top left above the store's proprietor. Both men in the photograph are unidentified. (Courtesy of WACC.)

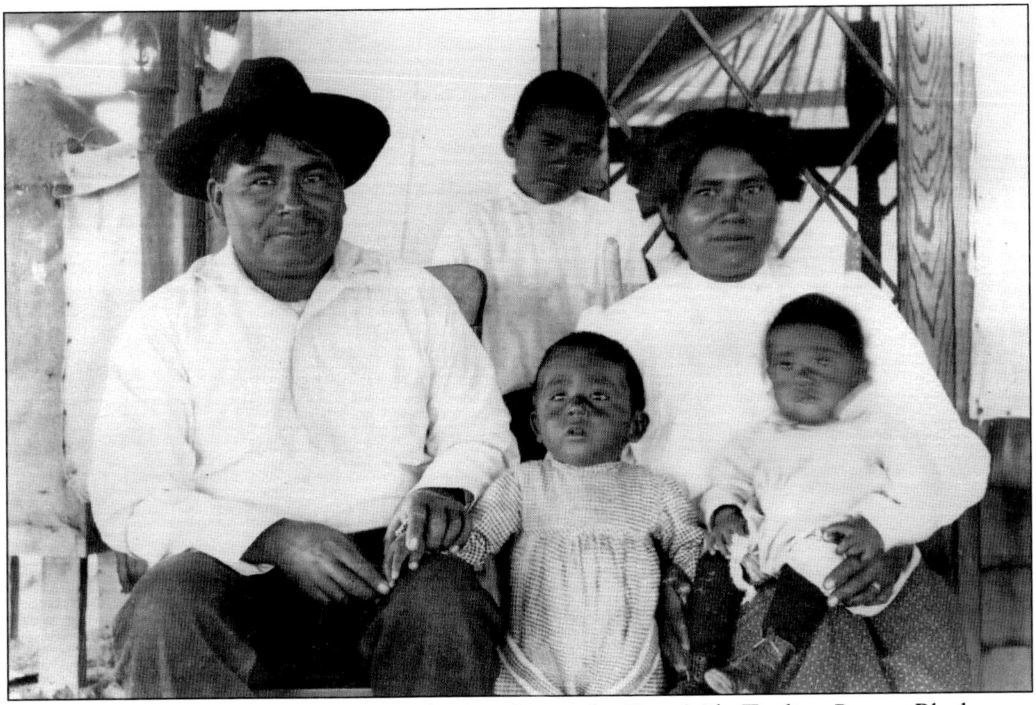

John Ben and his family were Pimas who lived near the Four Mile Trading Post at Blackwater about 1910. The Gila River Indian Community was established in 1859 and encompasses over 373,000 acres. (Courtesy of WACC.)

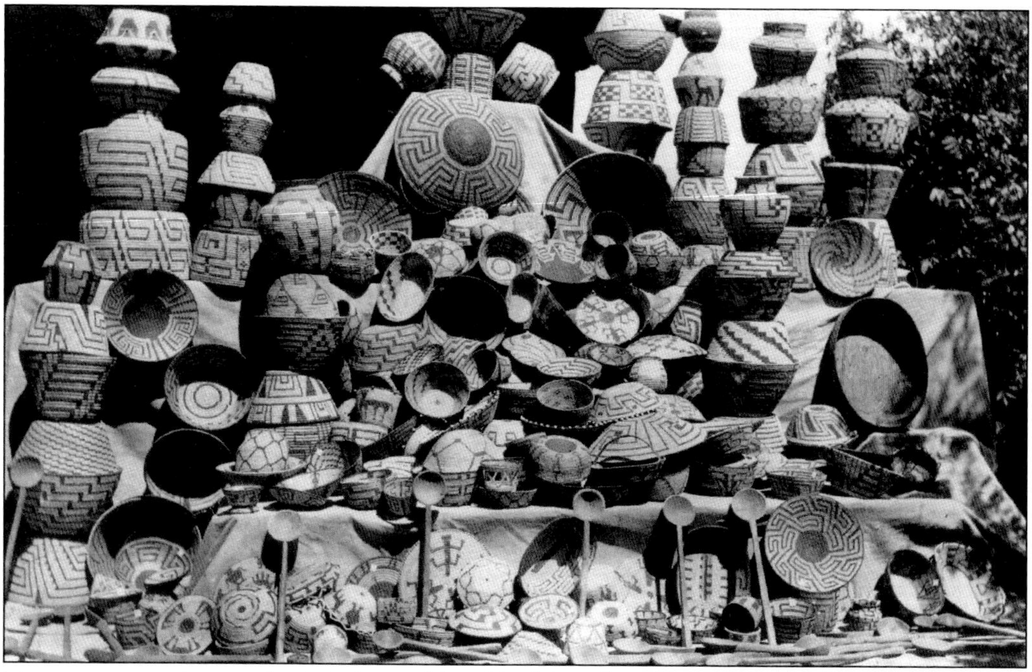

Pima women are known for their beautiful and highly collectible baskets. This 1906 collection of baskets at Blackwater Trading Post was considered a run-of-the-mill shipment. The baskets were extremely popular, both for practical and decorative purposes. Consequently, Pima baskets were shipped to stores and buyers across the country. (Courtesy of WACC.)

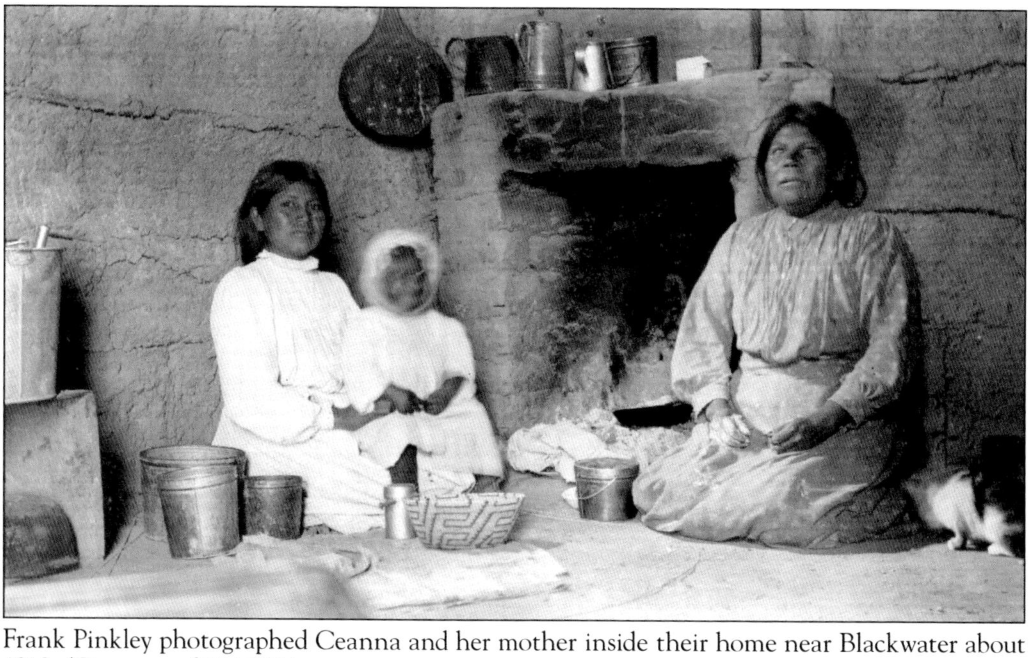

Frank Pinkley photographed Ceanna and her mother inside their home near Blackwater about 1912. (Courtesy of WACC.)

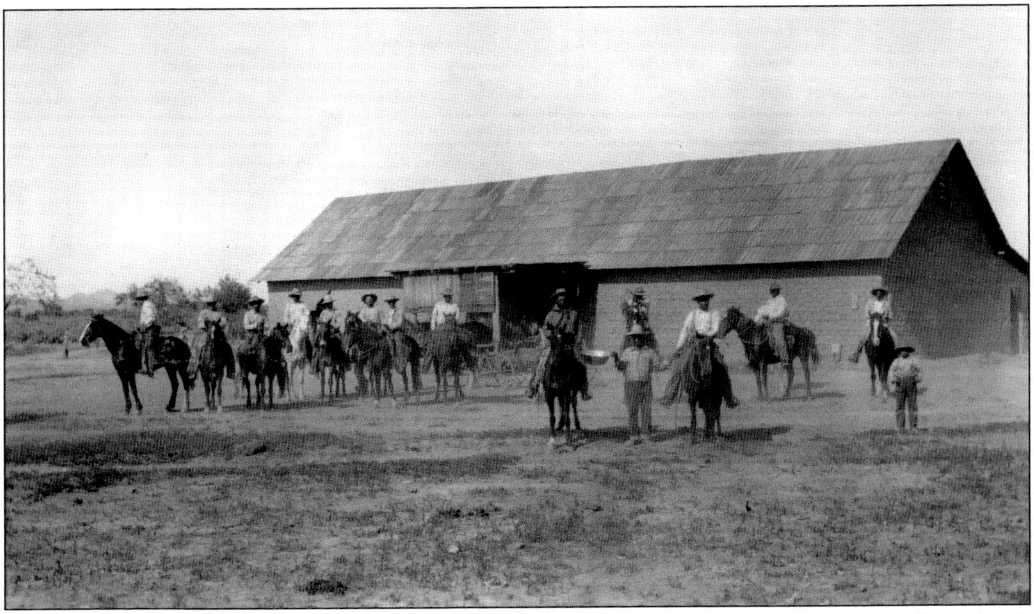

A group of cowboys in front of the Blackwater Trading Post prepares for a roundup, about 1912. (Courtesy of WACC.)

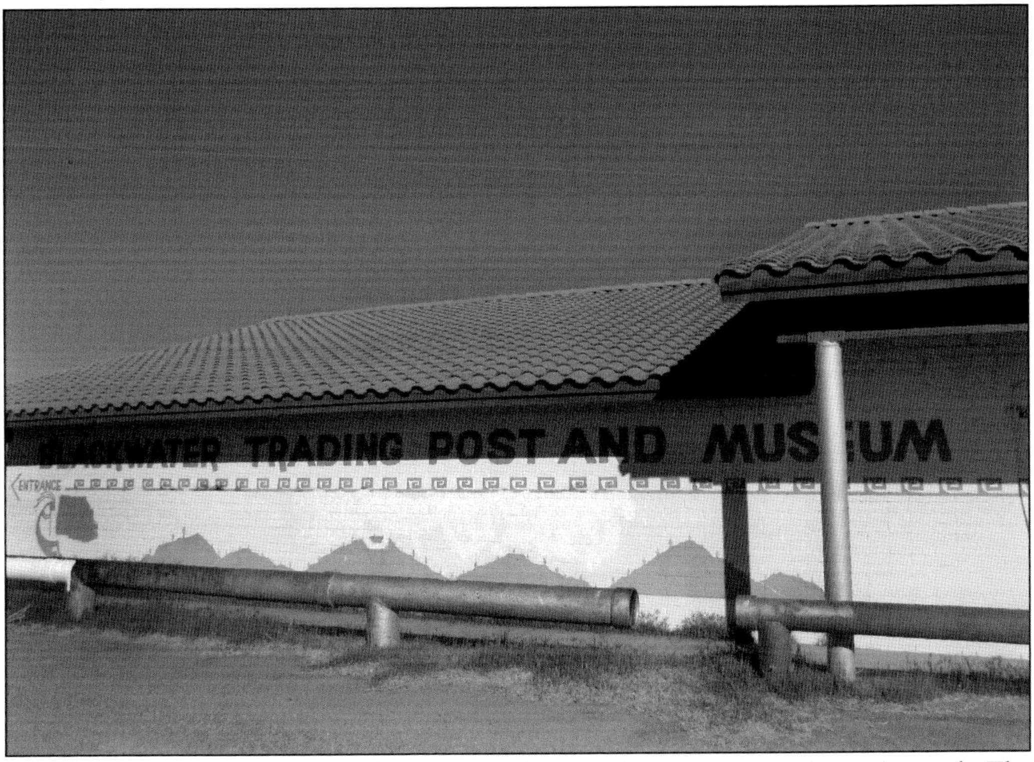

The original Blackwater Trading Post was abandoned and rebuilt a few miles to the south. The last owners sold the store and a large collection of historic baskets to the Gila River Indian Community for a future museum. At this time, the building is vacant, and plans for the museum are on hold.

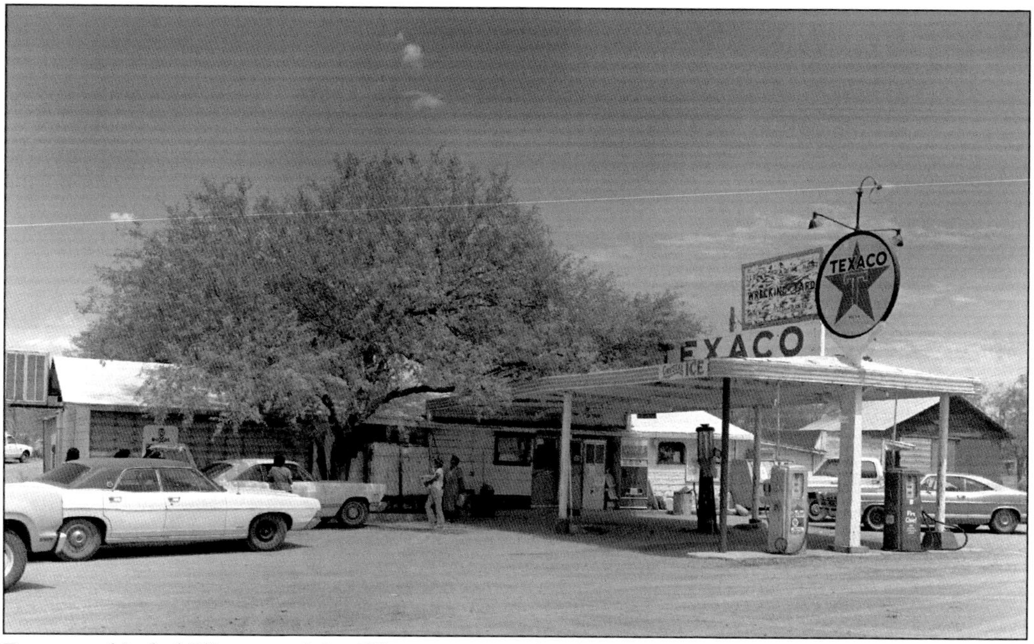

Ernest and Isabel Ellis owned the Olberg store north of Sacaton, near the old bridge over the Gila River, as seen in this 1975 photograph by Helga Teiwes. A local woman recalled going to Olberg Trading Post on horseback or wagon and walking to the store at Halloween for trick-or-treating because Isabel gave apples and oranges. There was a soda machine at the front of the store, and Isabel sat at the counter. She kept chickens that had the run of the store and a pet parrot. The Ellises' sons were mechanics, and there was a garage for automobile repairs. Olberg carried stovepipes, kerosene, hardware, and groceries, in addition to bags of seed during planting season. Local people traded loads of wood, leatherwork, and crafts. After the Ellis family left, the building remained vacant and eventually burned. (Above, courtesy of Arizona State Museum.)

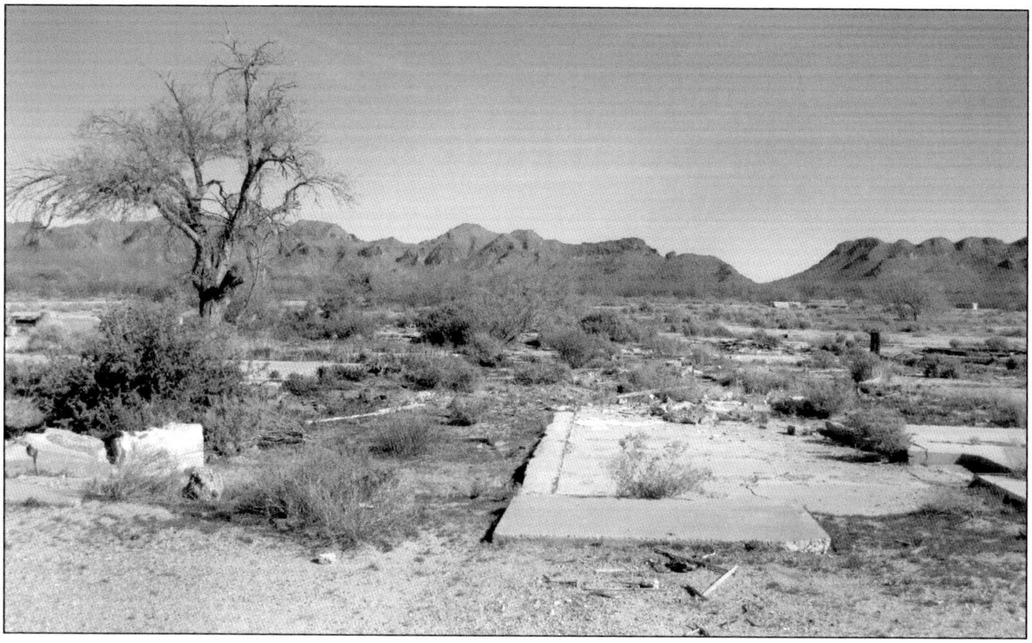

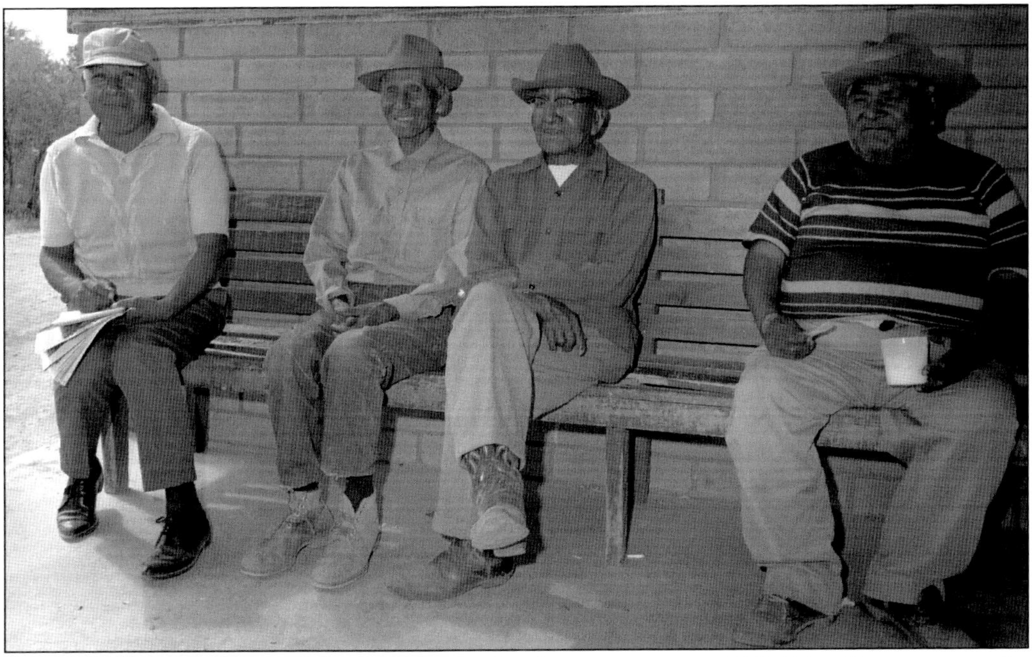

Helga Teiwes photographed these scenes at the Sacaton store in 1976. The Pima men on the bench in front of the store are, from left to right, Boyd Thompson, Chico Quarcho, Lewis Mac, and Scott Eldridge. Below, Jerry Ahmsaty carries a bag of groceries for a customer; he was the "carry-out boy." (Both, courtesy of Arizona State Museum.)

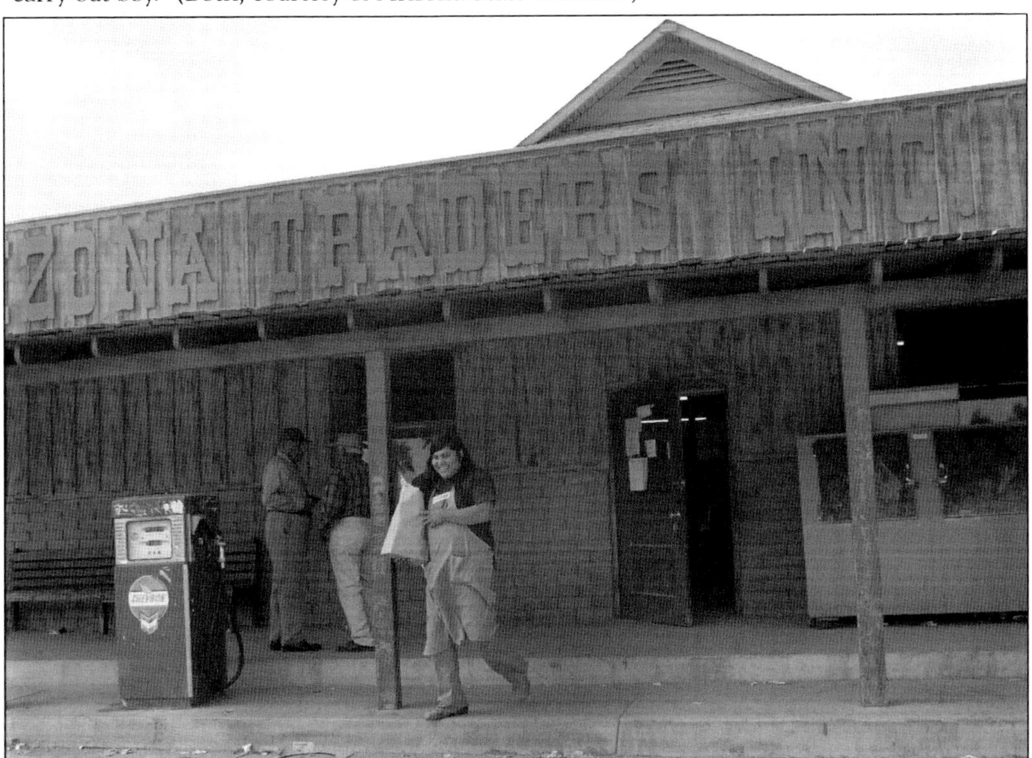

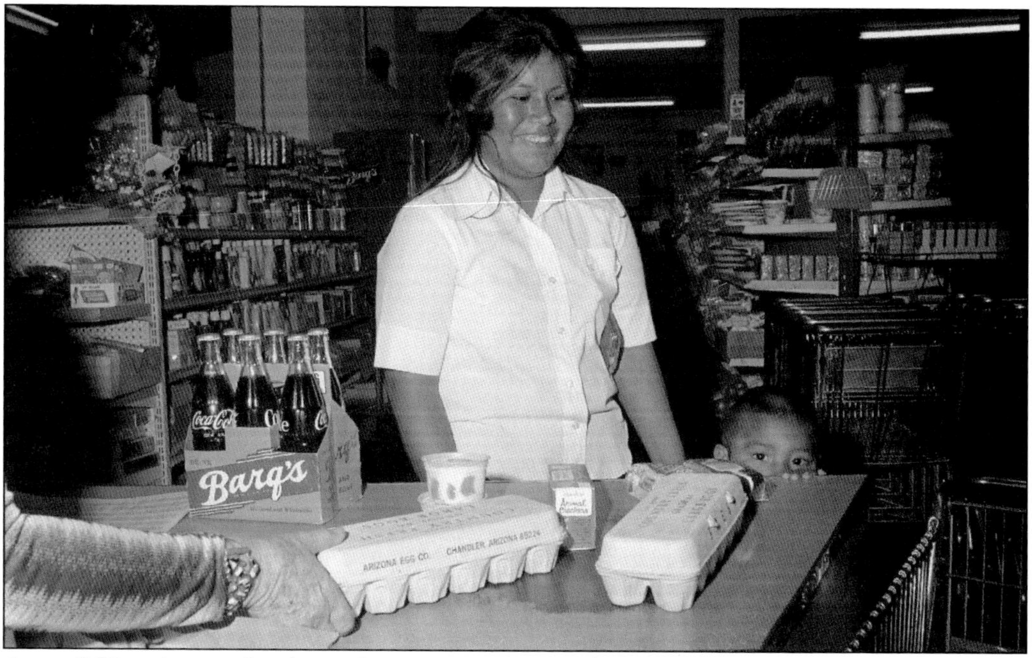

A small Pima boy peeks above the store counter at the Sacaton Trading Post as his mother purchases groceries while store employee Marlene Halbotson, hidden except for her arm, bags the purchases. Helga Teiwes took this photograph on the Gila River Indian Reservation in 1972. (Courtesy of Arizona State Museum.)

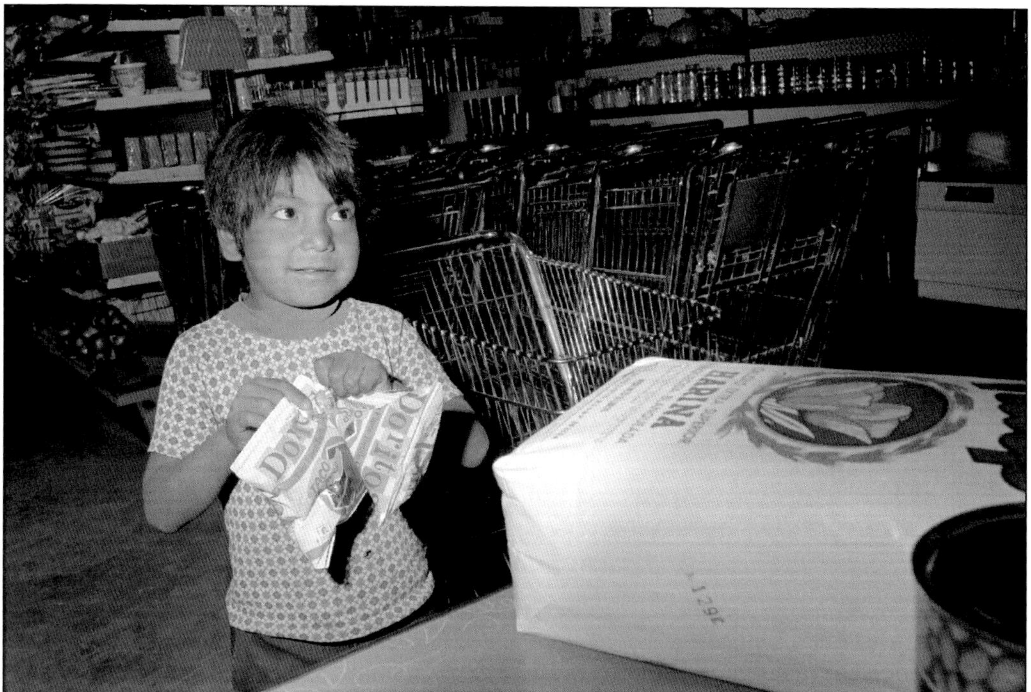

With a big grin, a Pima boy purchases two bags of Doritos at the Sacaton Trading Post in this 1972 photograph by Helga Teiwes. (Courtesy of Arizona State Museum.)

Five

Tohono O'odham
The Desert People

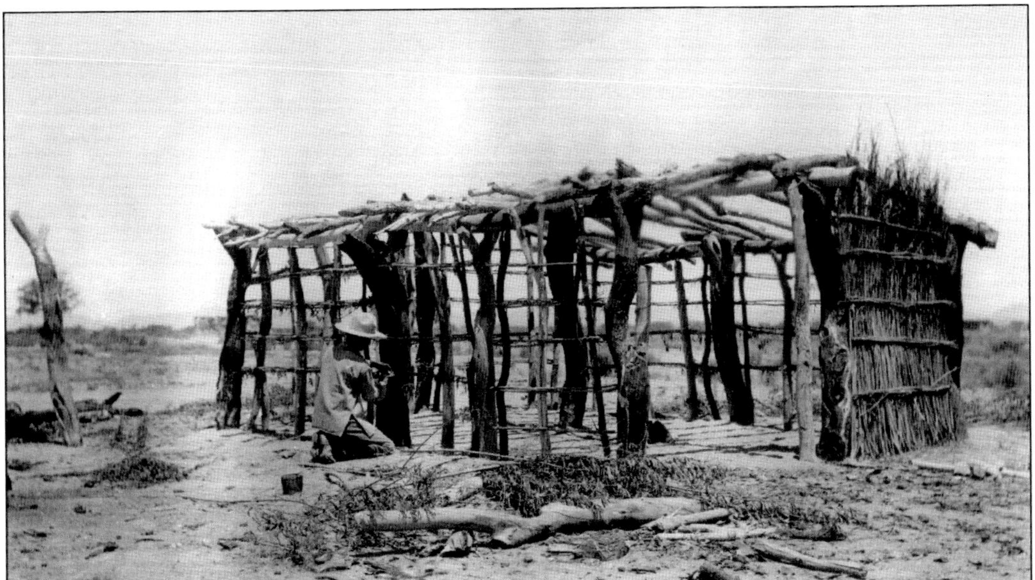

The Tohono O'odham Nation is located in the Sonoran Desert in south-central Arizona. At nearly three million acres, the reservation is comparable in size to the state of Connecticut. In earlier times, the Tohono O'odham people, formerly known as Papagos, moved seasonally from the desert to the mountain foothills. Houses were temporary structures, built with thin logs and covered with dirt and brush. This 1905 photograph shows a man building a framework for a Tohono O'odham house. (Courtesy of WACC.)

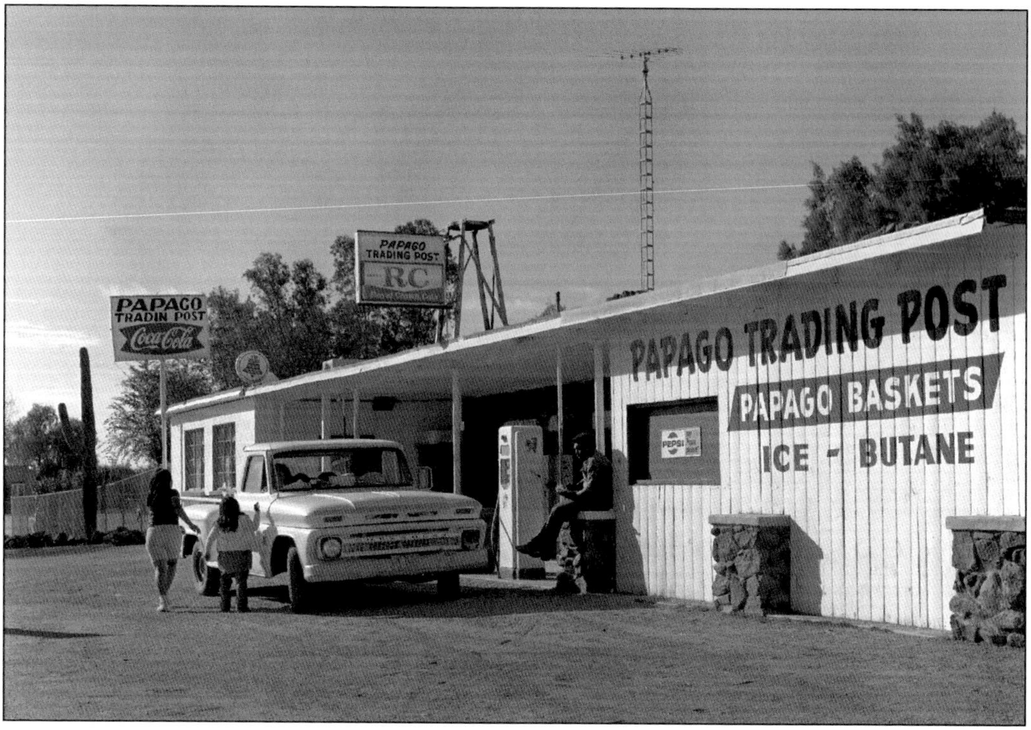

Sells, Arizona, is the headquarters of the Tohono O'odham Nation. In earlier years, there was a store on the hill to the west end of the town, as well as a store to the east, and they were known as the high and low stores. Helga Teiwes took this 1972 photograph of the Papago Trading Post. Aside from groceries and other dry goods, the stores carried a few locally made pots but were best known for buying and reselling the exquisite baskets woven by Tohono O'odham women. The 1903 photograph below shows an O'odham woman working on a basket. (Above, courtesy of Arizona State Museum; below, courtesy of WACC.)

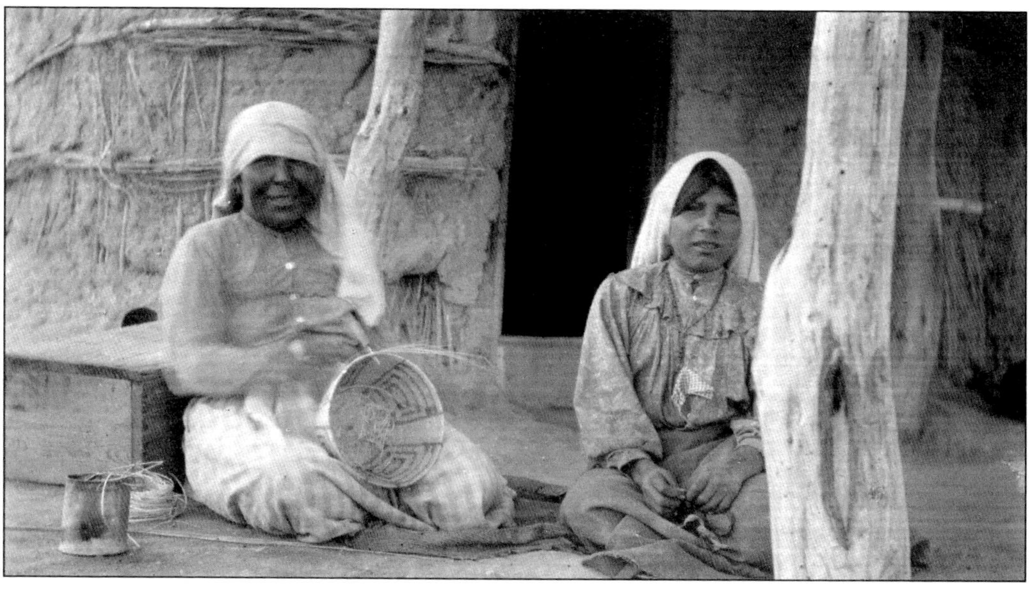

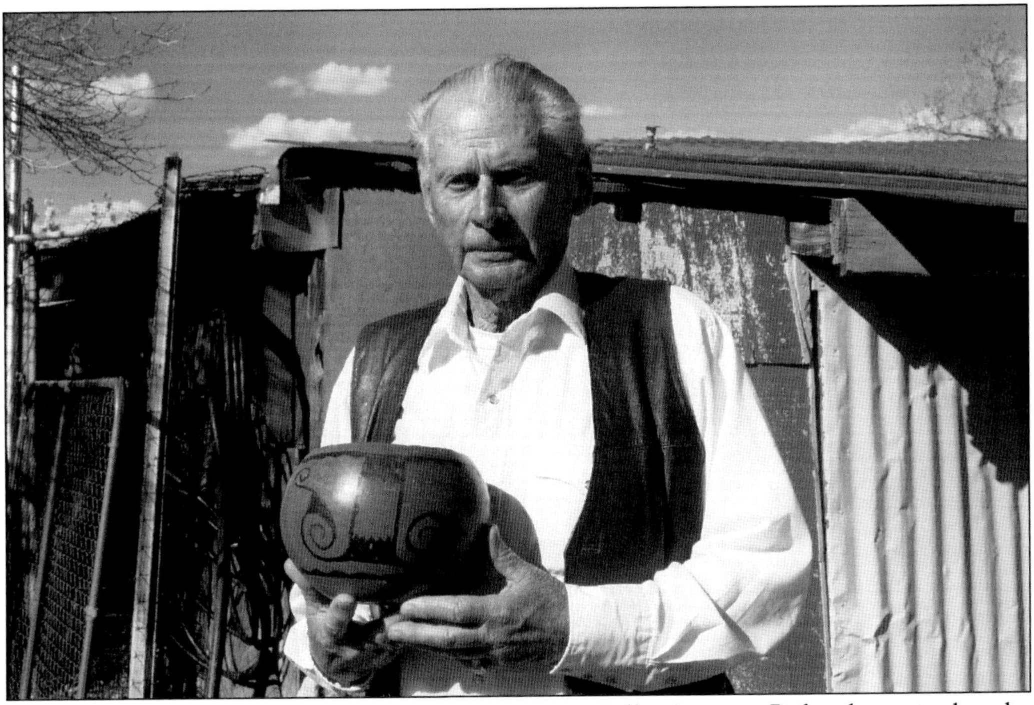

Joe Sestak operated a trading post and gas station in Sells, Arizona. Before he arrived at the Tohono O'odham Reservation, he had been a prospector, and he went to southern Arizona to investigate the mineral possibilities in the area. After Sestak acquired his store, he often traded gas for baskets and other arts. When he retired and left southern Arizona, he had acquired a huge collection of Tohono O'odham arts.

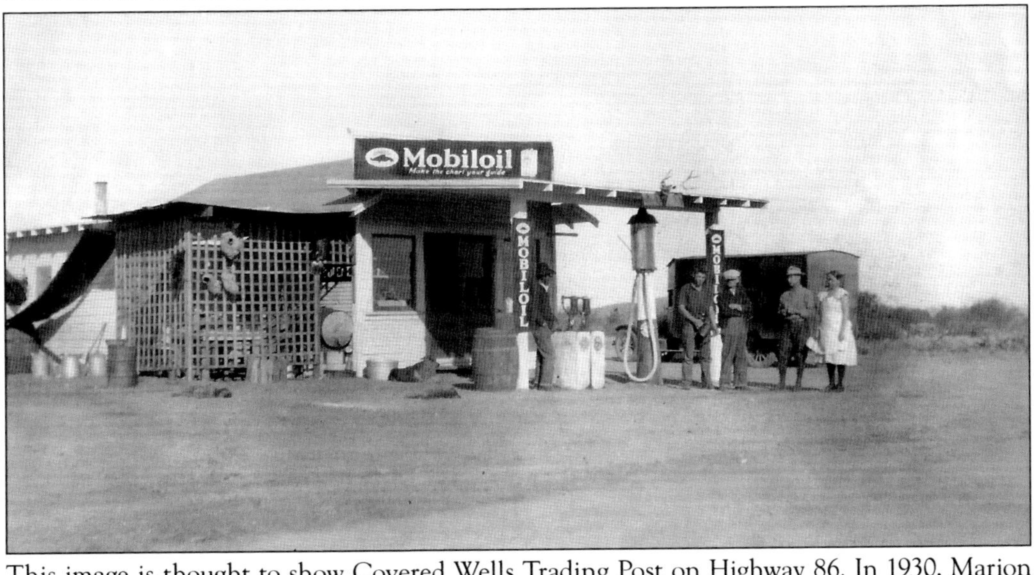

This image is thought to show Covered Wells Trading Post on Highway 86. In 1930, Marion Tracy, second from left, and his wife, Goldie, managed the store. Others in the photograph are unidentified. When this photograph was taken, the road in front of the store was just a dirt track through the desert. Covered Wells is about 85 miles west of Tucson. There is currently a small convenience store in the area.

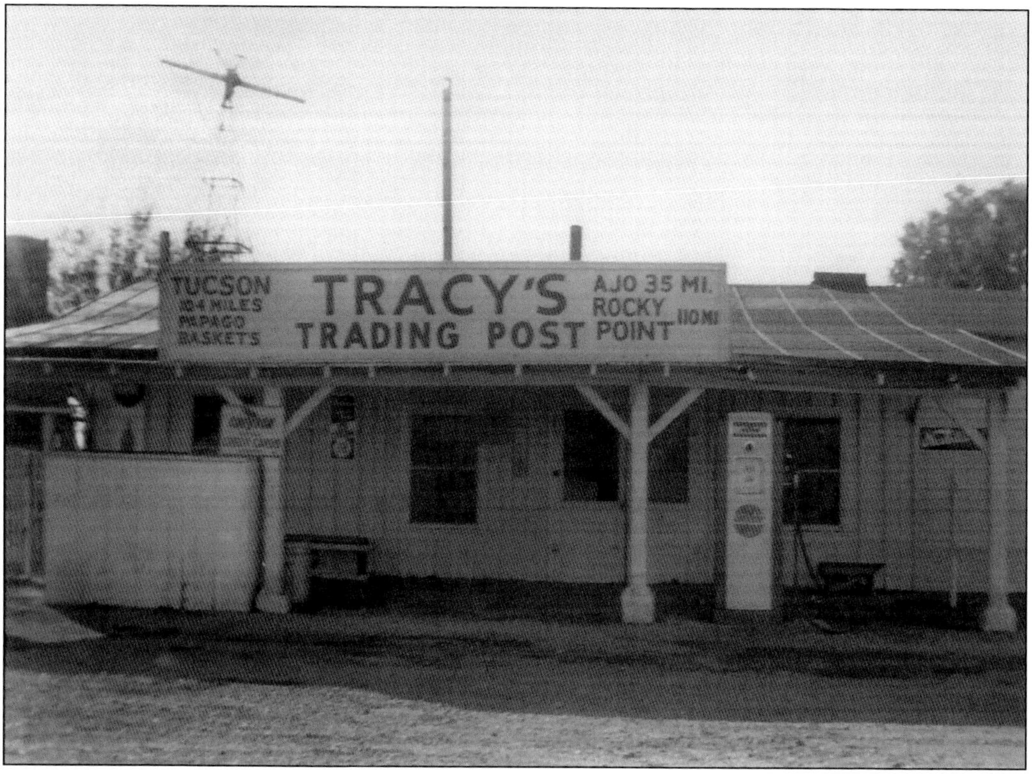

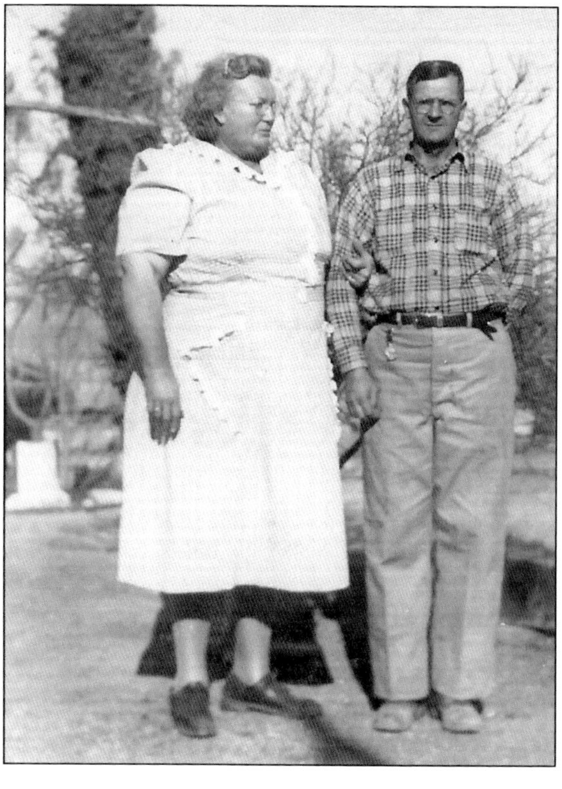

Marion and Goldie Tracy opened Tracy's Trading Post on Highway 86, 104 miles west of Tucson, in 1932. The original store along the dirt road was a tent, as were the living quarters. As part of their trading post license requirements, the Tracys were required to maintain a government well that supplied water to the store, as well as to local O'odham residents. Marion died in 1938, but Goldie stayed on managing the store. She was fluent in the O'odham language and often helped local people with transportation and basic nursing; she also contributed to local ceremonies and festivals. In 1941, Goldie married Jim Richmond, pictured with her at left, and operated Tracy's Trading Post until her retirement in 1967 when, because she was Anglo, she reluctantly had to leave the reservation.

Goldie Tracy Richmond is credited with keeping the Tohono O'odham basket-making art alive through the Depression years. She wrote letters to Indian curio shops around the country offering to sell quantities of O'odham baskets, at 5¢ to 25¢ apiece. Her niece Alice Fetty lived with Goldie in 1937 and recalled that they shipped nearly 20,000 baskets that year.

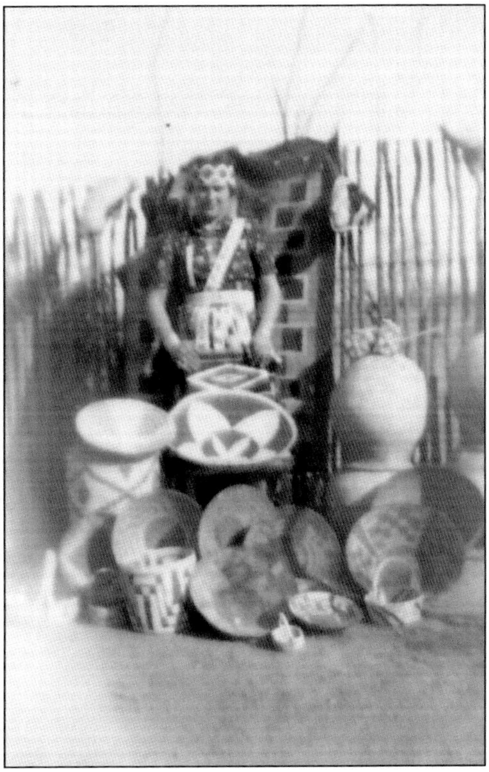

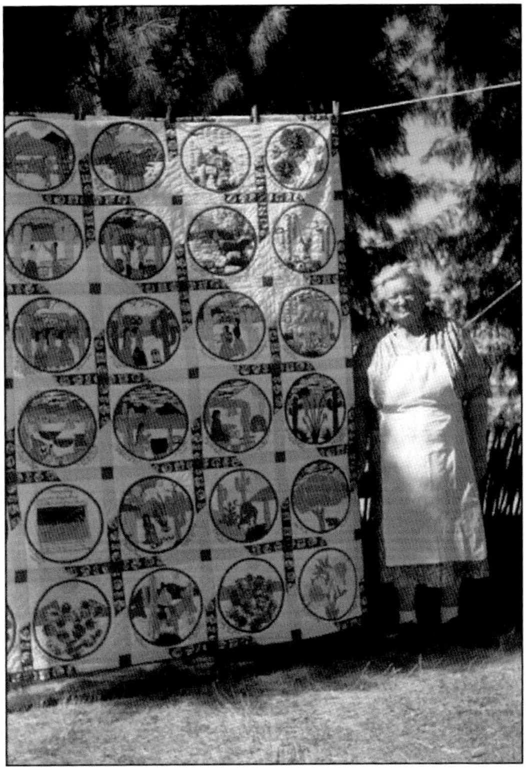

In addition to operating the trading post, Goldie Tracy Richmond also made quilts, but her quilts were not traditional; they were unique and noteworthy for her original designs that featured images of her Tohono O'odham neighbors and desert life, ceremonies and activities, and desert flowers and cacti. Goldie's *Papago Indian Activity Quilt* was named one of the 100 best quilts of the century and is featured in the book *The Twentieth Century's Best American Quilts: Celebrating 100 Years of the Art of Quiltmaking.* Several of her quilts are now in Arizona museum collections.

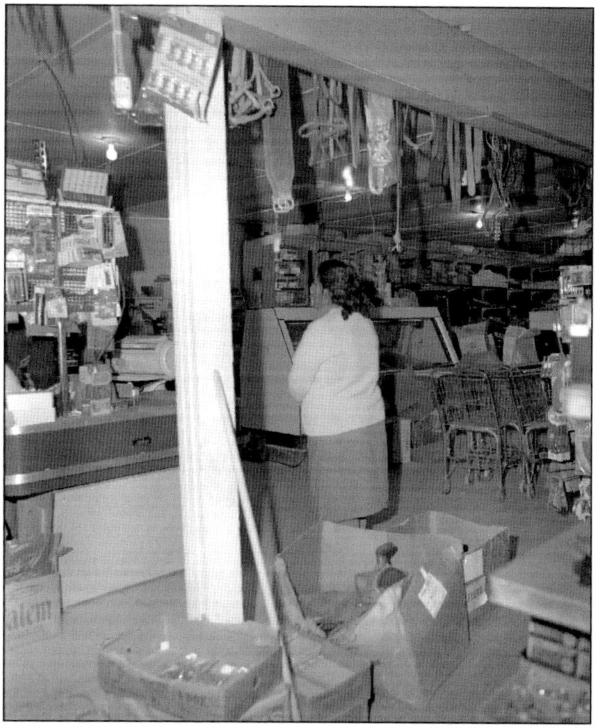

The Santa Rosa Trading Post was located on Highway 15 on the Tohono O'odham Reservation. The village of Santa Rosa, Kaij Mek, was an agricultural community. The trading post carried groceries and hardware, as well as Tohono O'odham baskets. Many O'odham men are horsemen, and the store also sold saddles, bridles, and other horse gear. As was the case among many Native Americans, the older people did not learn to read and write, and the trader often translated for local customers and also wrote letters for those people. Juan Gregario, shown in the 1972 photograph below, is signing what is likely a monthly credit voucher with his thumbprint. Both of these photographs are by Helga Teiwes. (Both, courtesy of Arizona State Museum.)

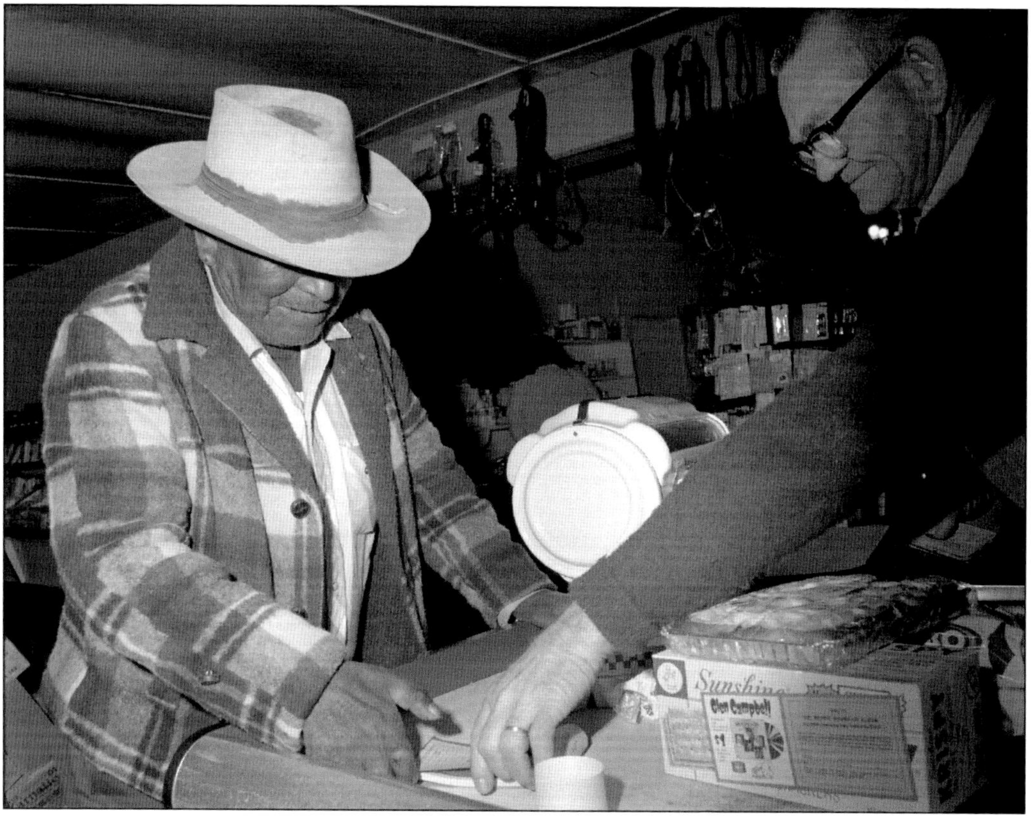

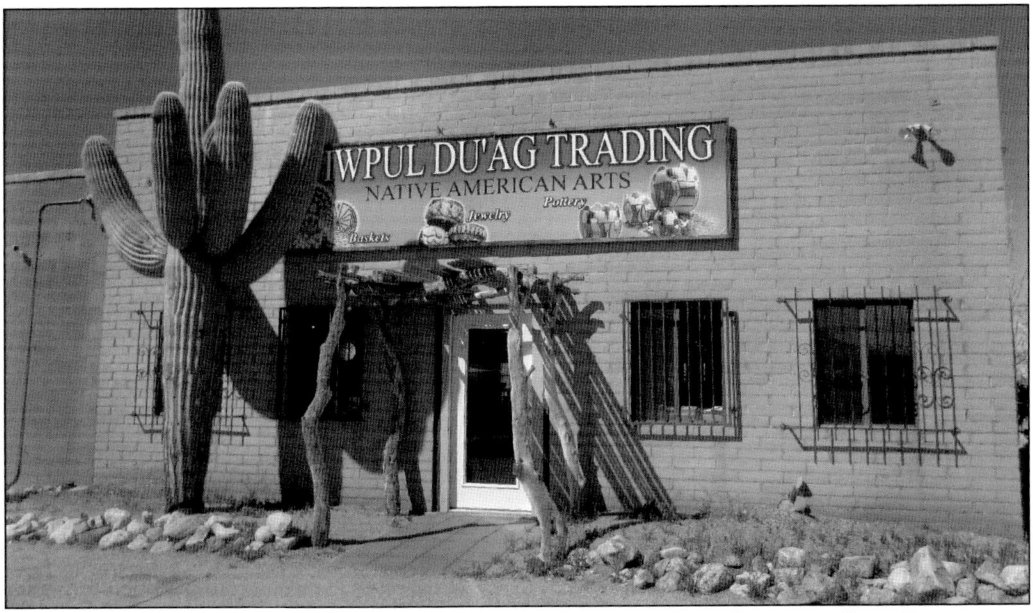

Wipul'dag Trading Post on Highway 86 on the eastern edge of the Tohono O'odham Reservation carries many beautiful O'odham arts. Inside the store, a visitor can purchase O'odham baskets, jewelry, pottery, and beautiful, original watercolors by O'odham artist Michael Chiago, as well as souvenir items such as T-shirts, man in the maze decals, and coffee mugs. There are also bundles of black devil's claw pods, which are used by weavers in the traditional baskets. At the west end of the building is the Coyote Store, which sells snacks, groceries, and wreaths of ribbon and artificial flowers that are used to mark the sites of casualties along the highway. It is believed that spirits of the deceased linger at these sites, and families decorate them with photographs, candles, and painted stones. These somber memorials also serve to remind motorists to drive safely and attentively.

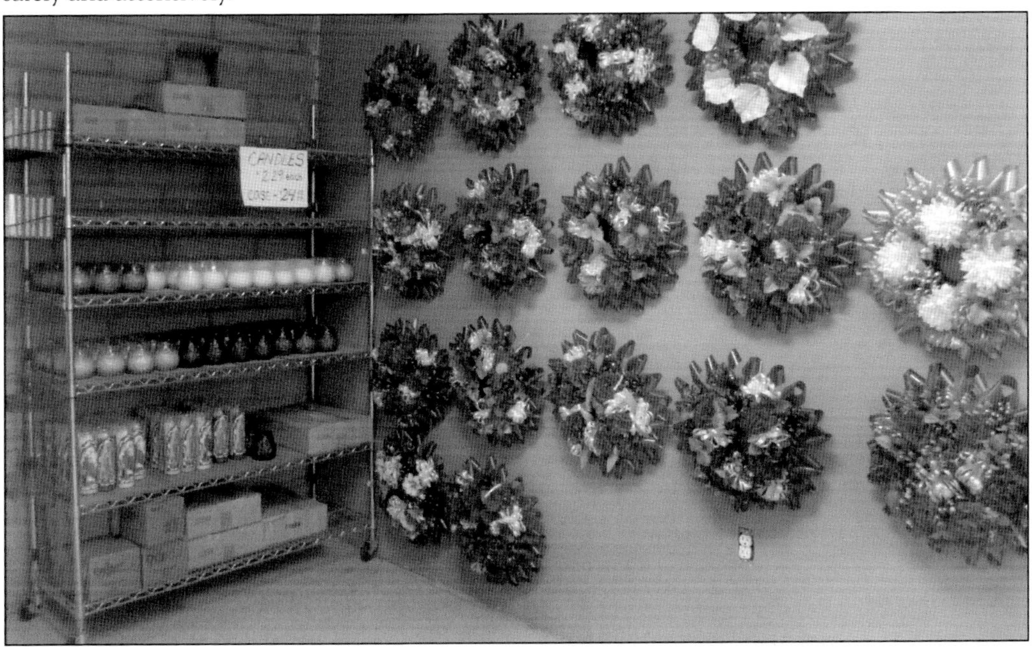

Bibliography

Berkholz, Richard C. *Old Trading Posts of the Four Corners*. Lake City, CO: Western Reflections Publishing Company, 2007.

Davis, Carolyn O'Bagy Davis. *Desert Trader: The Life and Quilts of Goldie Tracy Richmond*. Tucson, AZ: Sanpete Publications, 2012.

Eddington, Patrick, and Susan Makov. *Trading Post Guidebook*. Flagstaff, AZ: Northland Publishing, 1995.

Engels, Mary Tate, ed. *Tales from Wide Ruins*. Lubbock: Texas Tech University Press, 1996.

Gillmor, Frances, and Louisa Wade Wetherill. *Traders to the Navajo: The Story of the Wetherills of Kayenta*. Albuquerque: University of New Mexico Press, 1943.

Hegemann, Elizabeth Compton. *Navajo Trading Days*. Albuquerque: University of New Mexico Press, 1963.

Holloway, Winona J. *Riders to the Rainbow*. Live Oak, CA: Shadow Butte Press, 1998.

James, H.L. *Rugs & Posts The Story of Navajo Weaving and Indian Trading*. Atglen, PA: Schiffer Publishing, 1999.

Kane, Wanden M. *What Am I Doing Here?* Palmer Lake, CO: Filter Press, 1979.

Kennedy, John D. *A Good Trade: Three Generations of Life and Trading Around the Indian Capital Gallup, New Mexico*. Privately printed, 2009.

Kosik, Fran. *Native Roads The Complete Motoring Guide to the Navajo and Hopi Nations*. Flagstaff, AZ: Creative Solutions Publishing, 1996.

McNitt, Frank. *The Indian Traders*. Norman: University of Oklahoma Press, 1962.

Richardson, Gladwell. *Navajo Trader*. Tucson: University of Arizona Press, 1991.

Roberts, Willow. *Stokes Carson Twentieth-Century Trading on the Navajo Reservation*. Albuquerque: University of New Mexico Press, 1987.

Yost, Billie Williams. *Diamonds in the Desert*. Flagstaff, AZ: Silver Spruce Publishing, 1987.

Index